Criminological Research for Beginners

Criminological Research for Beginners is a comprehensive and engaging guide to research methods in Criminology. Written specifically for undergraduate students and novice researchers, this book has been designed as a practical guide to planning, conducting and reporting research in the subject. By first inviting readers to consider the importance of criminological research, the book places related methodology firmly in the context of students' broader study of Criminology, before moving on to provide a detailed guide to the practical processes of research.

It is common for Criminology undergraduates to feel intimidated at the prospect of conducting their own research, and these students typically struggle to see the relevance of research methods to their own studies. This book speaks directly to the needs of such students, and includes contemporary examples and case studies that bring this often thought of as dry subject to life, providing a thorough and accessible practical guide that students can return to at each stage of their research.

This book covers:

- An examination of the theoretical, political and ethical debates in criminological research
- A complete guide to planning criminological research, assisting student researchers in identifying their research questions, choosing their research methods and critiquing the available literature
- Guidance on the practicalities and processes of collecting data
- A discussion of the process of analysing data and writing up research.

Including an extensive glossary and supplemented with a companion website with extra examples, exercises and videos to further develop students' understanding, this book is essential reading for any undergraduate on a Criminological Research Methods course, or for anyone in need of practical guidance on any or every of the various stages involved in conducting thorough and effective criminological research.

Laura Caulfield PhD is Head of Research and Consultancy in the School of Society, Enterprise and Environment at Bath Spa University. She conducts research and lectures in the areas of criminal justice, criminal psychology and research methods. She is an expert in the evaluation of programmes for those involved in the criminal justice system and her work is currently focused on assessing the impact of the arts and other non-traditional programmes. In 2011 Laura was presented with a commendation award from the Howard League for Penal Reform for her research on the arts in prisons.

Jane Hill PhD has had a career in teaching Sociology and Criminology at undergraduate and postgraduate levels. She was Programme Director of BA Criminology at BCU when she retired in 2012. Jane has always had an interest in research methods and the philosophy of science. Her research has been in the areas of Child Protection, Community Justice and Restorative Justice.

Criminological Research for Beginners

A student's guide

Laura Caulfield and Jane Hill

Routledge
Taylor & Francis Group

LONDON AND NEW YORK

This edition published 2014
by Routledge
2 Park Square, Milton Park, Abingdon, Oxon, OX14 4RN

and by Routledge
711 Third Avenue, New York, NY 10017

Routledge is an imprint of the Taylor & Francis Group, an informa business

British Library Cataloguing in Publication Data
A catalogue record for this book is available from the British Library

Library of Congress Cataloging-in-Publication Data
Caulfield, Laura, 1981–.
   Criminological research for beginners: a student's guide/by Laura Caulfield PhD
   and Jane Hill PhD.
   pages cm
   Includes bibliographical references and index.
   1. Criminology – Research. 2. Criminology – Methodology.
   I. Hill, Jane, 1954–. II. Title.
   HV6024.5.C38 2014
   364.072 – dc23
   2013040610

ISBN: 978-0-415-50960-2 (hbk)
ISBN: 978-0-415-50961-9 (pbk)
ISBN: 978-0-203-49473-8 (ebk)

Typeset in Akzidenz Grotesk and Eurostile
by Florence Production Ltd, Stoodleigh, Devon, UK

MIX
Paper from
responsible sources
FSC
www.fsc.org   FSC® C013056

Printed and bound in Great Britain by
TJ International Ltd, Padstow, Cornwall

CONTENTS

List of figures	ix
List of tables	x
List of boxes	xi
Acknowledgements	xiii
Introduction	xiv
Visual tour	xvii

PART 1
The importance of criminological research — 1

Chapter 1 — The context of criminological research: power, knowledge, politics and values — 3

Chapter 2 — The significance of criminological research: understanding the philosophical roots of our claims to know about crime in society — 14

Chapter 3 — The ethics of criminological research — 27

PART 2
Getting going with criminological research — 41

Chapter 4 — Planning: Where do research ideas come from? How do we 'fine tune' them? — 43

Chapter 5 — Critiquing the literature and the process of writing your formal review — 55

Chapter 6 — Theories, methods and their relationship to theories of knowledge — 65

Chapter 7 — Preparing for the practical challenges of 'real-world' crime research — 89

PART 3
Doing criminological research: data collection   107

Chapter 8   Ethnographic approaches to research   109

Chapter 9   Questionnaires and surveys   124

Chapter 10   Using documentary and secondary data sources   138

PART 4
Doing criminological research: analysis and writing-up   151

Chapter 11   Analysing the data: quantitative analysis   153

Chapter 12   Analysing the data: qualitative analysis   179

Chapter 13   Analysing the data: documents, text and other data   195

Chapter 14   Writing up criminological research   209

Glossary   227
References   231
Index   239

LIST OF FIGURES

3.1	Ethics continuum	32
4.1	Interrogating your literature sources: policy documents	48
4.2	Interrogating your literature sources: academic texts	51
6.1	The dimensions of criminological research frameworks	67
6.2	The subjective/objective continuum	68
8.1	Researcher roles in observation studies	118
11.1	Standard deviation	157
14.1a	Example contents page from a qualitative dissertation	212
14.1b	Example contents page from a quantitative dissertation	212
14.2	A traditional report structure	213
14.3	Structuring your literature review	215

LIST OF TABLES

3.1	Upholding ethical principles	29
5.1	How to keep records of your reading	58
7.1	Participant recruitment strategies	98
7.2	Research in action: a summary of the research process in three English women's prisons	103
8.1	Data gathering via in-depth 'ethnographic' interviews	113
8.2	Data gathering via observation	122
9.1	Advantages and disadvantages of questionnaires and surveys	127
9.2	Advantages and disadvantages of closed and open-ended questions	130
10.1	Broad-ranging texts	141
11.1	Common types of study and statistical analyses	161

LIST OF BOXES

1.1	Student activity: the case of CCTV	5
1.2	Learning from experience	7
1.3	Identifying value positions	9
1.4	Official knowledge about crime – key questions	10
2.1	What are the characteristics of a 'good' piece of research?	15
2.2	Key terms explained	17
2.3	Key terms explained: *epistemology* and *ontology*	20
2.4	Student activity: can men carry out pro-feminist research?	23
2.5	Becoming a reflexive researcher	24
3.1	Learning from the past: real ethical dilemmas	31
3.2	Student activity: informed consent	33
3.3	Should confidentiality and anonymity ever be breached?	36
3.4	Can covert observational research be carried out ethically?	38
4.1	Breaking down concepts	45
4.2	Specifying concepts and identifying variables	48
4.3	Searching academic journals	50
4.4	Keeping track of your references	52
5.1	Critical reading	57
5.2	Student activity	62
6.1	Early theories of crime and punishment	71
6.2	Classicist ideas in use today	72
6.3	Were biological positivists able to avoid the use of values in their research into crime?	75
6.4	The study of suicide	75
6.5	The assumptions of the labelling perspective	79
6.6	Researching the crimes of the powerful	80
6.7	Policing the crisis	81
6.8	Using mixed methods to influence policy: Kelly *et al.* (1999)	83
7.1	Key term explained: Offender Assessment System	93
7.2	Research in action: piloting research with ex-offenders	95
7.3	Key term explained: the 'call-in system'	100
7.4	Critical activity	104
8.1	Student activity: critical ethnography	111

8.2	Student activity: when should I use in-depth interviewing methods?	112
8.3	Power and the interview process	116
8.4	Observation and theories of knowledge	119
9.1	Types of random samples	128
9.2	Spot the deliberate mistakes	135
10.1	Student activity	146
10.2	Analysing secondary data	147
10.3	Student activity: public and private prisons	148
11.1	Cause and effect in aggression and alcohol: dependent and independent variables	156
11.2	Research example	165
11.3	Reporting statistical tests	171
11.4	Research example	172
12.1	Transcribing interviews	182
12.2	Braun and Clarke's phases	186
12.3	Describing a thematic analysis in a method section of a research report	187
12.4	Coding activity	190
12.5	Getting started with NVivo	193
13.1	Suggestions for a qualitative content analysis coding manual	200
13.2	What to do when you have developed your initial codes	202
13.3	Jupp and Norris' discourse analytic research agenda	204
13.4	Activity	204
13.5	Getting started with using NVivo to help you manage documents	206
14.1	Our top three tips for successfully writing up criminological research	211
14.2	Example of relating the findings to the existing literature	218
14.3	Example conclusion	219
14.4	Example titles: domestic violence	220
14.5	Examples titles: female prison staff	220
14.6	Writing abstracts	221

ACKNOWLEDGEMENTS

LC: First, I owe immense gratitude to the students who so kindly allowed us to use examples of their work within this book. Their efforts and contributions have made this book a much richer resource. My co-author, JH, has been beyond brilliant and I have learnt from her as this project has progressed. I owe huge thanks to TG for supporting me through the challenges of producing this text, and for being so understanding when it so greatly impacted upon our social life! Last but not least, the team at Routledge have been superb – in particular Mike Travers, who has the patience of a saint.

JH: I feel privileged to have had 'nice work' for so many years. In my career as a lecturer I learnt so much from my students who constantly opened my eyes to what can so easily be taken for granted. I am grateful to them all for many of the lessons I have been able to incorporate in this text. LC has been a fantastic 'partner in crime', her enthusiasm, energy and friendship have made the process of producing this book a joy. To Dave, my life partner, I owe enormous thanks for his belief in me and uncrring support. Finally, I wish to thank the Routledge team for all their support and guidance in the production of this book.

INTRODUCTION

This textbook stems from our experience of teaching and doing research. Of all the aspects of doing a degree in criminology we know that students often find research methods modules the most daunting. We find this sad as research is *so* exciting and we hope that this book will help to foster in its readers some of the excitement we feel about research.

As the title suggests, this book is intended for beginners to research so we hope that it will make some thorny issues accessible to undergraduates who are just beginning their studies of crime. However, our teaching of postgraduate students in criminology has taught us that it is rare to find a post-graduate student who does not have some gaps in his/her knowledge of researching crime therefore we hope that this book will be of equal use to them. We have made reference throughout the book to pieces of research with which we are familiar and which raise interesting issues for discussion. It is our belief that it is important to learn from the work of others. Once you are able to assess the strengths and limitations of someone else's research then the chances are that you will be able to reflect upon your own work and make sure that your evidence and analyses are as convincing as possible. Whilst all research is subject to limitations, there is no doubt that some research is considerably more credible than others. Of course, some research might seem very convincing and compelling to the untrained eye and so we believe that it is important for students to acquire the skill of critique and to become conversant with the criteria by which different types of research are judged. Throughout the book we have tried to avoid oppositional ways of thinking about research (for example, quantitative versus qualitative) and instead we have encouraged readers to think about how the questions they ask are imbued with assumptions that will influence the mode of data gathering.

The text is structured around three key themes: the importance of criminological research; how to get going with criminological research; and how to do criminological research. Of course, these three themes are inter-related and we think that it is important to challenge the idea that doing research is a straightforward linear process. Doing research involves a constant process of reflection that is likely to involve the researcher in a process of going backwards and forwards through the various stages of research until s/he is happy that a consistent and logical approach has been achieved. For this reason we recommend that you go backwards and forwards through this text in order to remind yourselves of the key learning points from each chapter as you are in the process of doing your own research. Throughout the book we have recommended places where you might find it particularly useful to refer to other chapters.

Chapters 1–3 identify the importance of criminological research and attempt to reveal the ways in which politics and values are central to any consideration of crime in society. In Chapter 1 we look at the relationship between power and knowledge. We highlight the importance of being able to challenge what may appear to be common-sense policy responses to crimes, especially high-profile crimes that hit the press. We also encourage readers to think critically about crime statistics and to be aware of the processes that are involved in the production of those statistics. In Chapter 2 we introduce you to the philosophical underpinnings of research. You may feel the need to go over this chapter several times as this introduces some complex ideas. We are aware that it *is* difficult to get to grips with the philosophical issues that underpin all research in the social sciences and that if you are a beginner to research – whether undergraduate or postgraduate – these philosophical issues might seem at first like a complete bag of worms! The chapter encourages readers to think carefully about different theories of knowledge and to be mindful of the need to study crime from a variety of angles in order to gain a more complete understanding of the different types of crime within our society. In Chapter 3 we end this section of the text by considering the complex ethical issues to which criminological research gives rise. Whilst we point to the importance of the development of ethical principles in the research process, at the same time we caution against an overly rule-bound approach to ethics. By the end of this chapter you will become aware of the folly of following rules blindly, develop the skill of justifying your own ethical decisions, and be able to critique the decisions made by other researchers.

Chapters 4–7 are aimed at getting you started with your own research. We begin in Chapter 4 by getting you to think about your own theories and where they come from. In this chapter we aim to improve the clarity of your thinking and writing as well as provide you with practical tips that will enable you to carry out research in a thorough and logical manner. Chapter 5 moves on to the practical task of writing a literature review and helps you to distinguish between the different types of literature that you will need to consult in order to complete a piece of research. We focus on the importance of reading and writing critically rather than descriptively; we also alert you to the fact that although the review comes first in the writing-up stage of your research you will need to be sure to review and revise it as you go through the other elements of your study. In Chapter 6, therefore, we try to pull together all the elements of what we call a methodological (rather than method-led) approach to research in order that you will gain understanding of the relationship between theories of crime, theories of knowledge and the methods used to gain further knowledge. This is another complex chapter and you may find that that you will need to return to it on a regular basis in order to be sure that your final research report is consistent and logical in its approach. We end this section with Chapter 7 which takes you through the pros and cons of carrying out 'real-world' research with perpetrators or victims of crime, or people working with these groups. From the start, you should note that it is relatively unusual for undergraduate students to conduct this type of research, so this chapter serves two primary functions: the first is to provide you with understanding of the practical challenges involved in much of the research you read about as a student of criminology. This will allow you to develop your ability to think critically about the research you read about elsewhere in your studies. The second is to provide you with practical guidance on research processes applicable to all criminological research involving real people, including student samples. Of course, some undergraduate students do conduct the type of research outlined in this chapter, and so this chapter will be all the more important if you are one of these students.

The final sections of the book are about doing research. Here we move in to the practical tasks of data gathering and analysis. When reading this section you should always be mindful of the need to think about methods in relation to the theories of crime and theories of knowledge that we have discussed earlier in the book. We begin with in-depth methods of gaining data which are used in ethnographic studies of crime and move on to the construction of questionnaires and the use of secondary sources. The final chapters are concerned with data analysis and writing up your final research. As noted above, we have tried to avoid oppositional ways of thinking about research, and so you will find information relating to a variety of ways of collecting and analysing data. The guidance we provide is, for the most part, focused on the practicalities of 'doing' although we try to ensure you are reminded of how these practical lessons are situated within theories of crime and theories of knowledge. The practical guidance within this section of the book should enable you to understand how to robustly collect your own data, identify and critique existing data sources, and analyse this data. However, you should note that this book is a beginner's guide, and so as you become more skilled and advanced in your studies you may wish to supplement this section of the book with more advanced readings. Where relevant we recommend some of our favourites.

Of significant note, with reference to further resources, is the companion website for this book. We have developed a range of exciting resources and supplementary materials to complement each chapter of the book. Many of the resources are directly mentioned in the text and we encourage you to follow these links. However, readers will also find extra resources on the website that we hope will further enhance your engagement with the concepts presented in this book.

Finally, we have designed this book with you, the reader, in mind. Our years of teaching research methods have given us a thorough appreciation of the needs of students and the need to place research firmly within the context of your broader study of criminology. We hope this book helps you to appreciate the exciting and stimulating nature of criminological research!

Laura Caulfield and Jane Hill

VISUAL TOUR
(HOW TO USE THIS BOOK)

TEXTBOOK FEATURES

Listed below are the various pedagogical features that can be found both in the margins and within the main text, with visual examples of the boxes to look out for, and descriptions of what you can expect them to contain.

Goals of this chapter

Each chapter begins with a list of the key areas in which you can expect to gain knowledge through reading the chapter and completing its accompanying online resources.

Overview

Following the goals of the chapter, an overview is provided which summarises the key issues that will be covered in the chapter.

Boxed features

Boxed features appear throughout the text, containing helpful extra material for students, such as definitions of key terms, real-life examples, case studies, exercises, activities, discussion questions and useful tips.

BOX 1.4 **OFFICIAL KNOWLEDGE ABOUT CRIME – KEY QUESTIONS**

1. How far do you think that official crime statistics tell us the 'truth' about crime?
2. Are all crimes reported?
3. Do all reported crimes become official statistics?
4. Are all crimes recorded in the same way?
5. How would you explain the over-representation of some groups of people in prison?

Key learning points

Here the fundamental concepts covered by the chapter are listed, highlighting both best-practice research methods and potential pitfalls.

KEY LEARNING POINTS

- There is a tendency for beginners to criminological research to take a rather narrow view about how knowledge should be gathered. This reveals quite a lot about the power of scientific discourse in society.
- Criminological researchers must go beyond *common-sense* understanding of science in order to gain respect for their knowledge claims.
- All research will have strengths and limitations, the confidence we have in

Pause to think

Take a moment to 'read between the lines' consider the wider implications of the concepts, examples or themes being discussed in the chapter.

> **PAUSE TO THINK . . .**
>
> In fact the document doesn't tell us directly that much about crime but it is possible to 'read between the lines' by looking carefully at the ways in which language is used in the document. For example, the focus on marriage signals that some families are more likely to be perceived as a problem than others; the concern with 'dad-lessness' implies that lone motherhood is a problem. The ills of society are being placed squarely within 'dysfunctional' family relationships in this document but what does that term mean? Is a definition of a 'functional' family provided

Conclusion

Each chapter ends with the main conclusions that can be drawn from the concepts discussed in the chapter.

> **CONCLUSION**
>
> The processes of doing research are embroiled in relations of power, which should begin to alert us to the fallacy of notions of neutrality that surround debates about research. To say that there is a relationship between power and knowledge is not the same as saying that all knowledge produced within relationships of power should be dismissed. Rather, recognition of power/knowledge relationships should enable researchers to identify the ways in which issues are defined and in which

Glossary

Key terms that are highlighted in bold within the text can be found in the comprehensive glossary at the end of the book.

> **Absolute relativism**   When used in the context of research ethics this term refers to the view that there are no moral rights and wrongs, that is, what is right for some people can be understood to be wrong by others. Absolute relativism can be very problematic as it can lead to the position where oppressive practices can be justified.
>
> **Bivariate relationship**   A relationship between two variables.
>
> **Classicism**   A school of criminological thought based upon the work of Beccaria (1738–94) which assumes that people have free will to choose criminal or lawful solutions to their problems. It advocates swift punishment as a deterrent in order to make crime unattractive and illogical.

LINKS TO COMPANION WEBSITE FEATURES

Whenever you see one of the below boxed features in the margins of the book, containing the @ symbol, look for the related supplementary material for that chapter on the companion website at www.routledge.com/cw/caulfield. The related material will have the same title that appears in the box ('Assessing the impact of CCTV' in the first example below).

For instructors

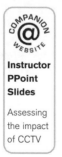

Instructor PPoint Slides

Assessing the impact of CCTV

Instructor exercise

Summar-ising an article

Instructor activity

Research workshop on gangs

Editable PowerPoint slides that instructors can adapt to fit their own teaching.

Sample exercises to set students that will allow them to consolidate their learning.

Suggested individual and group activities for instructors to offer students in lectures and seminars.

For students

Student video

What constitutes good research?

Student document

Secondary data sources

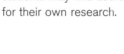

Student activity

Getting started with research

Video clips from a live student debate, featuring undergraduate and Masters students discussing their thoughts about how research should be carried out, ethical issues and their own research plans.

Links to various sources of secondary data that students may find useful for their own research.

Activites for students to carry out independently to explore different ways of carrying out research.

Student guide to ...

Holding effective interviews and focus groups

Student web links

Social data sources

Student quiz

Practical guidance on a variety of practical tasks such as moderating focus groups; constructing consent forms; reviewing articles.

URLs that link to a variety of useful social data sources.

Interactive multiple-choice quizzes, with an explanation of the correct answer upon completion of each question.

PART 1

The importance of criminological research

Chapter 1

The context of criminological research

Power, knowledge, politics and values

GOALS OF THIS CHAPTER

At the end of reading this chapter and by completing the online resources that accompany it, you will be able to:

1   understand the relationship between the context and processes of research;
2   identify some of the constraints that affect the process of research;
3   interrogate the relationship between power and knowledge;
4   begin to explore the role of values in criminological research.

OVERVIEW

- The research process can be limited by external social, economic and political factors, which can constrain the limits of any given research project.
- Beginning researchers need to be mindful of the sorts of issues that can make the task of doing research difficult, such as gaining access to a research setting, obtaining sufficient funds and convincing the fund holders that their research is worthwhile.
- Alongside the external factors it is also important to consider how researchers' own social and cultural backgrounds, as well as their positions within any given organisation, can be of significance when it comes to the questions asked, the process of data gathering, the interpretation of the data and indeed when it comes to the ways in which the findings are received.
- For those who are new to criminological research it is common to assume that researchers do not bring values and preconceptions to the research process. Indeed, it is likely that given the status and **common-sense** understandings of science in our society (as we shall see in Chapter 2), most people who are new to research will have the understandable, but rather naive, view that it is possible to carry out research without having to consider values at all.

- For the above reasons the chapter seeks to explain the relationship between power and knowledge in order to reveal the ways in which supposedly neutral research questions are shaped by political (both macro and micro) imperatives and financial constraints.

LEARNING FROM OTHERS

The context within which research takes place will have an impact upon the scope of the research as well as the questions that are asked. For this reason it is important that beginning researchers are taught to examine critically the research of others. Students should be encouraged to think about issues such as the economic and time constraints; the political climate in which research takes place; the imperatives of fund holders and the role of gatekeepers.

There will always be problems associated with time and money at whatever level research takes place. However, for beginners to research these limitations are especially relevant. It is therefore important that beginners *think small*. Most students who are starting research are unable to gain access to research funds. The positive aspect of this is that the problem of satisfying the priorities of fund holders is not usually something that impacts upon undergraduates and only impacts upon postgraduate students to a limited degree. This is an advantage for beginning researchers as they are often more free to explore issues that are of interest to themselves rather than to the fund holders. However, because students *will* experience economic and time constraints it is important to weigh up the merits of different forms of data collection not only in terms of their ability to answer the research questions/s in sufficient detail (see Chapter 6) but also in terms of cost and time. For example, it may be possible to use the internet to access people rather than spend time and money on travelling to interview people in person.

More advanced researchers will have access to funding from four key areas: government departments, research councils, charitable foundations and criminal justice agencies, such as police forces and prisons (Noaks and Wincup, 2004). Whilst beginners are unlikely to gain funds from these bodies it is important that early researchers examine different types of research in order to get an idea of the ways in which funders can impact upon the research process. For example, Home Office-funded research will be more likely to constrain research questions in order to ensure that the political imperatives of the day are given priority. As King and Wincup (2008: 55) have pointed out, this should be no surprise and although it is not, as they say, 'a scandal' it is something that should be borne in mind when applying for funding. If the desired end of a piece of research is to *challenge* policy in some way then an application to the Home Office for funding might not be the smartest move.

Whilst Home Office research is usually of a high quality it is unlikely to reveal a full picture of crime in our society. King and Wincup (2008: 55) are right to spell out the relationship between Home Office research and development and the political party in power. The task of thinking critically about the assumptions that underpin policies is not one that is usually given to those who are in receipt of government funding. The use of

BOX 1.1 STUDENT ACTIVITY: THE CASE OF CCTV

Take a look at Home Office Study 292, Gill and Spriggs 2005, https://www.**cctv**usergroup.com/downloads/file/**Martin**%20**gill**.pdf_

1   What are the main findings of the study?
2   Does anything surprise you about the conclusions of the researchers?
3   How far do you think that 'failure of implementation' is a reasonable explanation of the lack of success of CCTV as a tool through which to reduce crime?

Now look at Groombridge (2008) 'Stars of CCTV? How the Home Office wasted millions – a radical "Treasury Audit Commission" view', *Surveillance and Society*, 5(1): 73–80.

1   What might Groombridge's comments on Home Office Study 292 reveal about the context of research?
2   Why do you think that the study of the use of CCTV as a way of reducing crime has attracted so much funding?
3   Can you think of alternative research questions that might lead researchers to challenge the use of CCTV as a crime prevention strategy?

Instructor PPoint Slides

Assessing the impact of CCTV

CCTV as a form of situational crime prevention is a case in point. Over a number of years this has been the topic of Home Office research, which has been quite costly, yet the results of such research have been far from convincing.

The activity above should start you thinking about the need to weigh up the extent to which the concerns of any proposed research will match with those who hold the purse strings. It should also have given you an idea of the ways in which a response that has not been entirely successful can continue to attract funding and keep alternative responses off the agenda, which as Lukes' (2005) work demonstrates is an important dimension of power. Also the increasing **marketisation** of our universities is a significant development that is relevant to our discussion of the context within which research takes place. Increasingly some researchers might find themselves faced with the moral dilemma of whether to carry out 'safe' research that would be likely to attract funding and further their careers or to raise the challenging questions they would really like to answer through their research. Choosing the latter involves some risks in so far as it can be much more difficult to gain funding and public recognition – although we believe it is a risk worth taking in order to challenge the mounting constraints placed upon criminologists (see Hillyard *et al.,* 2004; Currie, 2007).

All funding bodies have a gatekeeper role (gatekeepers are those who control access to the research we wish to carry out) as they are able to make decisions regarding the research topics they are or are not willing to support. Even in small-scale, unfunded research however it is important to think carefully about the role of gatekeepers as they are part of the network of power relations within which research takes place. Gatekeepers will be concerned about the motives researchers may have in carrying out their research; they will want to know who and what it is for. They are often able to place limits on researchers' access to the people they might wish to interview or observe as part of their research. It is therefore important that you do some preliminary investigation about the agendas of any funding bodies to which you are considering making applications. Depending upon the type of research you wish to carry out, you will encounter gatekeepers not only when you are trying to secure funding but also when you are trying to secure access to participants. You will therefore need to think about how you will establish links with key individuals and build up relationships of trust. As Pole and Lampard (2002: 87) indicate, the relationship between researchers and gatekeepers can be key to the success of a study, therefore it is in the interests of researchers to build good relationships with these people. Gatekeepers who are working within criminal justice settings, for example in a Youth Offending Team, may well be sensitive if you appear to be critical of their practices.

One of us was involved in interviewing social work, educational and police professionals as part of the process of doing a PhD on the ways in which agencies work together in child protection cases. The interviews took place at a time when social workers had been criticised severely by the press as there had been a series of child abuse scandals during the 1980s. This wider context could not be ignored as it meant that there was deep distrust of researchers on the part of professionals who were in constant fear of being accused of either acting too soon or too late. It was therefore important that the researcher worked hard to reassure the participants in the research that her purpose was not to find evidence that agencies were failing to work together (the received wisdom from the many reports of inquiries) but rather to gain in-depth data about the complexities of working together. Access to the police was particularly difficult to gain as the gatekeeper (the Chief Constable in the area under study) would only allow one officer to be interviewed and permission was not given for the interview to be recorded. Whilst this meant that the data on police practices was very limited indeed the actions of the gatekeeper demonstrated the particular power of the police service to shape the knowledge that is produced about policing activities.

Similarly, in a later study Hill (2007) gained access to young black people who had been in custody through gatekeepers within Youth Offending Teams and other youth organisations. The gatekeepers were professionals who had good working relationships with the young offenders and they provided an important bridge between the researcher and the participants. However, the researcher had to work hard to convince the gatekeepers that the interviews with the young people should not be carried out in the presence of a criminal justice worker and was not always successful in this. Again, this highlights one of the ways in which power and knowledge are intimately linked and it indicates the need for a reflective discussion about these processes in the writing up of research.

Some research into crime involves gaining access to participants through gatekeepers who themselves have criminal careers. Whilst the context of such research differs from the examples given above there is nonetheless a power relationship which needs to be understood. Just as in the examples above the gatekeepers who have access to criminal worlds still have the power to define what can and can't be 'observed' or who can/cannot be interviewed. So although researchers can set agendas and control the foci of research they are, as Pole and Lampard (2002: 87) have noted, both 'powerful and powerless'. As we shall see in Chapter 3 such studies also give rise to ethical debates, which researchers need to think through before they embark upon their empirical research.

Do try to keep in mind that although gatekeepers are able to block research agendas that do not match with those of their organisation, their role often entails an analysis of how far researchers' proposals protect the interests of the proposed participants in their research. For example, it is now well known amongst social scientists in general that the powerful (usually white) research elites have frequently defined those with less power in society as 'problems' without giving any consideration to the different conditions of existence within which many of those so defined live their lives. For example, debates about the right of white academics within social science to carry out work on behalf of the state in black and Latino communities developed during the 1960s in the United States (see Blauner and Wellman, 1998) so they are in no way new, yet the issues that were raised back then continue to surface in the poorest communities in many western countries where associations are frequently made between rates of crime and 'people of colour'. It is therefore important that those who know and understand what life is like for some of the most excluded groups in society should be given a chance to talk about the 'problem of crime' as they experience it. This might mean that some charitable foundations will favour proposals from those who demonstrate their proximity to the issues they wish to research. This is not an issue of bias but rather an issue of *balance*. This will be discussed further in Chapter 2.

BOX 1.2 LEARNING FROM EXPERIENCE

Take a look at Fine and Weis (1998) 'Crime Stories: A Critical Look Through Race, Ethnicity and Gender', *Qualitative Studies in Education,* 11(3): 435–59.

This study used a life history approach through which it was revealed that the types of violence experienced or feared by young adults in poor urban communities in Jersey City and Buffalo in the US varied according to gender, ethnicity and 'race'. They did not set out to organise their data analyses around differences but, despite the participants' declarations about the irrelevance of ethnicity and gender, the narratives were suffused with the significance of gender and racial oppression in their lives.

The key findings from this study raised important questions about the way policies are formed. The researchers were concerned that although policies were supposedly developed on behalf of the poor they were not developed as a result of listening to the voices of *all* those people who made up the urban poor. Through the literature review Fine and Weis identified both qualitative and quantitative studies that produced knowledge suggesting that poverty increased the exposure to, experience of and propensity to be involved in violence amongst children and young adults. Their own research highlighted that policies reflected the narratives of poor white men. The findings of Fine and Weis showed that violence was a concern for all of the people in the communities they studied, but they also revealed that the commonality stopped there (1998: 455). Street violence perpetrated by the 'usual suspects' (black men) was the concern of white men who trusted the police within their communities. The violence of the white men, especially towards women within the domestic sphere, or of the police towards black men and Latinos, was a reality that the over-representation of people of colour within prisons served to deny. Domestic violence was experienced almost equally by women from each of the three groups of participants, although how they understood it and dealt with it varied between the groups, as did the police response. The significance of Fine and Weis' research is that it uncovered narratives that revealed the inter-relationship between the different types of violence (state, community and domestic) and provided an analysis through which they demonstrated the failure of policy to reflect the experiences of *all* urban poor people in the locations they studied. Furthermore, their analyses indicated that there were no winners because although the concerns of white males were taken seriously the failure to examine the inter-locking and simultaneous nature of oppressions resulted in policies that ultimately failed to improve life for *any* of the people living in the poor communities by increasing tensions.

Questions for new researchers to consider:

Student quiz

1   How does this research help us to understand the processes by which some offenders escape the label of 'criminal'?
     How does this study help us to identify hidden victims of crime?
2   Do recent tensions within British society suggest that Fine and Weis' analysis of violence in poor American neighbourhoods can inform policy research here?
3   Can you think of the ways in which media reports and the responses of politicians serve to shape the context within which much mainstream research on crime takes place?

The research by Fine and Weis (1998) revealed that in some states of America white victims' experiences of crime informed policy yet their research indicated that there were other victims within the communities they studied whose needs were not addressed. Furthermore, they identified an uncritical acceptance amongst the most oppressed groups of women who participated in that study that a punitive response to the men who were abusing them would address the problem of domestic violence even though their life experiences showed that this was not the case. This suggests that the insights of feminist research, which has suggested that not only should domestic violence be taken seriously but also that, in order to address the problem, the attitudes of some men towards women in society should be addressed at a deeper, structural level rather than at the individual level, had not seeped into public consciousness in the areas under study. This is an interesting finding given that within academic circles it has been acknowledged for some years that it is not really helpful to think about domestic violence simply as the acts of some individual (bad) men. Instead many academics began to look at the history of men's control over women and asked searching questions about the ways in which both men *and* women came to accept it as 'normal' (see Wright and Hill, 2004).

WHOSE VALUES? WHOSE JUDGEMENTS?

Stout *et al.* (2008: 6) argue that as crime is such a political issue criminologists have an ethical duty to 'expose the relationship between governmental agendas and knowledge production'. Therefore consideration of the context of criminological research will inevitably involve engagement with the role of values in the research process. New researchers in the area of criminology need to develop the skill of identifying the values upon which researchers make their judgements about the reasons for crime in society, which will in turn help them to understand how different responses to crime are justified. Once those values are identified then it is possible to assess the strength of the arguments put forward in any given piece of research as well as to consider whether there are other values that might lead to different and maybe better or more appropriate judgements about these issues. For example, a government that declares the only way to solve the problem of crime in society is to get tough with criminals may be operating with a theory that tough penalties serve to reduce crime by deterring criminals. However, it may be that politicians are responding to a perceived and perhaps media-led public disquiet about a supposed leniency towards criminals. In such a case the over-riding value position has nothing to do with deterrence and reducing crime but has more to do with satisfying a more basic desire for retribution.

BOX 1:3 IDENTIFYING VALUE POSITIONS

1   Do you think that harsher penalties are the most effective way to deter criminals?
2   Do you think that victims of crime are happier when offenders receive harsh sentences?
3   What are the sorts of crimes that are likely to create victims who are seriously harmed?
4   Are all crimes that result in serious harm responded to with harsh penalties?
5   Make a list of the reasons for your answers to these questions.

When considering the first question in Box 1.3 you will need to weigh up the evidence. As Carrabine *et al.* (2009: 296) have argued, whilst there is a long history of introducing severe penalties 'the results are modest at best'. It might also be the case that there are alternatives, such as improving social conditions, that will produce the desired end in a better way. As Lilly et al. (2011: 200−1) put it, 'scaring people straight' overlooks the positive ways in which the conformity needed to reduce crime can be brought about. Those who undertake research into crime have a duty to consider alternatives and to raise critical questions about what we take for granted – not least because harsh penalties are costly.

Your answers to the questions above will reveal much about your own experiences as well as the extent of your studies on crime. If you think that going to prison, for example, is one of the worst things that can happen then you might think that all people will think in the same way and therefore assume that prison is likely to be a good deterrent. However, if you have experienced prison in some way, directly or indirectly, you may be aware that these things are much less straightforward than they first appear. Similarly, if you have never been a victim of crime, or have little knowledge of victim perspectives, you may well think that a good reason for having tough penalties is to satisfy victims. When you begin to think about the answers to questions 3 and 4 above the extent of your knowledge about crime and victimisation will come into play. For those of you who are already aware that not only do victims of corporate crime exceed those of conventional crimes but also that the offenders are much less likely to receive harsh punishments, it is likely that you may already be starting to ask questions about the *circumstances* in which politicians advocate harsh punishments. The severity of the punishment does not seem to follow the extent of harm when we consider that the numbers of people who die or are injured as a result of corporate offences far exceed those who are killed or injured as a result of 'conventional' crime. Gaining awareness of the different ways in which various groups of offenders *and* victims are constructed will provide you with the tools to go beyond ideas that at first sight appear to be 'common sense' and therefore 'self-evidently' sensible. Research in the areas of corporate crime and victimisation reveal that the interests of those with most power (corporations) are often put before the interests of the victims, who in the case of these types of crime are often amongst the most disadvantaged in society (Tombs and Whyte, 2006).

Our understanding of the relationship between power, knowledge, politics and values would not be complete without an examination of the role official statistics play in our thinking about crime. In Britain the Home Office is the source of this important but, as we shall see, questionable information.

Instructor PPoint Slides

Hidden victims and the politics of crime research

BOX 1.4 OFFICIAL KNOWLEDGE ABOUT CRIME – KEY QUESTIONS

1   How far do you think that official crime statistics tell us the 'truth' about crime?
2   Are all crimes reported?
3   Do all reported crimes become official statistics?
4   Are all crimes recorded in the same way?
5   How would you explain the over-representation of some groups of people in prison?

When criminologists begin to raise questions about official crime statistics it becomes clear that they do not provide us with either a valid or reliable picture of crime (May, 2001; Carrabine *et al.* 2009). Before a criminal act becomes an officially recorded statistic a series of processes have to be completed, starting with the reporting of a crime. There are many reasons why crimes are not reported, ranging from the failure of a victim to realise that a crime has taken place through to a lack of trust in the police. Even if a crime is reported it may not become a statistic for a variety of reasons, such as the discretion of police or indeed because of discriminatory practices. It is not the purpose of this chapter to examine these processes in any detail but rather to alert you to the reasons why researchers should treat statistics with some caution. Indeed, it could be argued that official statistics can never tell us the 'facts' about crime but rather that they can tell us a great deal about *who* is most likely to be defined as criminal. As May (2001: 86–7) suggests, statistics are not independent of those who compile them, yet once a crime becomes a statistic a view of the world is generated that can be misleading and self-perpetuating. For example, if more black males are imprisoned for street crimes the result of this can be that people understand this as an indicator of black males' greater propensity to commit such crimes when in fact the fear that the statistics generate may have lead to increased reporting and increased policing of certain areas.

In recent years governments have taken an 'evidence-based' statistical approach to the study of crime within a performance target culture. Many of those who are concerned about crime and its impact upon society will want to do more than this by considering the complex and varying circumstances within which crimes take place. This has always been so within academic criminology. However, recent changes to the context of academic research have had the effect of relegating the role of theory to a subordinate position. As Tierney (2010: 330) has noted, a number of criminologists have pointed to this shift away from criminological theory and to the narrowing of the focus of criminological research. Indeed, it has been noted that there have been complaints that academic criminology has had little impact upon policy, although it is clear from Tierney's own historical account of the relationship between policy and research that the research that *does* impact policy is likely to be that which reflects the political imperatives of the time. This does not mean that all is lost and there is currently a rising commitment to public criminology (Tierney (2010: 330–1) which aims to impact upon the way public opinion about crime is formed. However, it is not easy for academics to swim against the political tide and Tierney cites Currie (2007) who articulates the powerful *disincentives* (Currie's emphasis) to raising public awareness through research that takes place within university research settings. As we have shown in this chapter already, academics may find it hard to challenge the politics of the day and may even be damaged by their efforts to do so because in order to gain their reputations as researchers they are reliant upon funding from bodies that have political allegiances.

CONCLUSION

The processes of doing research are embroiled in relations of power, which should begin to alert us to the fallacy of notions of neutrality that surround debates about research. To say that there is a relationship between power and knowledge is not the same as saying that all knowledge produced within relationships of power should be dismissed. Rather, recognition of power/knowledge relationships should enable researchers to identify the ways in which issues are defined and in whose interests; it should enable researchers to question why some issues are given high priority (for example street crime) and why others are consistently marginalised (for example domestic violence or corporate crimes). Researchers must ask searching questions about the reasons why some important theorising is ignored. Is it necessarily because the evidence is weak? Or is there more to it? Whilst there have been concerted efforts to take reports of domestic violence more seriously over recent years, there has been a simultaneous failure to address the problem. The fact that still about two women per week are killed in Britain at the hands of men is a poor reflection on our society and should be a source of some shame, yet this is not something that hits the headlines in a big way. Furthermore, the women who are often at the greatest risk are those whose partners or ex-partners have recently been released from prison. It is therefore not unreasonable to suggest that prison might not be the most appropriate response, or at least not the *only* response, that is needed to challenge this type of violence more generally.

The social location of researchers may serve to either increase or decrease the likelihood of being taken seriously by those who have the power to define 'the problem of crime'. For example, the issue of the way in which racial stereotypes are reproduced in political debates about crime can be explained by considering the ways in which the opinions of some researchers come to be seen as 'neutral' whilst those of other researchers are perceived to be 'biased' simply by virtue of the fact that they are put forward by a person who belongs to a minority group. In other words, it is important to understand how the views of those who have most power come to be perceived as 'normal' or even as representative of everyone in society, rather than of one group with one perspective amongst many.

⚹ KEY LEARNING POINTS

- When assessing the research of others and planning your own research you must be able to interrogate 'common sense'. In particular you should be able to identify the ways in which 'common sense' is constructed in media reporting about crime as this often forms part of the contextual backdrop to policy research.

- You need to learn how to judge the strength of evidence that is presented to the public. When a crime has been committed there is often a sense of moral outrage that is frequently fuelled by the media. Politicians will want to be seen to be responding to such outrage and they are quite likely to support harsh and inappropriate responses to crime in such circumstances, such as some of the custodial sentences meted out following the social disturbances in August 2011.

- It is your job as a researcher of crime to be mindful of the social processes outlined above and to identify, test out and question the theories that underpin responses to crime in society. Learning to critique the work of others (and by this is meant an assessment of the strengths and limitations of research) is an important first step in the process of doing research.

- Statistical evidence about crime rates is often the main way that people are convinced that changes need to be made – yet many people are unable to assess statistical information and instead they accept it in an uncritical way. Beginning researchers in criminology therefore need to be taught very early on how to raise important questions about the statistical information that often informs crime policy.

- New researchers should think carefully about where they will apply for funding, whether the questions they are asking are likely to be met with disapproval, and indeed whether they are sufficiently informed about their topic of concern to be considered the most appropriate person to carry out the research.

- Funders and the gatekeepers of research have the power to decide who should do what where. They can promote the theories which are in keeping with their macro and or micro political agendas as well as keep important issues off the agenda. Therefore a good strategy for all those researching crime is to assess the extent to which the ideals of the funding bodies match with their own theoretical assumptions. This means researching the agendas of the funding bodies before putting in applications. It will also be important to think through the feedback provided with unsuccessful applications in order to save time and energy in the future.

Student document

Article by Curry

Student document

Article by Hallsworth and Young

Chapter 2

The significance of criminological research

Understanding the philosophical roots of our claims to know about crime in society

GOALS OF THIS CHAPTER

At the end of reading this chapter and by completing the online resources that accompany it, you will be able to:

1 identify different ways of producing knowledge about crime;
2 begin to identify the relationship between theories of knowledge (*epistemologies*), theories of crime and methods;
3 judge the strength of claims 'to know';
4 think critically about crime.

OVERVIEW

- Research on crime can be carried out from within three key traditions.
- These traditions allow us to study crime from a variety of perspectives.
- Crime is a political issue therefore it does not make sense to claim 'neutrality'.
- Challenging neutrality is not a recipe for 'sloppy' research.
- For the above reasons we consider the importance of becoming a reflexive researcher and of thinking carefully about what is meant by 'objectivity'.
- The lessons from this chapter suggest that researchers need to think carefully about which knowledge claims are accepted, which ones are subordinated and on what grounds in order to challenge the stereotypes associated with stratifications such as ethnicity, gender, age and class.

In Chapter 1 we talked about the role of politics and values in research without mention of the different ways in which philosophical debates within social science in general have been divided on the issue of researcher neutrality. Many of you may well have thought that 'good' researchers must be neutral but you may not have thought about where that idea has come from or why you hold that view. This chapter seeks to ground our advice about how to do good quality criminological research in a discussion of theories of knowledge (**epistemology**). Theories about the nature of the world in which crimes take place (**ontology**) are also very important to the task of carrying out research, and as you will see as you progress through the book as a whole these two concepts are inter-related. We will talk about three basic theories of knowledge within which criminologists carry out their work: **positivism**, **interpretivism** and **critical criminological research**. We would include feminist criminological research under the heading of critical criminological research, with the exception of any approach that explains violence in terms of inherent biological differences, because these approaches seek to change the way we think about women's place in society and hence about the ways we come to understand crime.

You may also see references to post-modern research in some texts. Post-modernism is a term that is usually used to refer to a movement that commented on late twentieth-century culture and challenged the over-**determinism** of some Marxist structuralism in the social sciences and notions of truth. It is because of the refusal of post-modernists to arbitrate between competing 'truths' that we do not think these perspectives go beyond the insights of interpretivism. Similarly, whilst post-modernism acknowledges the place of values in research the assertion that all value positions are equal (see Neuman, 2006: 105) opens the door to oppression. We believe that post-modernism, whilst raising some important questions, is confusing in that it is characterised by extreme relativism that is simply not helpful when trying to understand and respond to the real problems that result from crime. As Harvey et al. (2000) note, post-modernists act as sceptics rather than critics. However, we would admit that post-modernism has a radical edge and that this perspective has highlighted some important issues. This is a topic to which you may wish to return further on in your studies but it is not one that we believe to be helpful at the early stages of research.

BOX 2.1 WHAT ARE THE CHARACTERISTICS OF A 'GOOD' PIECE OF RESEARCH?

Use this box to list what you think are the key features of a good piece of research. Return to your answers at the end of the chapter and then again when you have read the whole book! Has your opinion changed?

My notes . . .

Student video

Part 2 – values

Sometimes methodology textbooks dilute debates about research to a binary opposition between interpretivism and positivism, which use, respectively, qualitative and quantitative methods (for example look at http://www.ehow.com/info_8144495_qualitative-quantitative-research-methods.html). Other texts explain that the binary opposition between quantitative and qualitative methods hides the more nuanced views of many researchers these days, who utilise a variety of methods to obtain knowledge about the social world (e.g. Alexander *et al.,* 2008). However, we believe that it is important to have a basic understanding of the assumptions that underpin the three key theories of knowledge before beginning research as, even when researchers mix methods, they need to be clear about the assumptions they are making about the world they are researching and about the best way to carry out that research.

POSITIVISM

Students who are new to research are likely to have some understanding of what is meant by positivism – even if they are not familiar with the term. Positivism refers to an approach to research which largely copies the approach of science. The key assumptions are that there is a real world 'out there' that can be discovered or known. As positivists assume that it is possible to treat the social world in the same way as the natural world then the logical deduction from that premise is that the methods social scientists use should be the same as the methods used by 'natural' scientists. Natural scientists sometimes claim that they begin their research with the collection of 'facts'. Once facts have been collected (e.g. numbers and types of people who commit burglary), then it is assumed that theories can be developed from the facts. For example, if it was observed in many different places at different times that the main characteristic of a burglar was 'thinness' we could keep checking this out until we were sure that we had enough information to convince us that this characteristic is so significant that we could conclude that 'all burglars are thin'. This is what is known as 'the principle of **induction'** (see Chalmers, 2004: 41). Of course, it is easy to see that this is a frivolous example, although early criminologists did try to identify the physical features that were common to criminals (some of you may have heard of Lombroso, for example, who wrote *L'Uomo Delinquente [Criminal Man]* 1876). However, it may be that successful burglars do need to be reasonably slim and nimble in order to avoid being caught!

Induction involves a process of generalisation from a finite number of observations, which as the philosopher of science Karl Popper (1980) realised, is based upon flawed logic. For one thing what one person defines as 'thin' may not be the same as another so this means that in reality it is very difficult to observe in ways that exclude our values. More importantly, no matter how many times we confirm something we cannot really say that we have found 'the truth' because our next observation could always be the one that proves us wrong – the next burglar may be fat! Popper's view of science was therefore that researchers should maximise their chances of being proved wrong by setting up hypotheses and testing them out, rather than trying to gather evidence that confirms their theory. A method that begins with theory (rather than 'facts' or data) is called **deduction**. Popper did not think that we could collect facts that are free from values; we can say that 'facts' are always mediated by our values.

The criteria by which studies carried out in this framework are judged are reliability, representativeness, accuracy and validity (see also Chapter 9). It is assumed that research carried out within this framework can lead us to 'the objective truth' about crime and that it can explain why crimes occur. This approach to research will use quantitative methods as it is largely concerned with measuring concepts and with **correlations** between variables. It rejects interpretation as that is considered to be outside of science. This theory of knowledge also tends to take a deterministic approach which fails to acknowledge that human beings can act upon the world and are not simply acted upon. So for example, early biological positivists believed that criminals were born 'bad' and that they could be identified by their features. The implication of this is that criminals cannot change. A small proportion of radical feminists also asserted that men were 'by nature' more violent than women. This led them to the belief that the solution was for women to radically separate themselves from men and take control of reproduction (see Firestone 1970). This particular feminist perspective would not come under our definition of critical criminological research as this too denies the possibility of change and human agency. We call such assumptions *biological determinism*.

BOX 2.2 KEY TERMS EXPLAINED

Reliability: When positivists speak of reliability they are usually referring to the issue of whether the data are collected in the same way each time. In the previous chapter we suggested that crime statistics are *not* collected in the same way in all areas. As a simple rule of thumb think about whether you have been given sufficient information about how data were gathered in any given study in order for you to repeat the study in exactly the same way and come up with the same results.

Representativeness: This term relates to the issue of how far the data represent the group of people being researched. If researchers wish to generalise across the whole population of young people involved in crime in England, for example, it would be no use identifying a large group of 15-year-olds from one locality. Rather it would be necessary to specify what is meant by 'young people', e.g. 12–18 and to survey a cross-section from different areas – urban, suburban, rural, and from different class and cultural groups.

Accuracy: In order to have confidence in data collected we do need to know that researchers have made an effort to ensure that there are no mistakes in the mode of counting.

Validity: In positivism this term refers to the issue of whether the data collected actually measure the concepts being investigated. For example, if you wanted to test the theory that improved lighting in car parks reduced theft you would need to show that you had examined the levels of theft prior to the changes to the lighting and you would need to take into account other factors, for instance the installation of CCTV cameras to make valid claims about the benefits of improved lighting.

Some positivists assert that knowledge gained according to the rules of positivism is *superior* knowledge because it is not tainted by values or opinions. They believe that knowledge so derived can be used to control events in the future. As we shall see, and as we have already suggested to some extent in Chapter 1, the claims to superiority are open to question. This does not mean that studies carried out in this framework are not useful but rather that we need to be aware that just like any other framework it has limitations.

INTERPRETIVISM

As this name suggests interpretivists challenge the idea of an objective reality that can be grasped through research. They are more concerned with people's subjective understanding because they assert that the subject matter of the social world is completely different to that of the natural world. Thus their *ontological* assumptions differ from positivists'. In sociology and social psychology interpretivists have pointed out that as people are thinking and purposive beings it is entirely inappropriate to treat them as if they are 'things'. At its most extreme this framework asserts that reality can only be understood as consisting of those things of which we are conscious – the logic here being that if we are not conscious of something it does not exist in our experience. However, this extreme position is not held by everyone who works within this framework and we believe that such a position is problematic because things *do* exist beyond people's consciousness. For example, many of us may have been victims of crimes without knowing that a crime has taken place, such as the dilution of products like fresh juice or alcohol in a restaurant or bar. This sort of thing can happen on a grand scale and not be detected, but it does not mean that it has not happened. A more serious example is rape within marriage, which has only been a crime in England and Wales since 1992 yet women *were* being raped within marriage prior to that date and just because it was not then defined as a crime does not mean that their suffering was not a reality. However, a strength of the interpretivist approach is its ability to identify such suffering by speaking in depth to people and bringing the issue to light. (We will return to this when we consider the third approach, critical criminology.) Interpretivists have carried out important studies through which criminologists have gained knowledge about the ways in which those who break the law see the world. Some interesting examples are cited by Punch (2009: 179–81), who has documented some of the ways in which qualitative studies have revealed how police officers become corrupt. The various data reveal that corrupt cops rationalise their own criminality and construct their victims as deserving of their victimhood – in fact their rationalisations are just like those associated with the 'more usual' suspects.

Researchers operating within the interpretivist theory of knowledge contest the notion that knowledge derived from the positivist epistemology is superior. Instead they would argue that positivistic knowledge is simply a different kind of knowledge than that gained using qualitative methods. For interpretivists it is important to access the life worlds of those being studied in order to understand the meaning of their actions to them. This seems to us to be quite important if we are to address the issue of crime in society.

It is hard to carry out qualitative studies that are easily repeated. Criminologists who carry out studies within this framework prefer to talk to people in depth or to observe the life worlds of criminals. These data do not lend themselves to measurement therefore it is not appropriate to judge them by the criteria used to judge quantitative data. When the term validity is used in **qualitative research** it does not refer to the issue of how far the researcher has measured what s/he set out to measure but rather it refers to the question of whether the researcher has managed to convey an authentic account from the viewpoint of those being researched and whether the conclusions drawn by the researcher are plausible. Within this perspective the important issue is not so much whether a research participant tells 'the whole truth' but rather how a participant constructs the truth in different circumstances. This can reveal quite a lot about the decision-making processes that criminals go through prior to committing a crime. It can also reveal quite a lot about how criminals convince themselves that what they are doing is not wrong. Researchers can increase confidence in their findings if they are able to provide a detailed account of the ways in which their own role as the researcher may have impacted upon the findings. This is called **reflexivity** – see below.

CRITICAL CRIMINOLOGICAL RESEARCH

Critical criminologists are concerned with examining the ways in which we come to accept the world as it is. This means that the route to knowledge is via theoretical understanding of the mechanisms through which we make sense of our world. If we take the example of marital rape again, a concern of many feminists, it becomes apparent that there was for a long time an uncritical acceptance in society of men's rights to women's bodies once they were married. Without knowledge and understanding of the relations of power through which this view was maintained the law would not have been changed because the notion of a 'conjugal right' was accepted by both men *and* women (although not *all* men and women). It was only after considerable campaigns by feminist writers that the laws in relation to rape were changed. As Oakley (2002) has argued, definitions of crime have largely been formed by middle-class males and we might add oftentimes in the interests of that same group. One of us (the oldest!) has been shocked in recent years to find that many students were not only unaware of the fact that rape within marriage is a crime but that they were also puzzled by the notion of rape within marriage. This is an indication of the ways in which attitudes can remain untouched long after the legislation has changed. The ways in which these attitudes are formed are therefore of interest to critical researchers who are concerned with the ways in which oppressions are both produced and reproduced in our everyday lives through socialisation processes and media representations, for example. Critical criminologists' ontological position is that the social world is multi-layered and has hidden structures through which oppressive practices are maintained. These structures have real effects on people's lives therefore research has to expose them in order to bring about change.

As critical criminologists concern themselves with oppressive practices their research questions address issues such as why poor and black minority ethnic (BME) groups are over-represented in prison; why the crimes of the powerful attract lesser punishments (or perhaps no real punishment at all); why some victims are denied justice. This means that researchers within this perspective often take a longer, historical approach in order to examine the ways in which society has been organised over time and in whose interests. The *ontological* position is that reality is constructed in different ways in different times and places (so here they agree with interpretivists), but at the same time they try to show how these constructions have what we might call semi-permanence and how they impact upon people's lives, that is, these semi-permanent structures have real effects. In this sense there is, according to this view, a reality to discover, as positivists would assert − if for different purposes.

The purpose of critical criminology is to reveal the ways in which economic, political and social structures shape our definitions of crime (see White and Haines 2004: 203). There is always an acknowledgement of the political and moral dimension to research in this approach; therefore critical criminologists are unashamed to speak up about the values they hold. When researchers are overt about their value position it is possible for others to understand the grounds upon which they make their judgements whilst remaining free to agree or disagree. Unlike those in the other research traditions we have discussed, critical criminologists do not fight shy of speaking out about values − the ones they hold as well as those they believe to be problematic. Usually critical criminological researchers draw a line under the values that produce or reproduce oppression of those who have the least power in society. This means that research carried out within this framework will focus on the crimes of the powerful *as well as* on those of the less powerful. Critical criminology aims to explain the reasons why different types of crimes are committed within different social contexts and to explain why crimes are responded to differently according to where, when and who has committed them.

Student quiz

Theories of knowledge

Instructor PPoint Slides

Values and research

BOX 2.3 KEY TERMS EXPLAINED: *EPISTEMOLOGY AND ONTOLOGY*

Epistemology is a rather grand way of referring to a theory of knowledge. Social scientists have theorised for many years about the best way to gather knowledge on the social world and in the early days it was thought that social scientists should copy natural scientists. Today it is accepted that there is more than one way to produce knowledge and criminologists, like all social scientists, have to make decisions about the most appropriate way to obtain knowledge about the issue they wish to research. It is not useful to think about the different theories of knowledge as if they can be ordered from best to worst but instead it is a good idea to think about how each approach can lead to different types of knowledge that can help us to gain a fuller understanding of crime in society.

Ontology is another grand term that refers to theorists' assumptions about the nature of the social world and the people in it. It is often defined as referring to the 'nature of being'.

These explanations serve to provide the justification for radical changes to the ways in which we define and respond to crime with the aim of creating a 'more humane and equal society' (White and Haines: 2004: 211).

The methods used by critical criminological researchers will reflect the concerns they have and the questions they ask. This means that the quantitative/qualitative split is challenged by this group of researchers in favour of an approach that attempts to break down and offer alternatives for our conceptualisations of and responses to crime. Critical criminological researchers may well combine methods but they will want to go beyond both statistical measures and individual meanings in order to enhance theoretical understanding.

OBJECTIVITY: THE SECRET WEAPON

In Chapter 1 we alluded to the ways in which notions of value neutrality tend to be invoked as a way of demonstrating the superiority of some research over others. For researchers who do not carry out their research within a positivist framework it is important that they are able to defend their position when confronted with such comments. Edwards and Sheptycki (2009) have argued that criminologists need to understand both the politics and science of criminology; we believe that it is important to understand the relationship between these two issues as the invocation of 'science' is often the tool by which knowledge that challenges the status quo is undermined. Positivists talk about objectivity in research but when they use this term they are often also signifying value neutrality. If objectivity is deemed to be a sign of 'good' research then any research that can be labelled as 'subjective' will, by definition, be 'bad'.

Let's take a wander outside of criminology for a moment in order to borrow an analogy used by Lincoln and Cannella (2004) when considering the ways in which qualitative research in the US, which aimed to expose inequalities along the lines of class, gender, 'race' and sexual orientation in social life and schooling, was discredited. Their argument begins with recognition of the fact that serious philosophers have discredited the pursuit of objectivity as a key criterion with which to judge social research precisely because objectivity (presumably defined as value-neutrality) is an illusion. However, they argue that despite this the notion of objectivity is used as both a weapon – with which to discredit qualitative research – and a shield with which to protect those who claim superiority for their 'objective' scientific research from criticism.

Within social research general debates about the need to challenge sexism and racism in society raised important questions about the ways in which knowledge is produced. In particular, research that aimed to challenge the subordination of women and BME groups in society asked searching questions about whose science dominant knowledge has been based upon. Sandra Harding (1991: 87) grappled with science's 'insistence on its own absolute authority'. She made a strong argument against claims of value freedom by pointing to the consequences of scientific knowledge. She notes that some 'pure scientists' claim to have carried out actions in the name of science in ignorance of their possible consequences, a claim which she sees as evidence of incompetence rather than 'objectivity'. Harding (1991: 146) states that 'the best as well as the worst of the history of the natural sciences has been shaped by – or, more accurately, constructed through and within – political desires, interests and values'. It therefore is nonsensical to claim that objectivity can be achieved by *eliminating* values. Indeed Harding implies that if we do not admit to this nonsense then scientists are simply being allowed to abrogate responsibility for whatever follows from their knowledge claims.

Following the insights of the science historian Donna Haraway, Harding explains that the logic of value-free objectivity (which she calls *weak* objectivity) is that the only knowledge that counts is that which is obtained from 'no place at all' (the assumption being that a scientist can be 'every place at once') (Harding 1991: 153), which, she explains, is why Haraway used the phrase 'the God trick'. To put this simply, since we can't be all-seeing – like God – then we have to come at our research from different angles because we are all situated differently in society. So, the point is that those who have had most power to produce knowledge (historically this has been middle-class white men) have produced knowledge from one angle, which is not wide enough to gain a complete picture of our complex social lives. Therefore, if others with less power are allowed to do research from their angle then it is possible to build up a more complete picture of this complexity.

It is interesting that the association of objectivity with value-neutrality is so strong that some research has been criticised on what we believe are flawed grounds. For example, Claire Alexander (2000) has commented on reactions to her ethnographic study of Asian gangs. She submitted an article about the negative media portrayals of Asian communities in Britain to THES. The article had been agreed in principle with the editor but because she was late she dropped the article off in person. At this point it became apparent to Claire Alexander that the editor had not thought 'Dr Claire Alexander' would be an Asian woman. After the meeting the editor's view appeared to change and Claire Alexander was informed that her research was 'too subjective' because she was 'too close' to her subject matter. This experience led Alexander to argue for the explicit partiality of the ethnographic voice. She asks why white researchers are not accused of being 'too subjective' when they research white people. She might also have asked why it is assumed that all people who are grouped under one label are assumed to be 'alike' when if we think carefully about this we are more likely to acknowledge that there is diversity within as well as between the different groups that we label in society.

When second wave feminists asked 'What is the relationship between power and knowledge?' they were pointing to the fact that white men identified social problems and constructed research questions from their particular perspective. They thought that the knowledge they produced would help to solve problems for women not just men. Feminist studies drew attention to the ways in which subjectivity is crucial to the research design because only women can know what it is like to experience gender oppression. Knowledge that is produced from a standpoint is less – not more – distorted than knowledge that tries to erase or deny its partiality. It was, of course, important that white middle-class women were sensitised to the ways in which their claims about women's experiences needed to take account of differences between women – the same tools that had been used to question (white) male-centred knowledge needed to be used to question white female knowledge (see debates in Somekh and Lewin, 2009, and you might also want to look at original arguments by Sandra Harding, bell hooks and Patricia Hill-Collins). It was as a result of dialogues between different feminists that white middle-class feminists were sensitised to the fact that they could not and, we would argue, should not, try to speak on behalf of all women. Black women realised that their experiences were not the same as white women's experiences, even if there were some commonalities. In fact sexism was not usually the biggest problem for black women because the effects of racism in their lives often outweighed gender oppression. A recent illustration of this comes from the literature on the introduction of restorative justice in countries such as New Zealand, Australia and Canada where there are marginalised indigenous people. These studies have shown that western-style traditional criminal justice systems consistently failed to address the needs of indigenous people whereas the restorative responses within their own communities worked significantly better. However, when it came to issues such as domestic violence it became clear that women could not get justice in either system; in the state systems they were met with racist attitudes but in their own communities the gender inequalities were increased (see Nancarrow, 2006; Cameron, 2006; Daly and Stubbs, 2006). Without research from the perspective of these women such issues would not be identified and therefore would not be addressed.

Whilst the above provides a very over-simplified account of some complex arguments we hope to have conveyed that objectivity and value-neutrality should be seen as analytically distinct. Harding (1991) calls this *strong* objectivity because it allows researchers to be clear about their standpoint and it also acknowledges that the perspective of the researcher influences the knowledge that is produced. This acknowledgement of the partiality of *all* research is, of course, discomforting to those who have used their so-called 'neutral' science as a shield to protect them from critique and as a weapon with which to put down other forms of research. Studies that have aimed to address social problems, such as crime, have often left out the perspectives of the very people about whom they were supposedly concerned.

Cowburn's (2007) article engages with important epistemological debates which suggest that it is not necessarily the gender (and we could add 'race'/ethnicity/age/disability, etc.) of the researcher which is important to the task of uncovering oppressive practices through research but rather it is the *attitude* of the researcher. Not all male researchers behave in oppressive ways towards women and nor do all white researchers

---

BOX 2.4 STUDENT ACTIVITY: CAN MEN CARRY OUT PRO-FEMINIST RESEARCH?

Read Cowburn (2007) 'Men Researching Men in Prison: The Challenges for Pro-Feminist Research', *Howard Journal,* 46(3): 276–88.

Note down your reactions to Cowburn's discussion as you read. Try to jot down reasons why you agree/disagree with him.

behave in ways that oppress black people, although it is fair to say that many do not recognise their oppressive practices. This means that it is not enough to suggest that if research is carried out by a member of an oppressed group then that oppression will automatically be addressed. It *is* possible that some people who belong to groups whose voices are often subordinated to white males can reproduce their own oppression by failing to take a stand against some issues – and perhaps even by dismissing some issues as 'political correctness gone mad'. One of us has used this article in teaching and has been struck by the failure of some female as well as some male students to take issue with the fact that a Senior Officer in the prison said he would have to 'smack the bottom' of the female member of staff who allowed Cowburn to go unescorted to the lavatory (2007: 283). Several students saw this as 'harmless' and said the inclusion of this incident in the article was evidence of 'bias' on the part of the researcher. Did you think the same? We believe that these responses reveal the level of acceptance of some oppressive practices in society as well as a general misunderstanding of what is meant by bias. In fact Cowburn goes to great lengths to tell us about the way he carried out his research; he is a *reflexive* researcher.

Cowburn's discussion suggests that we need to think carefully about what we mean when we take a position in the process of doing research. He is not advocating taking sides in the sense of, for instance, taking the prisoners' sides over prison officers' (or vice versa). Rather he is grappling with the need to challenge oppressive practices, wherever they occur, that result in the subordination of the needs of whole groups of people. The logic of his discussion, in the context of his work relating to sex crimes, is that if we are to address properly crimes of a sexual nature then it is important to challenge sexism in general. It is because of sexism that some males are able to justify their crimes and that some female victims of rape are not believed. The fear of not being believed, or indeed of being constructed as partly responsible for the attack, is often enough to prevent women from speaking out at all about this crime. When this idea is coupled with racist ideas, for example about 'black hyper-sexuality', then the already

---

BOX 2.5 BECOMING A REFLEXIVE RESEARCHER

Recognising values in the work of others is an important element in the process of becoming a good reflexive researcher who has a heightened awareness of his/her own value positions. In everyday life people make decisions constantly that are shaped by the values they hold, but it is often the case that they are not conscious of where those values come from or even why they are held. Indeed, many people who are not involved in academic research have neither the time nor the inclination to reflect upon the values they hold so researchers are privileged in this respect. Cowburn provides a detailed account of the way in which he carried out his research, what he assumed, how his values impacted upon the whole process and how he made efforts to enable the reader to understand how and why he made his judgements.

difficult task of speaking out becomes even more difficult for black women than it is for white or Asian women. Without research that started from the perspective of different women this knowledge would not have been revealed.

Similarly, the kind of racism in society which is at the heart of beliefs about 'black people's inherent propensity to violence' will prevent female victims of non-sexual violence from speaking out. Unlike their white counterparts, black women will often weigh up whether it is worth speaking out because they are aware, in a way that white people do not need to be, that speaking out about violence will bring discredit to *all* 'black' communities. As we write there are concerns about racism in the ranks of Scotland Yard. It has emerged that a report written by Brian Piddick in 2004, when he was a Met commander, warned about the need for tougher action against officers who were discriminating against black people (Dodd, 2012). This report was buried and the warnings were ignored but the fact remains that police officers have operated with the false assumption that black people are more likely to be involved in crime, which has resulted in stop and search being used disproportionately against black people, which in turn has fuelled discontent and mistrust of the police in some communities.

Asian women who are victims of violence within the private sphere face yet another set of problems that differ from both black and white women's experiences. As Burman *et al.* (2004: 332) argue:

> Domestic violence emerges as something that can be overlooked or even excused for 'cultural reasons', as a homogenized absence; or alternatively as a pathologized presence, producing heightened visibility of minoritized women both within and outside their communities – since domestic violence brings them and their communities under particular scrutiny.

CAN/SHOULD WHITE PEOPLE DO RESEARCH ON BLACK PEOPLE?

Many black researchers have noted that being black does not necessarily mean that a researcher will challenge racial oppression. Indeed, an insight from feminism that has been relevant in researching race and racism is that people can reproduce their own oppressions. It is therefore more important that the researcher takes an overtly anti-racist stance. In my own recent experience researching black youth in the criminal justice system I was part of a team of largely white researchers – this was problematic because it was difficult to gain access to the research participants. It became clear from the data, however, that participants were not necessarily trusting of the black professionals with whom they had come into contact – they described black prison 'screws', for example, as worse than their white counterparts on some occasions. In interpreting such data it is necessary to think about the ways in which black people may internalise racial oppression as well as think about the difficulties involved in challenging the received wisdom of those with most power.

CONCLUSION

We have seen that criminological research can be carried out from within three key philosophical traditions, each of which produce different types of knowledge about our world. Criminology has been dominated by the positivist theory of knowledge but we have tried to show through our discussion of interpretivism and critical criminological research that this theory of knowledge has some significant limitations. This is not to say that positivism is bad and the other research traditions are good (they too have limitations) but rather to highlight the need to study the problem of crime in society from a variety of angles in order to gain a more complete picture of what is going on. Good researchers should be aware of the assumptions they are making and should provide reasons for their line of enquiry. This means that researchers should always take time to reflect upon the judgements they have made during the process of their research and be prepared to challenge their own preconceptions on the basis of new evidence.

KEY LEARNING POINTS

- There is a tendency for beginners to criminological research to take a rather narrow view about how knowledge should be gathered. This reveals quite a lot about the power of scientific discourse in society.
- Criminological researchers must go beyond *common-sense* understandings of science in order to gain respect for their knowledge claims.
- All research will have strengths and limitations, the confidence we have in any research should not depend upon the theory of knowledge that has informed the research but rather on the integrity of the researcher and her/his attention to detail about the research process.
- It is important to raise questions about the ways in which we define crime in society since definitions of crime reveal quite a lot about the moral values that underpin the law.
- If criminological researchers were to put aside their values in the research process then bad laws would not be changed and new ones would not be developed as, despite appearances, what counts as crime changes over time and from place to place. In other words there is *not* total consensus about what is right and what is wrong or about who should be defined as criminal. This means that it is important to take a critical position but this is not always a necessary condition for research.
- It is interesting that critical approaches to social research in general and to criminological research in particular are often constructed as 'biased', yet research that blames oppressed groups for their social conditions without taking a look at the impact of wider social structures on their lives could be said to hide behind a false neutrality.

Chapter 3

The ethics of criminological research

GOALS OF THIS CHAPTER

At the end of reading this chapter and by completing the online resources that accompany it, you will:

1   be aware of key ethical principles and of the Codes of Practice of the British Society of Criminology and other related professional associations;
2   be able to understand why it is important to take ethics seriously;
3   be able to identify the different stances on ethics;
4   be able to make judgements about what you consider to be/not to be acceptable practices within the context of criminological research;
5   be able to make wise ethical decisions when carrying out your own research.

OVERVIEW

- Ethical principles have been developed for good reasons.
- Professional associations, such as the British Society of Criminology, provide important ethical guidance with which researchers should make themselves familiar.
- However, blind adherence to a set of seemingly neutral principles can sometimes aid the concealment of personal and political motives that may run counter to the interests of research participants, researchers themselves or indeed to public interest in general.
- There are different stances on ethics that reflect the complexities of ethical decision-making. Ethical decisions are underpinned by different value positions so it is up to researchers to think carefully about and discuss their justifications for the conduct of their research process.
- New researchers should have knowledge and understanding of the bases upon which ethical judgements are made in the research of others in order to be better equipped to make the most appropriate ethical judgements themselves.

KEY ETHICAL PRINCIPLES

Since 'ethics is concerned with the attempt to formulate codes and principles of moral behaviour' (May, 2001: 59) then it is bound to be underpinned by values about what is good or bad conduct in research.

In previous chapters we have encouraged you to think about the moral dilemmas that face criminologists who wish to carry out the sort of research that might challenge those who hold the most power in society. In this chapter we will encourage you to think about ethics in a similar way. That is, we hope that by the end of the chapter you will not just think of ethics as a set of 'neutral' principles or guidelines that are to be followed in all circumstances, but as a set of principles that are underpinned by values, which are always open to question because the context of research varies.

We begin by outlining the key ethical principles that underpin professional associations' guidance on research ethics. Later in the chapter we shall develop a discussion about these key principles through which you will begin to gain more understanding of the complexities of ethical decision-making. You can think of these principles in the first instance as a set of rules, which should guide your research, but eventually we hope that you will gain a deeper understanding that will enable you to appreciate the different circumstances in which failure to adhere to some principles might be justified. There is an old saying one of us likes to use: 'rules are for the guidance of the wise and the observance of the foolish' which seems very pertinent to our discussion of ethics. We hope that you will eventually come to think of ethical principles as wise guidelines rather than rules that should be followed blindly in all circumstances. However, as the British Sociological Association ethical statement suggests (point 4, page 1) any departures from the main ethical principles should 'be the result of deliberation not ignorance'.

You can find the British Society of Criminology's code of ethics at http://britsoccrim.org/new/?q=node/22. More detailed guidance can be obtained from the British Sociological Association (http://www.britsoc.co.uk/media/27107/Statement ofEthicalPractice.pdf) and from the British Psychological Society (http://www.bps.org.uk) and from the Social Research Association (http://the-sra.org.uk/sra_resources/research-ethics/ethics-cases/).

In general criminological researchers must demonstrate that they are competent to carry out their chosen research project; that they have respect for everyone involved in the research process in any way; that they act responsibly at all times in order to avoid harm to participants, the research community and society in general. The various professional ethical guidance documents for social scientists have converted this general guidance into some clear principles, which are outlined in Table 3.1 below. However, we stress that new researchers should always discuss the ethical considerations with a lecturer/supervisor who will be able to offer guidance and a critical view. Whilst we encourage you to think carefully about the ethical issues to which research gives rise we do not think that it is appropriate to begin conducting research without having had the ethics of that research considered and approved by the lecturer/supervisor and, where appropriate, the university ethics committee.

Table 3.1 Upholding ethical principles

Principles	How to uphold them
Gain informed consent/ avoid deceit	• Provide as much information as is possible about your research to the proposed participants bearing in mind that it might sometimes be appropriate to withhold some information in order to ensure that participants do not change their normal behaviour.
	• Ask the participants to sign a form which provides proof that they consented to their role in the research process.
	• Make special provision for children and vulnerable adults – see below.
	• Do not be coercive.
	• Think carefully about the relationship between your research question and the methods needed to answer it. If you are unable to answer your research questions using overt methods you will need to weigh up the risks of using covert methods against the benefits to society of the knowledge likely to be produced.
	• If you decide that deception is your only option then it may be important in situations where the 'subjects' of research could be damaged by the findings to debrief those observed at the end of the data-gathering process.
Maintain confidentiality	• Sign a statement of confidentiality and give it to your participants.
	• Use pseudonyms.
	• Be careful about how you store data and destroy them as soon as possible.
	• Ensure that the data you publish do not help to reveal the identity of your participants (for example by describing the geographical location too precisely or by using a quotation that would facilitate the identity of the setting or key individuals).
Safeguard those involved in/ affected by the research – AVOID HARM	• Be aware of relevant laws, e.g. Human Rights Act, Data Protection Act.
	• Respect internet user agreements.
	• Provide information about help/support groups in research that is likely to raise sensitive issues.
	• Make sure that your participants are aware that they may withdraw at any time should the research begin to cause problems for them.
	• Do not take unnecessary risks that could result in avoidable physical or emotional harm to you, the research participants or the public in general.
	• Do not try to carry out research that takes you outside of your competence and could therefore bring disrepute to the community of researchers.
	• Do not accept funding from bodies that have objectives that differ from your own.
	• Use appropriate research techniques and do not make claims that go beyond your evidence.
	• Consider how your findings might be used/abused.

TAKING ETHICS SERIOUSLY

We need to take ethics seriously because no research should cause severe harm to human beings. If we are to continue to learn more about the problems that arise in our social world then it is important that researchers do their best to prevent any discredit to research communities. Unsurprisingly then, the over-riding justification that is usually provided for the development of ethical principles is that no-one should be harmed by research. This means that, irrespective of the questions asked, it is generally accepted that the human beings taking part in our research come first, even before the pursuit of knowledge, which is at the heart of all science – natural or social. If your research is likely to cause harm of any kind then this should (at least in the first instance) indicate the need to think again. As Bryman (2008: 146) notes, ethical considerations impinge on all scientific research but particularly in the social sciences.

In order to become an ethical researcher you will need to draw upon your own moral conscience and think about the consequences of the ways in which you are proposing to carry out your research. It will not be possible to second guess every eventuality that may arise in the process of your research at the proposal stage but taking the time to think through the possible ethical dilemmas as early as possible will at least ensure that any harms are minimal. As we have suggested in earlier chapters, it is a good idea to look at other people's research in order to familiarise yourself with some of the pitfalls which have beset other studies as this is a good way of avoiding similar mistakes in your own work. Reading about ethical decision-making will also clarify your own moral values and thereby allow you to present justifications for the ethical decisions you make in your research.

Taking ethics seriously does not *just* mean making sure that you think about ethics at the planning stage of research. Despite researchers' best efforts unforeseen ethical dilemmas may arise during the process of conducting research. These dilemmas arise precisely because no matter how hard we try we can never make accurate predictions in advance about human behaviour. Thus when an ethical dilemma arises mid-research the researcher will need to be careful to record the circumstances in which the dilemma arose, the decision she/he took and the justifications for that decision. As noted above, when researchers take the time to reflect upon and record their actions in relation to ethical dilemmas they will be helping new researchers to learn from their experiences.

Criminological research is a particularly thorny area because the issues crim-inologists wish to research are often highly sensitive and therefore the potential to harm is ever present. So far so good – but all this does beg the question of whether it is always possible to agree on what might constitute harm. Indeed, it might be necessary to construct what we might call a hierarchy of harms because some people may consider that certain (lesser) harms can be justified on the grounds that they reduce the likelihood of more serious harms occurring (or recurring) in the future. This implies that researchers need to be able to think through the consequences of their ethical decisions throughout the whole process of research in order to take account not just of the participants in the research but also of the group/s of people for whom the research is intended as well as the wider population which may be affected by the results. This means that making ethical decisions is a very complex process that, whilst guided by a set of principles, cannot be dealt with in a rule-bound way that assumes these principles can be followed in the same way in all times, places and contexts.

BOX 3.1 LEARNING FROM THE PAST: REAL ETHICAL DILEMMAS

Background

Before looking at ethics specifically in criminological research we want to introduce you to a world-famous social scientific study on obedience by Milgram (1963). This study is mentioned in a wide variety of social science research texts because, although it is an old study, it continues to inform debates about ethics in social research.

Milgram chose methods that included *deception.* The participants in his study believed that their role was to administer electric shocks to other participants in the research ('learners') when they made mistakes. In fact the learners were 'in on the act' so they were not research participants. Nor did they receive electric shocks but they put on an act to convince the real participants that they had.

As a result of your consideration of this study we hope that you will be better equipped to discuss and justify your own ethical decisions.

The context of Milgram's research

Milgram was interested to discover the extent to which people would obey an authority figure without question, even in circumstances where obedience would result in obvious harm to another human being. His interest in this topic was in part sparked by the seemingly 'blind obedience' of some German people during World War II who took part in Nazi atrocities.

Milgram made concerted efforts to weigh up the possible adverse effects of his chosen method of research. He sought advice from psychiatrists who were not of the opinion that the participants would be likely to administer the most severe 'shocks'. Milgram therefore decided that the psychological harm to the participants would be minimal. Milgram also ensured that he debriefed his participants and revealed his deceit so that he could minimise the ill-effects to the participants. A psychiatrist also saw the participants a year later and no problems were identified.

The participants' roles

Participants in Milgram's research were told the study was about the effects of punishment on learning. Their role was to administer 'electric shocks' to learners (who, they were led to believe, were also participants in the research) each time they made a mistake in a given learning activity. The researcher explained to these participants that the shocks were to increase in severity following each mistake. In situations where the learner cried out in 'pain' or complained of a serious medical condition, the researcher ordered the participants to continue with the shocks, which caused the participants to show signs of stress, such as sweating, nail-biting or trembling.

Whilst the experiment itself was tension-producing Milgram was happy that following the full de-briefing sessions the ill-effects of the experiment were short-lived. He believed that his experiment was ethically justifiable. What do you think? Try to provide reasons for your answer.

Now take a look at the more recent study by Cowburn (2007) to which we referred in Chapter 2. Was Cowburn behaving ethically in his interview with 'Martin'? Why/why not?

You can find further discussion of this on the companion website.

ETHICAL STANCES (OPENING CANS OF WORMS)

We have already hinted that there is more to ethics than following a set of rules. Having set out key principles and guidelines we are now going to explain why we believe that researchers should always consider the ethics of each individual piece of research on a case by case basis. This is sometimes called *situated* ethics or **consequentialism**. We prefer the latter term as it signals the need to consider the consequences of our ethical decisions, a process which allows us to weigh up benefits against harms. We hold this view because we are aware that in *some* contexts accepted ethical principles can not only serve to prevent the production of important knowledge (see Calvey, 2008), but also serve to maintain the interests of those who are already most powerful in society.

Some methodology textbooks go into long explanations about the different stances on ethics, which can serve to over-complicate the debates for those who are new to research. We prefer to think about a continuum, one end of which represents a universal position, in which it is assumed that the agreed ethical principles should be followed at all times as if they are inviolable rules, whilst the other end represents a position in which ethical principles can be thrown to the wind in the interests of knowledge production.

We do not believe that either of these positions at the extremes is tenable but, as we have already indicated, rather, we do think that there are contexts in which it may be justifiable to question the merits of some generally agreed ethical principles. Our position is underpinned by the belief that researchers should always be mindful of the consequences of their ethical decisions. We might assume that this is also the position of the largest social research funding council in the UK, the Economic and Social Research Council (ESRC) since, for example, as Calvey (2008: 907) observes, its Research Ethics Framework acknowledges that there are situations in which covert observation (a method of data collection which involves deception) may be justified. However, we are inclined to agree with Calvey's belief that 'covert research is effectively

Universalism   Consequentialism   Absolute relativism

Figure 3.1 Ethics continuum

stigmatised in the research world' (2008: 907) because in practice the proliferation of ethics committees, increased fears about risks and the increasing regulation of research have all served to privilege some forms of research over others rather than to alert new researchers to the situations in which any one of the generally agreed ethical principles might need to be questioned. As Carrabine *et al.* (2009: 42) have asked, 'is a criminologist working within tight ethical codes still able to conduct effective research into closed worlds ... such as the closed worlds of child sexual abuse, people trafficking or corporate crime?' We believe that new researchers should be taught to think critically about the contexts in which their research takes place so that they may be enabled to make wise ethical decisions.

Informed consent

With the above discussion in mind we now wish to examine the principle of informed consent. Whilst most research methods do not, at least overtly, challenge this principle, research which relies upon covert observational methods makes the notion of informed consent redundant. As some readers may be aware, much research on crime and 'deviance' has relied upon covert methods. For example, over the years covert observational studies have allowed researchers to reveal, amongst other things, detailed information about juvenile gangs (Parker, 1974); salesmen on the fiddle (Ditton, 1977); police practices (Holdaway, 1983); crack dealers (Jacobs, 2006); and trafficking in body parts (Scheper-Hughes, 2004). Unerring compliance with the principle of informed consent would rule out such research, which, we hope you will agree, would be detrimental to the study of crime. So, instead we wish to draw attention to some situations in which we believe adherence to this principle should be maintained whilst pointing to other situations where we believe the opposite position to be true. Furthermore, we wish to point out that the apparent adherence to the ethical principle of informed consent may serve to obscure the messiness, or what Calvey (2008: 907) calls the 'blurred reality', of fieldwork.

Quantitative techniques of data gathering lend themselves much more readily to the ethical principle of informed consent. In situations where researchers set up experiments in order to try to find out about the limits of human behaviour, for example, if a psychological study aimed to gain deeper understanding of the situations in which

---

BOX 3.2 STUDENT ACTIVITY: INFORMED CONSENT

Take another look at Cowburn's (2007) research on men in prison, to which we referred in Chapter 2.

Consider whether the participants in his research should have been informed about his concern with sexism. Try to provide ethical justifications for your view on this issue. In order to do this you should think about how far the means of research justified the ends and consider the extent to which other important ethical principles have been applied.

Student video

Part 1 – ethics discussion

human beings will become violent, they may well be able to gain meaningful consent, but if the participants were to be *fully* informed they might change their behaviour and thereby invalidate the experiment. In such circumstances the researcher has to weigh up whether/how far the deceit will result in harm to research participants, researchers or the public interest in general. Beins (2004: 44) states that 'there is good reason to believe that keeping participants ignorant of some aspects of the research has negligible effects on them in general'. We can deduce from this that there are degrees of deception, the most extreme of which are likely to occur in covert studies. Beins (2004) makes a useful distinction between active and passive deception in which the latter is seen as more justifiable since it does not involve the researcher in telling lies about what is going on (as in the Milgram study, cited above) but rather it involves withholding some information in order to avoid the problem of research participants changing their normal modes of behaviour (as in Cowburn's study). Passive deception can occur in any form of research but it is most likely to occur when qualitative methods, such as in-depth interviewing or overt observation, are utilised. This is the case because in situations where researchers are trying to access the meanings that participants give to their actions and possibly theorise about how these meanings may have come about (say through consideration of their acceptance of racist or sexist assumptions) revealing the full purpose of their study would very likely compromise the data.

Informed consent can only be gained, of course, when the participants are capable of providing it. Researchers therefore need to think about how they will deal with a situation in which the subjects of their research are unable to understand what the research is all about or what the consequences might be for them, that is special provision must be made to protect the rights of children and vulnerable adults by gaining consent from someone who has their interests at heart. Linda Moore (2011) provides a good discussion of her research with children in custody which outlines some of the difficulties involved in gaining consent from children. Where doubts about a child's ability to give meaningful consent arise she advises that researchers seek the advice of professionals.

Informed consent constitutes an important aspect of many types of research but there is no doubt that there are situations in which the gaining of consent may render the research ineffective. Where the research topic suggests that meaningful and useful data could not be gained other than through the use of covert methods then researchers should try as far as possible to weigh up the risks involved in carrying out their chosen study. When this method of data gathering is chosen it is especially important that the researcher should be more acutely aware of the ethical dilemmas that may arise in the process of their research. Furthermore they should be capable of defending their actions. Note that the most common defence of the use of covert methods relies upon adherence to another ethical principle, confidentiality, which we shall discuss below.

Producing an informed consent form

In studies where it is appropriate to gain informed consent you will need to produce a form which you and your participants should sign. In general your form should include the following:

- the title of your study;
- name/s and contact details of the researchers;
- a clear and concise description of the purpose of your research;
- an outline of the possible benefits or risks of taking part;
- your guarantee of anonymity and confidentiality (note that you will need to remember to store the form safely in order to maintain anonymity);
- your guarantee to respect the participants' rights to withdraw at any time (which you should sign);
- agreement sections which relate to the collection and storage of data.

Some people produce two forms, one which informs the participants and a consent form. We think it makes things clearer if the information is on one form but follow your university's guidance on this point. Most universities will provide students with guidance on producing a consent form. We also recommend that you look at the examples we have provided on the companion website.

Student guide to ... Consent forms

Of course, it is possible that your research may involve the participation of children or vulnerable adults. In these circumstances it is not possible to gain their informed consent so you will need to consider who can be approached to give consent on their behalf. Sometimes organisations will have their own rules and procedures and it is your duty as a researcher to find out what these are and make sure that you follow them. It is also your responsibility to undergo a Disclosure and Barring Service (DBS) check when conducting research with children or vulnerable adults.

Student guide to ... Informing participants and interview protocols

Note that as your research progresses you may realise that the original purpose of your study has changed (this is why good researchers keep a reflexive journal so that they can record the reasons for any shifts in purpose or perspective). In such circumstances you would need to decide whether you would need to produce another consent form for your research participants. Whilst **reflexivity** about ethics is seen as a must for those carrying out covert studies as Calvey (2008: 909) points out 'covert practices are routinely glossed over in sanitised overt accounts'.

Confidentiality and anonymity

We have seen above that the principle of informed consent is not applied in a universal way to all research. Where informed consent is obtained it is usual for the researcher to guarantee confidentiality and anonymity in order to ensure that participants and, where applicable, the organisations to which they belong cannot be harmed as a result of taking part in the research. When using covert methods a researcher will not have provided any such guarantee but this does not mean that s/he can ignore the issue of confidentiality and anonymity. Indeed, this principle may well be even more important in such circumstances since the topics of covert research are far more likely to reveal information that could impact negatively upon the 'subjects' of the research as well as upon the researchers involved in the study, those who belong to the wider research community and where applicable the organisation in which the research is taking place. It is therefore incumbent upon researchers to try to identify as far as possible any situations in which they think confidentiality could be compromised.

BOX 3.3 SHOULD CONFIDENTIALITY AND ANONYMITY EVER BE BREACHED?

Consider these two studies and decide whether the decisions made by the researchers were ethical:

1   There have been several covert studies in which researchers have recorded their observations of illegal activities amongst bouncers in nightclubs. One such study, which one of us has often discussed with students, is Sanders' (2005) study of the supply and use of ecstasy in a London nightclub, which used the method of covert participant observation. Sanders witnessed bouncers supplying ecstasy to punters in the club – but he was not involved in this activity himself. As this was a covert study there was no formal agreement to maintain confidentiality although Sanders chose to do so. Was this a good ethical decision? Why/why not?

2   Piper (2005) has discussed the issue of confidentiality in a study in which she was involved. The study was concerned with the topic of children harming animals. Her discussion reflects upon a dispute that arose at the steering group phase of the study when the question of what should be done if a child, who had been promised anonymity and confidentiality, disclosed that s/he harmed animals because s/he was being abused. Most of the group agreed that in such a case confidentiality should not be maintained. How would you deal with a situation of this sort? Give reasons for your answer.

Student document

Suggested readings

The discussions to which the cases in Box 3.3 give rise illustrate the ethical dilemmas which beset social researchers. They also illustrate that the ethical principles with which researchers are encouraged to operate cannot be viewed as a 'one size fits all' way of addressing these dilemmas. It can be seen from these examples that the *context* of the research must always be at the forefront of the researcher's mind when making ethical decisions. For example, there is a world of difference between maintaining the confidentiality of someone who is observed breaking the law in public and breaking the confidentiality of a child who has disclosed abuse to a researcher in the process of participating in research.

In the first case the context of the research is the key to the process of ethical decision-making. Here the methods chosen by the researcher would make no difference to the freely chosen actions of those being observed as the setting is a public place. It is therefore safe to assume that the people being observed would be involved in those activities whether the researcher was there or not. Berg (2004: 52) suggests that if the research project itself does not increase or cause risk to the participants then it may be considered ethical. Of course, it would be another matter entirely if the researcher got involved with the drug dealing not least because this would bring disrepute to research communities in general. However, some researchers may decide that research of this nature is not for them as there may be risks to researchers or their families that they are not prepared to take. This is completely fine but we believe that if decisions were to be taken by ethics committees that some subjects are inappropriate for academic study it would rule out much important research on crime and indeed would serve to maintain inequalities of power.

In the second case we must look again to the research context, this time the important issue is that the participants are children. It would not be ethical for a researcher to maintain confidentiality when confronted with the disclosure of abuse from a child. This is because any harm that may subsequently come to that child as a result of inaction on the part of the researcher would not be justifiable since responsible adults who are working with children have a statutory responsibility to report suspected abuse. When the participants in research are children then the adults who are involved in the research must intervene to protect the child. However, when constructing the consent form it is a good idea to construct a paragraph which spells out the situations in which breaches of confidentiality would be permitted. In the research by Piper *et al.* (cited by Piper 2005: 60) the following phrase was used:

> I can promise confidentiality on anything you may tell me except on anything that leads me to be concerned for your own or another's safety, in which case I must do whatever is necessary to ensure that you or the person being harmed is protected.

In this particular piece of research confidentiality *was* maintained with regard to children's disclosures of any harms done to animals. Whilst, as Piper (2005) acknowledges, some members of the RSPCA did not agree with this at first, it was decided that it would be unethical to get children to admit to doing something wrong only to end up reporting them. It is important to note that some organisations may require exceptions to maintaining confidentiality. For example, HM Prison Service stipulates that researchers report criminal activity, self-harm and any breaking of prison rules to a member of prison staff. Some organisations may also have standard templates for consent forms and participant information forms.

Avoiding harm

'No generic formula or guidelines exist for assessing the likely benefit or risk of various types of social enquiry. Nonetheless, social researchers must be sensitive to the possible consequences of their work and should as far as possible, guard against predictably harmful effects' (SRA, 2003: 17).

In order to avoid harm, researchers must do two key things:

1   At the design stage think through and identify the harms to which their chosen methods of study may give rise and ensure that all practical steps are taken to demonstrate that their choice of actions can be justified ethically by avoiding undue harm. (Refer to Table 3.1 above.)
2   When/if unforeseen ethical dilemmas arise in the process of research the decisions that are made in response to these dilemmas should be documented and reflected upon in the research methodology as this will help others to make wise ethical decisions in the future.

BOX 3.4 CAN COVERT OBSERVATIONAL RESEARCH BE CARRIED OUT ETHICALLY?

At the time of writing 11 care home workers have been convicted of ill-treating patients in the Winterbourne View private care home. These convictions were made possible by undercover filming of abuse, which when made public on BBC's *Panorama* in 2011 was distressing for the families of those who were abused. However, as Ramesh (2012) reports, as a result of this undercover investigation by the BBC the abuses have come to be understood as 'disability hate crimes' and the Care Quality Commission, the National Health Service Regulator, has made changes which should improve the response to complaints about abuse to patients and has facilitated the setting up of a specialist whistle-blowing team.

Calvey (2008: 914) has noted that there is a huge public appetite for covert documentaries while at the same time academics within the social sciences are being increasingly regulated.

1   Why do you think this is?
2   Should covert observational methods be used as 'teaching material for cases of failed or bad ethics' (Calvey, 2008: 914)? Or instead should teachers be encouraging students to think carefully about the ethical issues to which different covert observational studies have given rise in order that they may carry out important criminological studies using this method in the most ethical way possible?
3   How might an academic go about researching disability hate crimes using covert observation?
4   What are the ethical dilemmas to which such a study might lead?
5   How might these dilemmas be resolved?

We have seen from our discussion so far that the avoidance of harm may require us to challenge some well-established ethical principles. This does not mean that these principles are not important but rather that our adherence to them should be context dependent. Gaining knowledge and understanding of the contexts in which ethical principles may be breached justifiably will avoid complacency amongst researchers that is sometimes (albeit inadvertently) encouraged by a 'tick box' approach to ethics. As May (2001: 67) has noted, the drawing up of and conformity with ethical guidelines is a beginning. From these beginnings many debates will continue to flow. As a general rule we would say that a simple guiding mantra for ethical research is to follow the principles unless to do so would incur undue harms. In such circumstances researchers need to ensure that they justify their actions by explaining how ethical principles may sometimes come into conflict with each other. They should demonstrate the ways in which their decision to breach a principle will reduce harm. Murphy and Dingwall (2001: 340 cited by Flick 2009: 38) for example have argued that ethical codes that are not method sensitive may not only constrain research but may also increase the risk of harm to participants by 'blunting the ethnographers' sensitivities to the method-specific issues which do arise'.

Universities will have their own ethical guidelines and committees. It is up to researchers to convince these committees that they have thought carefully about how they will avoid undue harm in their research. Whilst harm to participants is a particularly important issue, harms to academic institutions, to wider social organisations, to public interests and indeed to the researchers themselves should all be considered. As the guidance in Table 3.1 demonstrates, researchers can avoid undue harm by being as informed as possible in advance of their studies. In criminological research, where there is a strong likelihood that the research will be of a sensitive nature, it is important to acknowledge that even where participants give their consent to trawl over difficult events the researcher has a duty to have identified organisations or professionals who can be called upon if any participants suffer from any ill-effects as a result of their participation. This signals that you have gone beyond simple compliance with an ethical principle. Our experiences on ethics committees suggest that researchers will sometimes downplay the risk of harm to themselves. However, it is important to note that in such circumstances this may cause difficulties for the research institution as research managers and universities might ultimately be held responsible for something that happens to a researcher. However, all research will involve some degree of risk and if ethical codes become inviolable rules then the 'flavour' of research will be vanilla.

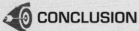 ## CONCLUSION

Instructor activity

Identifying ethical issues in research

Criminological research raises some particularly complex ethical issues. We have tried to convey the importance of the development of ethical principles in the research process whilst at the same time suggesting that an overly rule-bound approach to ethics may be counter-productive in some contexts. We have suggested that it is useful to think of a continuum of ethical stances and we hope to have conveyed that there are problems for criminological research at both extremes. The research examples we have provided should have helped you to identify the circumstances in which ethical principles may conflict with each other, which in turn should enable you to develop the skills of justifying your own ethical decisions and critiquing the decisions made by other researchers.

Student quiz

Ethics

KEY LEARNING POINTS

- It is very important that researchers reduce the possibility of undue harm resulting from their research. For this reason researchers should be familiar with ethical principles.
- There are different stances on ethics but we have suggested that the consequentialist stance enables researchers to be cognisant of the ways in which ethical principles can conflict with each other in some contexts.
- The research examples demonstrate that there are particular concerns about covert research methods because these are said to negate the principle of informed consent and to be based upon deceit. However, unless we examine the *context* of research these concerns cannot be understood properly.
- From the above it follows that ethical principles have been developed with good reason but also that it is unwise to follow them in a rule-bound way as this will rule out some research methods through which important knowledge about crime has been produced.

PART 2

Getting going with criminological research

Chapter 4

Planning

Where do research ideas come from? How do we 'fine tune' them?

GOALS OF THIS CHAPTER

At the end of reading this chapter and by completing the online resources that accompany it, you will:

1   begin to recognise where your own ideas originate;
2   be aware of the ways in which you theorise about crime in your everyday lives and reflect upon those theories;
3   be able to specify general concepts;
4   be aware of the importance of background reading;
5   begin to translate your ideas into research questions;
6   be aware of the purposes of a literature review.

OVERVIEW

*   This chapter will encourage you to think about where your ideas about crime come from. What we choose to research is likely to be influenced by our own life experiences. We may have been a victim of crime in the past or we may even have been involved in the perpetration of crime in either a direct or indirect way. The ideas we hold about what is right or wrong are influenced by our families, the friends we keep, our level of education, etc. So the questions we choose to ask will be influenced by what we think we know and by what we believe already.
*   However, a good researcher needs to demonstrate that s/he has more than 'everyday' or 'common-sense' knowledge about his/her chosen topic of research therefore it is important that you examine the work of others in order to reflect upon and refine your own ideas for research.
*   Once you have done some initial background reading you will have expanded your knowledge of your chosen research topic. It is also likely that in the light of the new knowledge encountered through the first stage of the literature review process you may discover that you are beginning to challenge the views you held previously. This is just the beginning of your exploration . . .

GETTING STARTED: IDEAS (CONCEPTS) AND THEORIES

In Chapter 2 we introduced you to the different theories of knowledge within which criminological research has been carried out. We demonstrated that the ways in which researchers' theories about how the social world should be defined and about what is the best way to gather knowledge on the social world will influence the questions that we seek to answer through our research. In this chapter we are concerned with where our ideas (or concepts) come from and the relationship of these ideas to lower levels of theory – what we might call specific theories – about crime.

Crime is a social problem therefore you do not need to be a criminology student to have opinions about crime. However, as a serious researcher you will need to have a good understanding of where your ideas have come from and you will need to reflect upon the reasons you hold particular viewpoints. A research idea may develop from a profound personal experience, such as being the victim of a violent crime or from a wider concern with an issue that you feel strongly about, for example trafficking in nuclear arms. However, it is important to be realistic about what can and cannot be achieved within a research project. It is better to 'think small' in the early days of research as in this way it will be easier to demonstrate that you can do a competent study which you are able to defend.

To carry out a competent study you must demonstrate your understanding of theory. Whilst the word theory might make some students feel anxious, it is good to remember that theorising is a common feature of our lives, it is not just something academics do. However, unlike lay people, academics try to produce convincing evidence to support their theories and they learn how to identify the strengths and limitations of existing evidence by critiquing the available literature, through which they demonstrate their knowledge of their chosen research area – more of this later. As we have suggested, very often our research ideas take root from our day-to-day experiences. For example, we may be travelling on a bus or a train and overhear someone say something like: 'families are not the same as they used to be, couples are not committed to each other anymore and that's why we see so many kids getting into trouble' or 'crime has increased in our area ever since we started letting all these foreigners come to work here'. Whether we agree with such ideas or not will depend upon many factors, such as who we associate with, where we live, what newspapers we read and our level of education. We hear these sorts of things because people in their everyday lives are trying to make sense of what is happening in their world. However, such explanations of different types of crime are not usually based upon systematic theorising but rather they have often been gleaned from rather similar and often unreliable sources.

As a new researcher you will need to think about how you can move from the unsystematic form of theorising that is often a feature of everyday life, to what is a more 'privileged' form of theorising (after all most people do not have the time to think about things in the way that academics can) that takes place within an academic setting.

In academic research a sound theory is usually based upon a set of ideas that we have about something. Criminologists use theories in order to attempt to find explanations for the phenomena that we refer to collectively as 'crime', yet the term crime encompasses many forms of lawbreaking from individual illegal drug use to organised corporate crime. Those who study crime may be concerned with why different crimes happen but they may also be concerned with the reasons why some behaviours come to be defined as criminal. For example, who decides that using the drug cannabis is illegal but using the drugs alcohol or tobacco is not? On what basis is such a decision made? Contrary to what many people think it does not necessarily have to be on the basis of harm, as Nutt (2009) has argued, yet even his scientific evidence has not been enough to convince politicians. Nutt struggled to explain that the view expressed by many politicians, that you cannot compare the harms of an illegal substance with those of a legal one, is illogical. Indeed Professor Nutt was sacked in 2009 by the then Home Secretary Alan Johnson because his evidence did not 'fit' with political imperatives, yet these same politicians are likely to call for 'a more scientific' approach to research when social scientists carry out **qualitative research** on drug use in society. So researchers need to become mindful of the ways in which our understanding of crime in society might be shaped by an often ill-informed public perception, oftentimes gained from biased or partial media reporting and a perceived need on the part of politicians to respond to that public perception.

The above discussion suggests that it is important for criminological researchers to break crime down into several categories in order to provide more meaningful knowledge of and explanations for the many acts that constitute crime in society. For example, in everyday life when people say things like 'crime has got worse' there is an assumption that we all know what is meant by this because there is a tendency to understand the term 'crime' to mean street crimes. Researchers have to be much more precise than this so that there can be no doubt about the phenomenon which they wish to study. This is important because in general people get their ideas about crime from various media, which focus more on street crimes. This skews our thinking about crime and serves to mystify the many other crimes which should cause us concern. Once we understand this we can quickly see the need to break down our ideas more precisely in order to improve our research design. As Neuman (2011: 57) puts it, 'simple is better'.

To illustrate how you can make the move from everyday to academic theorising it is helpful to have an example. Let's start with an idea that has taken hold in society, such as the linkage of family breakdown with crime. This is an idea that has been taken up by politicians across the political spectrum, for example family breakdown remains an indicator of risk in the assessment tools used by Youth Justice Services (see for example Smith, 2006) and it is an assumption embodied in the statement used in the Conservative policy document *Breakthrough Britain* (Centre for Social Justice, 2007) that crime is strongly correlated with family breakdown.

BOX 4.1 BREAKING DOWN CONCEPTS

Crime and family breakdown are two key concepts that might inform a piece of research. Try to think how you could clarify these concepts in order to make research aims clear.

As a starting point for the exercise in Box 4.1 we might expect that you would have interrogated the concept of crime itself since, as we have already demonstrated in Chapter 2, crime changes over time and across space so the concept (or idea) of crime is best understood as a *social construction*. It is therefore a good idea to *specify* the types of crime that are being linked to family breakdown rather than to speak of crime in general. Through the process of breaking crime down into categories, for example, street theft, you will be able to pave the way for theory testing. Similarly we might expect that family breakdown would need to be more clearly defined. Families 'break down' for a variety of reasons: there could be a death in the family; a family member comes to need full-time care; a divorce or separation. The reasons for divorce or separation might vary too, for example you might suppose that if a couple split up because of violence it could be more likely that the children would become involved in violent crime. This is a process that can help you to narrow down your area of research. The more you clarify your ideas in this way then the better placed you will be to identify the focus of your research and test out your ideas. In qualitative research this process of conceptualising is ongoing, researchers will often come up with new definitions of concepts in the process of analysis (see Chapter 13). In **quantitative research** this process is important because clear definitions are needed in order to **operationalise** concepts, that is make them measurable (see Chapter 9).

Instructor exercise

Summary of article by Curry

THE INFORMAL LITERATURE REVIEW: BACKGROUND READING

Instructor exercise

Summary of article by Hallsworth and Young

Researchers always demonstrate that they are familiar with the existing knowledge surrounding their research topic. You should begin the process of reviewing the literature on your chosen topic as soon as possible as this will enable you to avoid replicating things that have been done already. By the time you get to the end of the full process of review you should be in a position to construct your final question for research. But where do you start? At first it is likely that your research ideas are rather vague and you may well need to discuss these with your supervisor in order to avoid starting the impossible or just to get an idea of where to look in the first instance. There is such an array of literature that it can be very bewildering at first and your interest in a topic may start with the sort of literature that is not usually associated with academia, such as television programmes. Your study may well benefit from 'literature' gained from films or TV, especially as crime is such a popular entertainment topic. There will also be plentiful news media resources. However, it is important to review academic journals (refereed journals are best, that is those that are reviewed by other academics, but there are also some useful non-refereed publications, such as *Criminal Justice Matters,* that may provide you with a quick and useful insight into a topic); academic books, official documents, organisational documents (sometimes called 'grey' literature) – for instance documents that you might find if you have worked as a volunteer in an organisation like the National Association for the Care and Resettlement of Offenders (NACRO).

Student activity

Getting started with summarising

Tips for sifting the literature

The most obvious place to begin is with the title of a resource, which will usually tell you quite a lot about the content. Here is a good example: *Unmasking the Crimes of the Powerful: Scrutinising States and Corporations*. Of course, as you become familiar with different writers you will also begin to get an idea of the perspective of the authors. For example the title above is a book by Tombs and Whyte (2003) who write from a critical perspective influenced by Marxist analyses. You will often find a précis on the back cover of books which will help you to ascertain its relevance to your study. You can also scan the index to identify the topics that may be most useful to you. A refereed journal article will always include an abstract that will provide detail of the study's purpose, methods and findings. You might also look at the introduction and conclusion to assess its relevance.

> **TIP**
>
> The internet is a wonderful source of information but you must be discerning. You need to ensure that the sources you cite are reputable, at worst you could be accessing sites that are operated by hate groups (Berg, 2004) so take care. Here are some tips to help you be discerning: Look for the author's name – if there isn't one be very cautious, if there is have you heard of him/her? If not, look that person up to find out what else s/he has written. Can you discern the agenda of the author? For example are there assumptions about gender or ethnicity that you find worrying or offensive? Can you find out the reason the internet site exists and how long it has existed? Also when was it last updated? Does the author mention other writers that you have heard of and provide evidence to back up what is being said?

Where shall I start?

We think that it is helpful for students to be given an idea of what is involved in the process of refining research ideas and this is indeed what many lecturers do when they talk about their own research or when they encourage postgraduate research students to speak to undergraduates about their progress in research. Those who are new to research are inclined to think of the process in a linear way when in reality the process is quite messy. In order to demonstrate how this process might begin we are going to return to the example used above in which we began to think about a statement in the policy document *Breakthrough Britain*, which asserts an association between family breakdown and crime as part of a justification for supporting marriage through changes to state support.

We would like you to imagine that you heard something about the crime/family breakdown aspect of the policy document on the news and that this sparked an interest in the topic, which you thought you might pursue as part of your course – note that interest in a topic can be ignited for a variety of reasons, for example because you agreed with the connections that were being made or because you thought there were some problems with attributing crime to 'family breakdown' and you wanted to find out more. It is often worth looking at documents of this kind because they tell us quite a lot about which crimes are constructed by governments as the most pressing as well as about the ways in which those who are involved in certain crimes are perceived. As Radzinowicz

(1999: 469, cited by Garland and Sparks 2000: 192) pointed out, there is a disturbing gap between criminology and criminal policy and unfortunately despite the wealth of criminological knowledge a rather populist political approach holds sway. So there is a constant need for criminologists to challenge the assumptions made by politicians and for them to question the grounds upon which policies are implemented.

BOX 4.2 SPECIFYING CONCEPTS AND IDENTIFYING VARIABLES

Using the insights gained from the exercise in Box 4.1 specify what you mean by the concept of family breakdown and jot down some of the crimes that you think might be linked to it. Try to give reasons for the association. Next, try to think of other variables that might help to explain the crimes you believe to be linked with family breakdown (as you have defined it).

Now take a look at the document *Breakthrough Britain* (available at: http://www.centreforsocialjustice.org.uk/publications/breakthrough-britain-family-breakdown). What evidence is provided in the document for the proposition that there is a *strong* (our emphasis) correlation between crime and family breakdown? How would you assess the *strength* of the evidence provided for this theory within the document?

Figure 4.1 Interrogating your literature sources: policy documents

Your initial thinking, as revealed through the above exercise, will depend upon your own experiences and/or upon some previous reading. It is always useful to do an exercise such as the one above with others because when we compare our thoughts with those of other people we can often start to identify the ideas that we take for granted. The initial reading of the document should have enabled you to identify the evidence provided by the authors and the ways in which that evidence is used to justify policy proposals.

Some of you may have used the 'find' facility on the computer as a quick way of identifying where the key concepts (crime and family breakdown) that are of interest to you are used in the document. This should also have enabled you to discern the ways in which the concepts were defined.

PAUSE TO THINK . . .

In fact the document doesn't tell us directly that much about crime but it is possible to 'read between the lines' by looking carefully at the ways in which language is used in the document. For example, the focus on marriage signals that some families are more likely to be perceived as a problem than others; the concern with 'dad-lessness' implies that lone motherhood is a problem. The ills of society are being placed squarely within 'dysfunctional' family relationships in this document but what does that term mean? Is a definition of a 'functional' family provided or hinted at? Which crimes is the report concerned about? *Which* family members are the foci of concern? Are there any contradictions in the arguments? If you raised questions for yourself in this way you can give yourself a pat on the back as this means that you are already starting to read critically.

It is also important that you recognise that the document is political therefore you need to think about what you have read in context. Might it be that 'family' is being used in an ideological way to support a particular view of welfare? Are the correlations between crime and family breakdown being overdrawn? Of course, just because you are embarking upon a piece of criminological research this does not mean that you will not have political views yourself, but these views should not stop you from thinking carefully about the strength of the evidence that is provided to justify policies that purport (at least in part) to reduce crime in society – whichever party is putting them forward. As Denscombe (2002: 35) says 'personal interest should not act as a blinker that unduly narrows the focus of research'. So it will be important to look for the source of the evidence that is used in the document you have read and to think about how it has been collected and used rather than to accept it because you think you agree with what is being said.

Where next?

You are only just getting into the research process having pursued one idea by looking at a policy document. There is a whole lot more background reading to do before your ideas can become more concrete. It is important to remember that doing research is a creative enterprise (Berg, 2004). If you are following a thread of ideas that you find interesting the chances are that you will enjoy reading around the topic until your 'criminological imagination' is developed. A useful next step might be to search for further statistical information – but remember the caution we recommended in Chapter 1 in relation to official crime statistics – or for responses to the document. For example, Gingerbread, Barnado's and Child Poverty Action Group provided a joint response to *Breakthrough Britain:* http://www.gingerbread.org.uk/uploads/media/17/6863.pdf, which, whilst welcoming some aspects of the report, challenged the assumption that the tax and benefit system favours lone parents; the view that lone parenthood of itself leads to poor outcomes for children; suggested that where there is conflict in families separation might lead to better outcomes for children. These 'snippets' of information are useful as they give you some idea of other variables that may need to be considered in your study, for example, having looked at the evidence provided in this document you might deduce that poverty or conflict could be more significant indicators of crime-related problems than family breakdown.

BOX 4.3 SEARCHING ACADEMIC JOURNALS

Go to your university library page and conduct a search of the *British Journal of Criminology* that might help you to gain more information about the variables that can lead to crime amongst young people. Use the key concepts we have been focusing on so far as your starting point. What did you find? How did you decide which articles might be useful?

It is highly likely that you will have found Juby and Farrington's (2001) article 'Disentangling the Link Between Disrupted Families and Delinquency'. A quick look at the abstracts of the articles would have helped you to identify this as an article that might be particularly useful. You should now read it as carefully as possible and try to identify the key concepts and theories that are being used, discussed or developed and to identify the theory of knowledge (**epistemology**) within which the study has been carried out. It is also a good idea to look at the citations that have been included too, as these will provide you with further relevant sources of reading which are likely to lead to more ideas to follow up for your own study. Any study will have limitations. Often the authors will point out some of these – as Juby and Farrington (2001) do. However, you might also wish to think about how a move from one theory of knowledge to another might open up other possibilities for future research. For example, as we noted earlier, the variables that have been associated with delinquency in positivistic research have been translated into risk factors that are used in assessments within the Youth Justice System to predict where intervention should take place (the Risk Factors Prevention Paradigm or RFPP). If you were to pursue further background reading in the area we have been discussing you would soon have discovered that this is the case and that there are differing perspectives on the merits of this. A logical place to search would be *Youth Justice*, a journal in which if you were to do a search you would find an article by O'Mahony (2009) 'The Risk Factors Prevention Paradigm and the Causes of Youth Crime: A Deceptively Useful Analysis?' in which he discusses some of the problems with using scientific approaches within the social sciences where constructs are imprecise and culturally variable. He points to the importance of challenging notions of 'culture-free' risk factors because the ways in which gender and 'race' are socially constructed are very important to our understanding of why some (young) people get involved in crime. There is thus a suggestion that it might be important to carry out studies from within an interpretivist framework in order to gain a more nuanced understanding of the reasons young people turn to crime. Furthermore, O'Mahony (2009: 112) points to the ways in which the RFPP fails to take account of adult onset offending such as white-collar crimes and domestic violence – a discovery which, at this early stage of research, could take you off in another direction . . .

Figure 4.2 Interrogating your literature sources: academic texts

BOX 4.4 KEEPING TRACK OF YOUR REFERENCES

Note that from the minute you begin to do your background reading you should keep track of your references. Set up a file on your computer and make sure that you always record what you have read using the Harvard system. Many universities now have packages such as Endnote and help is often provided in university libraries.

This is the way to reference the journal article:

Juby, H. and Farrington, D. P. (2001) 'Disentangling the Link Between Disrupted Families and Delinquency', *British Journal of Criminology,* 41(1): 22–40.

Look up the Harvard referencing system and note the different conventions for each type of resource. You will probably find that your own university or university library has a guide to Harvard referencing that you can access. However, below you can find a link to a 'How to write references' guide from Birmingham City University: http://library.bcu.ac.uk/references.pdf

Student activity

Getting started with referencing

Instructor exercise

Referencing

TIP

A common mistake amongst beginners to research is to place journal article titles in italics. An easy way to remember which part of a journal reference should be italicised is to remind yourself that the different articles in a journal are like book chapters therefore the title should be in inverted commas. The title of the journal itself – like a book title – should be in italics.

TRANSLATING IDEAS INTO QUESTIONS

Eventually we hope that through the process of careful background reading you will be equipped to raise quite a few questions about the studies you have looked at, which will in turn have enabled you to construct some research aims. You could decide, for example, that your aim is to explore the reasons why more boys than girls get involved in delinquent activities or to critically examine the way in which the term family breakdown is used to support youth crime policies. Both of these aims could have emerged from some of the literature that we have mentioned above. Eventually, in your attempts to fulfil your aims, your research question/s will emerge, for example we could ask 'How does the term "family breakdown" serve to mystify more salient reasons for youth crimes?' Alternatively you could decide to set up a **hypothesis** (to test a theory) such as 'youth crime will be lower in local communities where there is affordable leisure'. This implies that you would need to carry out multi-variate analysis in order to ascertain whether the **independent variable** 'affordable leisure' is significant – see Chapters 6 and 9. A decision to look at boys compared to girls suggests that gender constructions will be an important element of the research and that you have found some materials that question the use of gender-neutral risk categories (see above). Note that a critical examination does not necessarily imply that your study belongs to what we have termed the critical theory of knowledge although the process of taking a concept apart (deconstruction) might well move you into that research tradition as the research progresses (hence the importance of keeping a reflexive journal). However, if your study explicitly sets out to explain the ways in which a concept might serve to hide relations of power and oppression you will be operating overtly with a set of values that will form part of your analysis – see Chapter 2. As you continue to review the literature and indeed begin the data collection process you may find that you need to refine your research question. This is a normal part of research and any refinements should be discussed in your methodology.

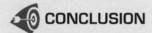 **CONCLUSION**

Research is a creative enterprise in so far as you need to think 'outside the box' in order to raise interesting questions that may not have been asked before. This chapter should have enabled you to start thinking about your own views on crime and why you hold them. It is hoped that it has also encouraged you to start talking to others about their views as this is a good way of identifying the ways in which your own life experiences might influence the way you think. It is a good idea to start practising writing clear definitions of the concepts that are of concern to you so that by the time you carry out your own research project you will be able to make the limits of your concerns apparent. It is extremely important that you begin background reading as early as possible and that you become adept at discerning reliable sources. Your background reading will help you to construct questions for research and even though your question may eventually shift a little this process will lead to the more focused reading that is needed to write the formal literature review. In other words, by the time you have done your background reading you should have a fair idea of what you are trying to achieve and how you will achieve it.

KEY LEARNING POINTS

- Think small when you begin research as this will help to ensure that you stay focused.
- Reflect upon your own viewpoints and try to articulate why you hold specific views.
- Always try to go beyond *common-sense* knowledge by reading around the subject in a critical manner.
- Use shortcuts, such as reading abstracts, to assess the relevance of your sources.
- Keep good records of your sources and don't forget to record page numbers if you are writing down direct quotations.
- Be methodical when making notes using the headings suggested to organise your thinking.
- Remember that although your review comes first in the presentation of your final research, in reality you will find that you are 'tweaking' it throughout the whole research process.

Chapter 5

Critiquing the literature and the process of writing your formal review

GOALS OF THIS CHAPTER

At the end of reading this chapter and by completing the online resources that accompany it, you will:

1 be able to distinguish between different types of literature;
2 understand what it means to critique the literature;
3 be aware of the ways in which researchers use different theoretical perspectives;
4 be aware of the need to make your own standpoint clear through your discussion of the standpoints of others;
5 be able to write your review in a coherent, structured and appropriate style;
6 be aware of the importance of **reflexivity** in the process of writing a review.

OVERVIEW

- The process of writing a review is ongoing throughout research in the sense that it will constantly be refined as your ideas develop.
- The quality of a review is enhanced by a researcher's ability to distinguish between different types of literature – empirical, theoretical and methodological. It is therefore important that researchers continue to develop the skill of critical *reading*.
- Familiarity with the work of others enables researchers to establish and justify their own standpoints on their chosen topics of research.

CRITIQUING THE LITERATURE

Researchers carry out a review of the literature to inform and refine their research questions, as discussed in Chapter 4, and also because they need to demonstrate their awareness of the state of knowledge on their chosen topic. It is really important that reviews are critical as this will ensure that you demonstrate your ability to *analyse* the sources you have identified as important as opposed to just describing them. As Bell and Opie (2002: 137, citing Haywood and Wragg, 1982: 2) point out, it is fairly easy to produce a descriptive review but it's quite another thing to produce a review which demonstrates 'that the writer has studied existing work in the field with insight'. In practice this means that when you are preparing to write your review notes you should not simply outline what has been said but you should also record your own response to what has been said, such as what might be missing or which authors disagree with that position. So, we now turn to the task of helping you to read critically as this in turn will enable you to make the move from descriptive to analytical writing. You will need to read theoretical literature as well as empirical studies so that you become familiar with the ways in which researchers use theory in their research. Empirical studies will, of course, include discussions of methodology too, which will include important references that you should note as you will need to chase up some of these so that eventually you will be able to justify your own methodological approach – more on this in Chapter 6.

We think that it is a good idea to produce a table on which to record the key information gained from each piece of literature. You should also record your own thoughts on each piece – even if you shift your position after further reading, these comments will be a useful start to the writing process. We suggest that you use the following headings:

1   Literature source
2   Key concepts
3   Theoretical perspectives
4   Key quotations/ideas
5   Methods used (where relevant)
6   Theory of knowledge
7   Political standpoints (if relevant)
8   Research questions
9   Key findings
10   Your own critical comments

TIP

Make sure that if your review notes include direct quotations/ key ideas you also keep a record of the page number where the quotation/idea appears. You don't want to be accused of **plagiarism** nor will you want to be chasing up page numbers later on when you have returned books or lost articles, etc.

BOX 5.1 CRITICAL READING

Imagine that you have done your background reading and that you have decided to carry out a piece of research on male sex offenders' accounts of their offending with a view to exploring the origins of their techniques of neutralisation (Matza, 1964). Construct a table using the ten headings outlined above. Return to the article 'Men Researching Men in Prison' (Cowburn, 2007). As you read these pages try to make notes under all the headings you think are relevant. You should also try to read actively, that is ask yourself questions about what you have read as you go along. For example, what was Cowburn trying to do? How did he go about it? Were you convinced by his justifications? Why/why not? It will even be important to identify any aspects of the reading that have confused you as this will signal that you need to chase up some further references to gain deeper understanding. Note that it may help you to return to Chapter 2 when considering Cowburn's theory of knowledge.

Now consider the tables below and compare them with your own.

Cowburn provided a synthesised account of the theoretical, empirical and methodological literature that has influenced his work on sex offenders. He demonstrated the importance of including a discussion of these key elements in any piece of research since such details enable those who are reading the research to understand the basis upon which judgements were made in the research process. Although the article is actually concerned with the difficulties encountered by male researchers in the data collection process it is a useful article to review because it provides such a lot of detail about the assumptions behind his previous research and in particular it provides a very detailed account of the reasons why he has chosen a critical epistemological approach. This article certainly demonstrates the importance of the three key aspects of literature that should be included in a review.

When you compare your notes with those in the table above it is likely that you will identify some gaps in your knowledge but everyone will come to this task with different levels of information. For example, those readers who have studied sociology or social psychology may be familiar with Goffman's work, but for those readers who are completely new to social science it would not have been possible to give a name to one of the theoretical perspectives (*symbolic interactionism*) that has influenced the conduct of Cowburn's research. Goffman's work influenced thinking about crime because he raised questions about the ways in which people can be defined as 'deviant' by the professionals who are in charge of them. He also tried to explain the ways in which those who were acting in a 'deviant' way could appear 'normal'. Cowburn drew upon Goffman's ideas about the 'use and avoidance of the rules of interaction' (Carrabine *et al.,* 2009) in order to avoid possible conflict with those who were working in the prison in which he carried out his study. So Goffman's theories are relevant to Cowburn's collection of data rather than to the analysis.

Table 5.1 How to keep records of your reading

Literature source	Key concepts	Theoretical perspective	Key quotations/ideas	Methods
Cowburn (2007)'Men Researching Men in Prison', *The Howard Journal*, 46(3): 276–88	Male power (how it is used to oppress) Masculinities Sexism **Hegemony** 'Playing it Cool' Situational Withdrawal (Goffman)	Sex offenders are not simply members of 'deviant' population – sex offending has its roots in society where there is a continuum of male behaviours which may account for some men becoming sex offenders – seems to be influenced by radical feminism here? This may be useful	Critique thus combines a number of elements: a critical relation to the topic, encompassing a self-**reflexivity** of the author and the topic, and the consideration of the social bases of knowledge; a commitment to the political emancipation of both women and men; and where appropriate, empirical inquiry not just assertion and speculation. (Hearn, 1998: 801 cited by Cowburn, 2007: 277) Women disrupt the close association between the prison officer role and the performance of masculinity; if women are allowed to do the job, and if they can do it as well as their male counterparts, the job is 'no longer a viable resource for constructing masculinity' (Martin and Jurik, 1996: 175; Crawley, 2004: 195)	Used life histories and observation in his previous research. Only 9 interviews so rather limited in scope. Interviewing methods are linked to the insights of interactionism (see Goffman)

It would thus appear that sexist harassment of women workers plays a central part in maintaining the hegemony of men in prisons (p281)

Theory of knowledge	Political standpoint	Research questions/aims	Key findings	Comments
Critical – strong objectivity, tries to challenge oppressive ways of being male; preconceptions of researcher should be explicit	Pro-feminist Anti-sexist Commitment to the political emancipation of both women and men (Hearn, 1998)	A discussion of Cowburn's previous research – article is concerned with the problems encountered by male researchers doing research in prison setting. Aims to understand masculinities and sexism in prison	There are challenges at two levels: 1. Theoretical – there is a need to understand the standpoint of the researcher in order to challenge 'dominant' knowledge; 2. Empirical – (Cowburn thinks this is the most important) how should the researcher conduct him/herself to get the best data? Avoid confrontation, be non-collusive, critique some dominant male practices at the publication stage. Challenges polarities – does not agree with Liebling (2001) that researchers are either on the side of the prison or on the side of the prisoners – Cowburn notes that his work does not fit easily on either side of that polarity	Cowburn had problems listening to the accounts of some sex offenders who tried to justify their actions – should he have intervened in Martin's case? Not sure whether Cowburn's confrontational stance could have had a negative impact on the data? But Cowburn's intervention seemed reasonable as Martin was trying to justify something that couldn't be justified. Cowburn put a different scenario to Martin in an attempt to make him see the problem with his justification for abusing his daughters – it seemed to work as it made him uncomfortable – not sure whether it was ethical but I thought it was a good way of widening our understanding of how an offender can convince himself that it is OK to carry on offending.

Cowburn's discussion of his theoretical perspective is explicit about the influence of feminism upon the way he carries out the research as he acknowledged the role of feminism in challenging theories of knowledge that claimed neutrality. He also acknowledged the importance of lower level theories about gender and crime. We can tell this because Cowburn talks about masculinities (not masculinity) and because of his references to theorists such as Hearn, Butler and Connell — although again this depends upon the extent of your knowledge of authors writing in similar areas.

Note that in Cowburn (2007) we are not told a great deal about the ways in which gender theories influenced his own data analyses, but he was clearly trying to challenge oppressive ways of being male.

CASE STUDY: SAMANTHA'S PROGRESS

Samantha is (an imaginary) student who has already read a good deal of literature on the topic outlined in Box 5.1. She has made notes on them all, using the table we suggest above. She has underlined comments made in recent articles, which refer to the dearth of literature (Blagden and Pemberton, 2010; Mann, 2012). She has noted also that Blagden and Pemberton (2010) and Mann (2012) have included useful discussions of some of the practical and ethical issues relating to carrying out research in prison, which she has compared with Cowburn's account and she has noted that this will be useful when she discusses her methodology. There is an asterisk in her margin reminding her to discuss the issue of confidentiality (see Chapter 3) in her methodology chapter. Samantha noted that in the more recent studies she has read the authors were concerned with the issue of offenders taking responsibility for their actions, even though in some senses Blagden and Pemberton saw the offenders as vulnerable. She compared this article with Lacombe's (2008) **critique** of the treatment of sex offenders in a risk society and with Wilson and Jones' (2008) discussion of offenders' use of the internet to access extreme pornography. She noted that Lacombe's historical account of the treatment of sex offenders referred to the now 'discredited' view that offenders were monsters who could not control their behaviour yet the therapy involved their acceptance of the view 'once a sex offender always a sex offender'. She made a note that she was unsure about this. Lacombe also referred to the assumption made by therapists that sex offenders have fantasies which they will eventually act upon — Lacombe questioned this but Samantha noted that Wilson and Jones (2008) said a little more about this issue and identified the circumstances in which sex offenders might act upon their fantasies. However, she put a question mark in the margin as she was unsure of her own view on this.

Samantha was interested to see that in both Mann's (2012) and Blagden and Pemberton's (2010) accounts of their interviews with sex offenders there was evidence

> ### KEY TERM
>
> **Critique** — this term should not be confused with criticism. Rather critique means identifying the strengths and weaknesses and it usually involves making your own original points that are based upon your wider knowledge of the topic.

that the offenders tried to justify or minimise the effects of their crimes. This set her thinking about *why* they might do this and she was reminded of something she had read in Cowburn's article – the view that sex offending has its roots in 'normal' society. This is a view that she found challenging but interesting. Indeed, it occurred to her then that Wilson and Jones (2008) had also mentioned the 'normality' of sexualised images of children in advertising etc., so she chased up this idea by exploring the feminist literature. She spoke to some of her lecturers and eventually one of them suggested that she might find an old but quite important piece of feminist literature helpful. The article was MacLeod, M. And Saraga, E. (1988) 'Challenging the Orthodoxy: Towards Feminist Theory and Praxis', *Feminist Review,* 28, Spring: 16–55, which Samantha thought was relevant to the point Cowburn was making. She discovered that the authors documented some of the ways in which male professionals constructed men as biologically driven rather than as responsible for their actions. In some cases child sexual abuse was explained as a result of family dysfunction – where dysfunction stood for problems with *maternal* behaviour, such as losing the desire to have sex. Samantha made a critical comment about this in her table as it didn't really make sense to her. She was aware of the 'bad press' that feminism often gets and up until this point she thought she agreed with some of the criticisms. The more she read the more she came to understand that the idea that men are biologically driven was coming largely from men who were trying to explain sexual violence. This seemed strange to her as she had a recollection that some feminists were criticised for the mantra 'all men are rapists' but this was certainly not what the feminist writers she was reading seemed to be saying. Rather they were saying that men *can* control their urges but if they grow up believing that they cannot then perhaps it is no surprise that some men will try to excuse their behaviour.

With very little searching Samantha also found references to Carol Smart (1989:67) who documented the ways in which in courts sexual abuse was often put down to women's frigidity. A quick Google enabled her to find reports of how Judge Cassell, in his summing up of a case of child sexual abuse in 1990, suggested that as the abuser's wife was pregnant and not having sex with her husband, the husband was 'understandably driven' to have sex with his 12-year-old stepdaughter. Samantha was quite shocked by this and she raised the following question in her notes – 'Were these the same men who resisted feminist theorising? They are assuming men can't help it'. She spoke to her supervisor about this, who explained that there were several different feminist perspectives. One of the most radical perspectives suggested the separation of men from women on the grounds that men are 'naturally' more violent than women. He went on to explain that this reasoning was based upon a biologically determinist premise that was criticised by most feminists. He also told Samantha that he thought she was correct to note that the male theorists who explained abuse in terms of *women's* failure to satisfy men were making the same error. So from this Samantha gained a more nuanced understanding of different feminist perspectives and her supervisor explained that media representations of feminists were usually based on a caricature image of the most extreme (although small in number) feminists.

Samantha chased up the references to Jeff Hearn's work, cited by Cowburn, and found that he had similar concerns to the feminist writers. His work, influenced by feminism, alerted her to the fact that gender should include discussions of masculinity

Instructor
activity

Critiquing
a research
article

as well as femininity. Samantha also looked up some of the literature on child abuse and she found Nigel Parton's work in her university library in which she discovered a quotation that she thought was important: in parliament David Hinchcliffe, on 27 April 1989, stated that the roots of sexual violence were 'not so much in deviant family and sexual values but in 'normal' ones ... we need to address in particular male socialisation, sexual attitudes and expectations of women in society' (cited by Parton, 1991: 166). Samantha came to the conclusion that this older literature was highly relevant to her research as the little evidence that was available suggested that the same justifications are being made today by sex offenders.

Student
activity

Planning a
review

Samantha decided to carry out life history interviews that explored with the offenders the ways in which they constructed their masculinity. She thought that although some interviews had been carried out in prison with sex offenders none of them had sufficiently explored the relationship between their constructions of masculinity and their offending. She also decided that Matza's (1964) concept of neutralisation was still relevant today when considering sex offences.

Student
guide to
...

Reviewing
articles

BOX 5.2 STUDENT ACTIVITY

Identify the key elements of Samantha's progress with her literature review. Do you think that she left anything important out of the process? Follow up some of the references at the end of this chapter and make some critical comments of your own. How would you have proceeded with research on this topic?

GETTING DOWN TO WRITING

Like any other piece of work a literature review has an introduction, a main body and a conclusion. We suggest that you provide an introduction which explains why you think your chosen research area is important, for example, in the case study we used above 'Samantha' could have decided that the official programmes open to sex offenders fail to take account of the meanings that they give to their offending behaviour but instead *impose* meaning onto their behaviour, which they have to accept (see Lacombe, 2008). However, we think that the best introductions are often written at the end of the writing process so we would not necessarily recommend that you begin this task before you have written the main body of the review. This does not negate the need to have a good idea of why you think your chosen topic is worthy of research.

The case study included above outlined, albeit very briefly, some key elements in the process of writing the main body of a review. It is very important to compare and contrast the literature and to revise and reconsider your critical comments as you move back and forth between new and old – but relevant – studies. The more you read the more likely you are to be able to make sensible critical comments when you begin to write.

Once you have got to this stage in your review you will be very familiar with the literature and you should be able to organise it in a logical way and get writing. There are several ways to do this but in general you will start by setting the scene and then you will work your way from broadly related research, through which you set the context, through to the specific research that has influenced your study most so that you finally end up with the formulation of your own clear statement of the research aims. This is usually referred to as the 'inverted pyramid' approach (see Chapter 15 for a visual representation of this). It is important to remember however, that the structure and justification will be based upon *your* research purposes and therefore you will need to take time to make sure that this is the best way of presenting the literature you have read. A straightforward chronological approach might be ideal when you are taking a historical approach to your study, perhaps in a situation where you are looking at something like the circumstances in which laws change in relation to specific issues such as drug use, for example. You will need to make a judgement depending upon your chosen topic but often a chronological account can lead to a boring and somewhat incoherent review. Within the inverted pyramid approach it is also possible to organise the literature thematically. Try to take the time to identify key ideas which you can then group together and discuss critically – preferably in order of importance. It is also quite helpful to use headings which act as 'signposts' for the reader.

Remember that it is not a good idea to spend a long time discussing something that has only limited application to your research, in other words the length of your discussion on each theme should be proportionate to the importance of the topic. In practice this means that your review is far more than a summary of the state of knowledge in your chosen area. Rather it should provide a synthesis of ideas that perhaps have not been linked before. Note that although you will have a separate methodology chapter/section to your research you will need to discuss the significance of researching the same topic in different ways within your review. As we have indicated already, research only appears to be a linear process so although the review comes before methods you do need to display your knowledge of methodology literature in your review.

> **TIP**
>
> Colour code the key ideas you have identified in each of the articles in order to help you to organise your review more coherently into key themes.

Once you have made your decision about the structure of your review you should take another look at your critical comments. When you present the different literatures you should spell out the implications of the knowledge that you are including and you should try to identify what you think is missing and how your research might fill that gap. Ensure that you make links between those perspectives that are similar – you can use words or phrases like similarly, in the same vein, additionally, etc. When you introduce studies that present different views you should use words like however, or conversely. We think that it is also very important that you make your own 'voice' clear. So, although at this stage in the research you are writing about the views of others, you should nevertheless make comments as you go from which the reader will be able to identify *your* perspective. This is why it is so important to read critically and make notes about your own response to the materials you are reading as you go along. For example, you may have identified that the literature provides quite conflicting knowledge on your chosen topic. You therefore need to comment on the reasons why there is such conflicting evidence and explain the reasons why you are more convinced by some than others. *Don't sit on the fence!* Keep your aims in mind at all times in order to maintain your focus and remember, as Denscombe (2002: 51) has reminded us, that the literature review is your opportunity to 'enhance the credibility of your research in the eyes of those who read it and who might be influenced by its findings'.

Your conclusion should sum up the major agreements and disagreements as well as your general conclusions about the research that has had the most influence upon your research design. You should end up with a clear statement about where your own study is going and how it will add to the existing knowledge. And finally, don't forget:

- that it's OK to use headings in a review – in fact it often helps;
- to write clearly and succinctly – imagine the reader knows nothing;
- to proof-read;
- to check all your references are included;
- to revisit and review your own critical comments throughout the process of carrying out and writing up your research.

CONCLUSION

In order to write a convincing literature review you should ensure that you consult relevant texts through which you demonstrate your knowledge of your chosen research topic. A good review will not simply describe the existing state of knowledge but it will also critique that knowledge in a way that makes the researcher's perspective explicit. In order to write critically it is necessary to *read* critically, that is to make notes of your thoughts and responses to the reading materials as you go along. It is worth putting time and effort into the preparation of the review as it is this process that will help you to consolidate your own ideas.

KEY LEARNING POINTS

- There are three key types of literature: empirical, theoretical and methodological.
- Critique involves the identification of *strengths* as well as weaknesses.
- It is important to develop strategies to help you write your review in a methodical way. We have recommended that you produce a table in which to record key aspects of the literature that you have identified as important to your research.
- You will produce the first draft of your review quite early in the research process but don't forget that it is very important to continue reading as your research progresses. You will need to revisit and revise your review before you finally complete your research.

Chapter 6

Theories, methods and their relationship to theories of knowledge

GOALS OF THIS CHAPTER

At the end of reading this chapter and by completing the online resources that accompany it, you will be:

1 familiar with different theories about crime and with the assumptions that underpin them;
2 able to understand the relationship between theories of crime, theories of knowledge and methods;
3 able to identify the methods that are most appropriate to the research questions you might wish to answer;
4 able to understand the difference between methods (the *how* of research) and *methodology* (not just the *how* but also the *why*).

OVERVIEW

- This chapter will help you to pull together the knowledge that you have gained through your reading of the early chapters in this text in order that you will be ready to 'get going' with research.
- It will focus specifically on some of the key criminological theories that have been developed over time.
- Through a series of practical exercises it will help you to understand the relationship between theories of crime, theories of knowledge and their relationship to the methods of criminological research.
- By the end of the chapter you should have the ability to identify the methods that are appropriate to your own research questions and to justify your choices.

DEVELOPING A METHODOLOGICAL APPROACH TO THE STUDY OF CRIME

Most criminological textbooks provide expansive discussions of different theories of crime, but it is true to say that more often than not theories are discussed with very little reference to either theories of knowledge or methods. Where methods are discussed it is usually in a chapter that is separate from the discussion of theory. The relationship between theories and methods, therefore, is quite often ignored and can lead to the false impression that the methods researchers use are unrelated to the questions they ask.

Criminology has been influenced by a range of disciplines within medicine and social science. Garland (1994) spoke of three key perspectives: sociological, psychoanalytic and administrative criminology. Sociological criminology is concerned with the relationship between the individual and society. Psychoanalytic criminology draws upon the work of Freud and the role of the unconscious and conscious mind. This approach focuses upon individuals and the ways in which the development of personality might influence the propensity to commit crimes. Administrative criminology focuses largely on crime prevention strategies rather than on the individuals who commit crimes. This perspective treats individuals as rational calculators who will weigh up the pros and cons of criminal acts. Each of these broad strands is influenced by a set of assumptions about the nature of the social world in which crimes take place as well as about human 'nature'. In turn these assumptions will influence the questions researchers ask as well as their decisions about the most appropriate way to gather knowledge that will help them answer them – as we saw in Chapter 2. Our main job in this chapter is to enable you to identify the assumptions which underpin various criminological theories. Once you are able to unpick these underlying assumptions you will soon be able to understand how they in turn have influenced the types of research projects in which criminologists have been involved. It is this process that will enable you to understand why research has been carried out in a particular way but, more importantly it should help you to think about your own research purposes in a deeper way.

THE DIMENSIONS OF CRIMINOLOGICAL RESEARCH

Burrell and Morgan (1992) in their book *Sociological Paradigms and Organisational Analysis* developed a matrix onto which they mapped perspectives within sociological thought along two axes. We propose to adapt this here in order to enable you to identify the underlying assumptions of key criminological theories and related penal and victim theories. Burrell and Morgan identified four sociological paradigms (or frameworks) which we believe to be helpful to the task of understanding the philosophical assumptions behind the three key criminological perspectives. However, we also wish to reveal the importance of moving in and out of frameworks as a device through which to confirm or challenge what we (think we) know. This process helps us to work out not only what our views are but also why we hold them and our reasons for changing them. Once you are able to do this you should also be able to produce better critiques of the work of others and more convincing justifications for your own research. As we noted in Chapter 1, crime is a political concept therefore, as Stout *et al.* (2008: 6) have so eloquently put it, criminology should not just be about problem solving on behalf of the state (administrative criminology) but it should also be about different ways of raising issues for debate that may challenge the state. In order for researchers to carry out both of these important tasks it is essential that they gain understanding of the ways in which assumptions about what in general any social science is/should be – and indeed what society is/should be – shape the knowledge about crime that is produced.

The study of crime is largely influenced by sociological and psychological theorising and through these disciplines our knowledge and understanding of crime has been widened considerably. It is for this reason that criminologists need to have an awareness of the assumptions that have underpinned this theorising. Sociology, as the name suggests, is concerned with the social, whereas psychology is largely concerned with individuals (although note that there are different perspectives within psychology and also that social psychology and interactionist sociology have much in common). Sociology has frequently been discussed in relation to two key concepts: order and change, both of which are relevant to any discussion of crime in society. Early social theorists grappled with two key questions: How does change come about? And how is order maintained? For change to come about human beings have to be considered as capable of acting upon their social world. For order to be maintained there has to be some acceptance of social regulation. The concepts of order and change have often been

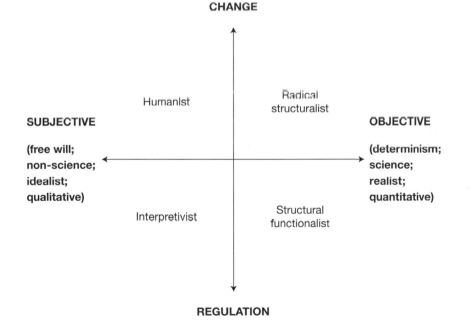

Figure 6.1 The dimensions of criminological research frameworks (adapted from Burrell and Morgan 1992)

perceived as polar opposites (as the two extremes in the change/regulation continuum in Figure 6.1). The key questions about order and change are linked to, but separate from, another set of assumptions relating to four important debates about **ontology**, **epistemology**, human nature and methodology that together make up the subjective/objective continuum in Figure 6.1 above. Researchers need to decide:

- whether or not they think that there is a tangible social world that can be discovered through research (ontology);
- whether or not they think that science provides the appropriate tools with which to research the social world and if so what form of science they are talking about. Some key questions we raised in Chapter 2 for example were what do we mean when we talk about objectivity? Can it be achieved? If so, how? Is science inductive, deductive or both? (epistemology);
- whether human beings can be said to have free will? If so, to what extent? (human nature debates);
- what sorts of methods are appropriate to their aims and research question/s (methods debates).

These are all questions with which social scientists in general are familiar and which will therefore underpin any research into crime. Following Burrell and Morgan (1992) we can represent the questions embodied within the subjective/objective continuum in the following way:

Whilst you will see that like Burrell and Morgan we have set up oppositional concepts it is our intention to demonstrate that as criminological research has progressed the debates that have ensued have facilitated ways of overcoming oppositional modes of thinking. However, the frameworks do provide us with a useful heuristic device through which researchers can become aware of the assumptions they are making and thereby become more logical in their arguments and research decisions.

The sociologist Anthony Giddens (1979) attempted to overcome the polarisation of structure and action. These concepts are linked to our consideration of the order/change continuum. Giddens (1979) pointed out that structure does not simply

Idealism	ONTOLOGY	Realism
Anti-science	EPISTEMOLOGY	Pro-science (however defined)
Free will	HUMAN 'NATURE'	Determinism
Unstructured (e.g. ethnographic interviews and observation)	METHODS	Structured (e.g. experiments and large-scale surveys)

Subjective ◄───────────────────────────────────► **Objective**

Figure 6.2 The subjective/objective continuum (adapted from Burrell and Morgan, 1992)

constrain action rather it is involved in action. An example we might use when discussing research on crime is the way in which the structure of the law might actually lead people to question why a given act is defined as criminal. In a later work (1990: 221) Giddens outlined the range of phenomena that constraint includes. He explained, for example, that human activities often take place within institutional settings, which can either mobilise or limit the human capacity to act. Furthermore, he explained how the more institutions are grounded in our everyday routines the more difficult they are to change. Finally, and perhaps most importantly for criminologists, Giddens noted the ways in which sanctions are used to limit people's options. Thus, as we explained in Chapter 1, crimes are defined and responded to within relations of power, which result in the constraint of only *some* people's actions. What we hope that you will soon realise is that this does not mean that the functionalist paradigm (by which we mean the scientific approach to research that assumes society functions in a similar way to the human body in so far as each part contributes to the whole) produced knowledge that was 'wrong' or of no use but rather that it produced only partial knowledge that led to important further debates. As we saw in Chapter 2 such insights are key to **critical criminological researchers** as they are concerned with bringing about change and therefore with the need to understand and reveal the relations of power within which crimes are defined and within which crimes and society's response to them take place.

We can plot different types of research at various points between the two extremes of the regulation/change continuum on the basis of whether their main concern is with the maintenance of social order in society as it is or with the development of a more equal society. Thus we can see that doing research involves questions not just about methods – *how* we do research – but also about *why* we have chosen to do our research in a particular way. A *methodological* approach to criminological research therefore involves the need to understand the relationship between theories of crime, theories of knowledge and methods. Research into crime has most commonly been concerned with order and regulation in society, after all if some behaviour is defined as a problem to society then it is logical to want to regulate that behaviour. However, what we know is that there is not always agreement about the sorts of behaviour that should be defined as a problem. For example, homosexuality was once defined as illegal in the UK and continues to be illegal in some countries. It was only as a result of wider debates within social science that attitudes to homosexuality were changed. Without the acknowledgement of the human capacity to change the way we think about things that we take for granted there would be little chance that the way we define and respond to crime could ever change. The history of crime however, demonstrates that in fact the way we define and respond to crime *does* change – even if changes may come about rather more slowly than some researchers would like. This does seem to indicate that it is not logical to polarise regulation and change but rather to examine the issues that may inhibit or facilitate change and to examine the contexts in which change might be more appropriate than adherence to the status quo.

You may have already deduced from your reading of Chapter 2 that discussions of **interpretivism** and **positivism** are often centred on another polarisation, objectivity and subjectivity, or we might say science or anti-science. We attempted to show how it might be helpful to see the constant interplay between objectivity and subjectivity by being more precise about what we mean by objectivity and by keeping this concept separate from the concept of value-neutrality. We did this in order to include the third theory of knowledge, critical criminological research, within our discussion. When you start plotting the assumptions made by different theorists on the matrix in Figure 6.1 we hope that you will be able to identify a pattern that will enable you to discuss the assumptions that this group of theorists tend to make. Keep in mind the fact that debates about theories of knowledge centre on the extent to which the social world can be studied in the same way as the natural world as well as on the issue of what is understood by the term 'truth'.

PAUSE TO THINK . . .

- Can we find 'the truth' about crime once and for all?
- Is truth always mediated by our experiences and therefore a relative concept? (Refer back to Chapter 2.)

Once you get the hang of identifying the philosophical assumptions that theorists make you should begin to understand that the delineations between the different research traditions are not as neat as many 'standard textbooks' suggest. Furthermore, the exercises outlined below should help you to identify some of the contradictions and flaws that can always be found in theories. Once you are able to do this you will in turn be able to make and express judgements about the reasons why some theories are stronger than others. Thus, when you come to do your own research you will be far better equipped to:

- make suitable choices about the literature which is to inform your study;
- discuss the theories that have informed your own studies;
- comment upon the strengths as well as the limitations of the theories that have informed your work in order to explain the ways in which your research will address the gaps in existing knowledge;
- express the reasons why the methods you have chosen are appropriate to the questions you want to answer. (This means that as well as being able to *describe* the methods that you use in your own research you should also be able to *justify* your choice of methods and explain *why* you carried out your research in a particular way.)

THE BEGINNINGS OF CRIMINOLOGY: CLASSICISM AND POSITIVISM

You will be able to find detailed accounts of early criminology in many of the textbooks available from your university library. Furthermore it is highly likely that your degree course will have begun with an outline of the main criminological theories. Our aim here is not to reiterate those theories in detail but instead to get you thinking about what they assume. The two sets of ideas outlined in brief in Box 6.1 both continue to influence the ways in which crime is researched today. This first mapping exercise will have shown

BOX 6.1 EARLY THEORIES OF CRIME AND PUNISHMENT

Using the knowledge gained in Chapter 2, think carefully about the following before reading on:

1   The Italian economist Beccaria was a key theorist of the classical school of criminology. He believed that crime could be understood through reason, that is, it was assumed that people are capable of calculating the risks of their actions (Lilly *et al.*, 2011). Similarly, the British philosopher Bentham (1789/ 1970: 1, cited by Valier, 2002: 10) theorised that humans aim to avoid pain and maximise pleasure. These ideas underpinned the deterrence and retributive theories of punishment. According to Beccaria, if human behaviour is overly controlled it is likely that crime will increase rather than decrease therefore it was deemed important that punishments should 'fit the crimes'.

2   Lombroso (1876) theorised that some people were 'born' criminals and that the criminal 'type' could be distinguished from the non-criminal 'type' by their physical features. Criminal anthropologists of the day tried to identify the significant physical features, such as weight and size of the brain, closely set eyebrows, large cheek bones, amongst others. Galton (1883: 15, cited by Valier, 2002: 19) described criminal types as lacking conscience and self control, these are mental conditions which, he theorised, were hereditary. The goals of these researchers were focused upon what could be observed and/or measured.

- Where would you 'map' these two sets of ideas in terms of their assumptions about free will/**determinism**? Try to give reasons for the position you choose.
- What theory of knowledge is implied by each set of ideas?
- Where would you place each set of ideas on the regulation/change continuum? Why?
- What are the implications of all the above for the choice of research methods?
- What do these theories leave out?

you (quite quickly, we hope) that they represent opposite ends of the free will/ determinism continuum. **Classicism** assumes that because human beings are rational beings they are all equally capable of making decisions that are in their best interests – but we might want to add the caveat 'not in circumstances of their own choosing' to invoke Karl Marx. It is not necessary to be a Marxist to acknowledge that it might be very important to know something about the circumstances in which people commit crimes but since the pleasure/pain principle of classicism did not take account of social inequalities in society many criminologists today see the theory as incomplete. According to classicist theories all criminals should be treated in the same way irrespective of what we would call extenuating circumstances. Thus someone who stole food because his/her family is starving would be treated in the same way as someone who stole food despite having plenty. At heart the classicists expressed a theory of *punishment* which they viewed as deterrence; theories of crime causation were not their concern nor were the motivations of criminals. Instead classicists reduced criminals to calculators of risk.

BOX 6.2 CLASSICIST IDEAS IN USE TODAY

Look up rational choice theory and situational crime prevention, both of which come under the heading of administrative criminology.

- What do these perspectives assume about both criminals and victims?
- Do these assumptions take account sufficiently of people's different life experiences?
- What types of research methods can be used to support rational choice theory?
- What would be the likely attitude of such researchers to the official crime statistics?
- What are the strengths and limitations of such research?

In opposition to classicism the early positivists (we like to refer to these as *biological or individual* positivists) did not assume that human beings were in control of their actions because they theorised that crimes were only committed by those who were somehow 'defective'. In other words the causes of crime lay not in the way in which society was organised – or as in the case of the classicist argument in the way in which people were controlled – but rather in the biological make-up of each person. Thus experts were required to identify those people who, as prisoners of their own biology, could not be held responsible for their crimes. Of course, this also implies that they could not be reformed and therefore this perspective was used to justify, at best, shutting prisoners away indefinitely in poor conditions or, at worst, the death penalty. Whilst Lombroso's focus on physical characteristics became the focus of critique (including in his own work), biologically deterministic theories continued into the twentieth century. The shift in focus to supposed hereditary mental conditions became known as the eugenics movement, a science defined by Galton (1883) as 'the science of improving stock' (cited by Valier, 2002: 19). As a result of this approach some of the most brutal forms of social control were justified, for example in the United States there were mass sterilisations of people defined as 'feebleminded' and in some states 'psychosurgeries' (Lilly *et al.*, 2011), such as frontal lobotomies, were permitted up until the 1970s. For Europeans the worst examples of the impact of the study of inherited characteristics was seen in Nazi Germany.

As the biological positivist theory of knowledge assumes that the (social) problem of crime can be understood best by copying the methods of natural science it can be seen that there is a clear relationship between this assumption and the ways in which they chose to treat their subject matter (criminals). Whilst criminals, like non-criminals, are thinking, conscious human beings there is an assumption that they should be treated as if they are 'things' (or non-human) for the purposes of research. That is, their feelings and motives are excluded from the process of study. Thus you should be able to discern the relationship between ontology, epistemology and the choice of research methods made by early positivists who assumed that motives lie outside the enterprise of science.

Whilst classicism focused upon individuals' free will and their ability to make choices, it too failed to focus upon people's explanations of their crimes. Rather classicism assumed that there is an abstract human nature that is inherently selfish and hedonistic. For this reason classicists focused upon crime prevention. Early classicism assumed that crime would be prevented if controls were not so restricting as to cause rebellion. Put simply, the more restrictions there are in society the less pleasure people would have and the more laws would be broken, an idea which is summed up in Lilly *et al.*'s phrase (2011) 'bad laws make bad people'. This said, in cases of serious violent crime, it was argued that punishment should be meted out quickly and that citizens should be aware of the crimes that carry harsh punishments so as to ensure that they would be clear about the certainty of the punishment following such crimes. So, whilst on the one hand the classicists' focus upon free will seems in stark contrast to the determinism of biological positivism, on the other hand, when we explore the assumptions that classicists held about 'human nature', it is possible to discern determinism, albeit in a different guise, since 'human nature' was assumed to be universally selfish and hedonistic and therefore in need of constant control. Classicists believed that it was necessary for states to be open about the moral codes that underpinned the laws in society and that there should be consensus about the need for the laws that exist. Their concern was not to explain crime but rather to prevent it by ensuring that most people adhered to the social controls.

PAUSE TO THINK . . .

Do those who break the law always act out of self-interest? Can you think of examples of crimes that might be said to stem from different motivations?

LEARNING FROM THE PAST

The early biological and sociological positivists have to be understood in the context of their time and place. The idea that social issues could be studied in the same way as natural science stemmed from the success of science in solving problems in the natural world. Indeed the word positivism represents the optimistic view that the world could be changed for the better . . . but did this mean for the better of all? When we examine the work of early theorists it is possible to discern a whole host of assumptions that we might wish to challenge in our current society. For example, what we would now understand as sexist, classist and racist assumptions can be seen in hindsight to have underpinned the work of Lombroso (1920: 151):

> Women have many traits in common with children; that their moral sense is deficient; that they are revengeful, jealous ... In ordinary cases these defects are neutralised by piety, maternity, want of passion, sexual coldness, weakness, and an underdeveloped conscience.

For Lombroso, white middle-class males were assumed to be at the pinnacle of evolution therefore any characteristics that were not held in common with these men were thought to be the ones that would facilitate the identification of the criminal classes. When explaining female crime Lombroso believed that the further removed a woman was from white middle-class definitions of 'femininity' the more likely she was to be criminal. This is a view that was also present in the work of psychologists such as Thomas (1907) and Freud (1920) – see discussion by Klein (1973) – which is evident in the words of Thomas (1907: 112, cited by Klein, 1973):

> What we look for most in the female is femininity, and when we find the opposite in her we must conclude, as a rule, that there must be some anomaly ... Virility was one of the special features of the savage woman ... in the portraits of red Indian and Negro beauties, whom it is difficult to recognise for women, so huge are their jaws and cheekbones, so hard and coarse their features, and the same is often the case in their crania and brains.

PAUSE TO THINK . . .

Examine newspaper reports of female-perpetrated crimes.

- Can you identify some of the assumptions of early positivists in the ways in which female criminality is reported today?
- How might criminological researchers challenge such ideas?

The sociologist Emile Durkheim is famous for the way in which he applied the methods of science to the study of social life. His important study of suicide (1970) provides us with a very detailed account of how he arrived at the view that suicide, which seems like one of the most individual acts that can be committed, is caused by forces that are outside of the individual. Note that in Durkheim's time (1858–1917) suicide was against the law, which is no longer the case. In this study Durkheim tried to follow the rules of natural science very closely and it took him a great deal of time to come up with the conclusion that lack of integration in society was the cause of what he called *egoistic* suicide; lack of security about the rules that govern society was the external cause of what Durkheim called *anomic* suicide. These were the two forms of suicide which, according to Durkheim, were prevalent in modern industrial societies. It is

BOX 6.3 **WERE BIOLOGICAL POSITIVISTS ABLE TO AVOID THE USE OF VALUES IN THEIR RESEARCH INTO CRIME?**

Do some further reading about:

1   how Lombroso explained female criminality;
2   the 'types' of people who were identified as in need of treatment by scientists in the eugenics movement.

What was assumed by these theorists?

Look up critiques of Wilson and Herrnstein's (1985) *Crime and Human Nature* and Herrnstein and Murray's (1994) *The Bell Curve: Intelligence and Class Structure in American Life.*

Did these much later studies suggest that the authors were able to carry out their work in such a way as to exclude their ideological views?

BOX 6.4 **THE STUDY OF SUICIDE**

Research the debates about Durkheim's method in the study of suicide.

*   Do you think that he managed to keep his values out of the research process? Provide reasons for your answer and make an evaluative comment.
*   What assumptions did Durkheim make about the official statistics on suicide?
*   Have all those who have researched suicide made the same assumptions about the official statistics?
*   Choose a specific crime and identify the official statistics on the prevalence of this crime. Think of a research question that relates to this particular type of crime and try to articulate the way in which your research question will shape your perspective on the official statistics.

Hint: You may need to refer to Chapter 1 in order to refresh your memory about the different assumptions that theorists have made about official statistics.

interesting to research the debates on the study of suicide because they reveal the ways in which studies from different epistemological positions widen our understanding of this phenomenon.

Whilst we have suggested that positivism implied some optimism about the possibility of manipulating causal variables in an attempt to reduce crime in society, a focus on the individual's characteristics (biological positivism) can lead to the justification of drastic measures to control behaviour. For example in the past surgery and electric shock treatment were justified and today drug treatments are used to control behaviour in children as young as two. A focus on social conditions led to entirely different solutions to the problem of crime, which involved the manipulation of social variables, such as widening access to education or action against poverty. The sociologist Emile Durkheim, who is often considered to be an archetypal positivist, for example assumed that crime is a normal, indeed healthy, aspect of social life (Durkheim, 1982). For Durkheim crime served a positive function because laws signal the moral values of society. When individuals break laws the social response serves to maintain the 'moral' society. However, there may be occasions, especially when groups break the law, when the social response is to question the morality of the law (rather than the lawbreakers). In these cases crime functions to change the status quo and to change perceptions of what is/is not moral. As Carrabine *et al.* (2009) point out this is the paradox of functionalism. We believe, however, that this paradox demonstrates the fallacy of labelling a *theorist* because the whole reason for developing theories is to test them out and revise them in the light of new information – this is the nature of research and it means that theorists can provide more nuanced explanations or shift their ground in the light of new evidence (if you are interested you might want to look at Durkheim's work as a whole and consider to what extent it is appropriate to refer to him as 'a positivist').

Researchers take account of and build upon the work of others. The influential American sociologist Robert Merton, for example, drew upon the work of Durkheim to develop a theory of crime that he linked to the strains of living in the American society of his time. As Tierney (2010) has pointed out, Merton posited a link between the lack of opportunities to achieve, legitimately, the American dream of material success and the incidences of crime. It follows from this that if the legitimate means of success are improved, say through wider access to further education, then crimes will be reduced. However, the theory has several shortcomings – for example, many crimes are committed by those who *have* achieved material success; there are differences of opinion about what are the most important cultural values; violent crimes cannot be explained by Merton's theory and, as we shall see shortly, as cultural criminology has highlighted, some crimes may give the perpetrators pleasure – or 'a buzz' as we might say colloquially. This said, Box (1983) argued that if Merton's anomie theory was applied to the study of corporate crimes some of the most well-known criticisms would be addressed.

POSITIVISM TODAY

We have seen so far that the focus of analysis for biological positivism was the individual mind or body. These perspectives generally failed to take account of the impact of the social context of crime. Later positivistic schools of thought shifted the focus of attention from individuals to the social conditions in which crimes are committed. This did not necessarily signal a shift away from determinism but rather a shift in theorising about what the determining factors leading to crime might be. To put this in more formal language there was a shift in the theories of causation, that is, a shift from a focus on the individual to a focus on society, but not a shift in the *epistemological* or *ontological* positions. For some commentators a problem with sociological positivism's assumption that the causes of crime lie outside of the individual is that it allows criminals to abrogate responsibility for their actions. This is why many social researchers today talk about *reasons* rather than causes because it is only through an examination of the *relationship* between individuals and society that we are able to get a more nuanced understanding of why different forms of crime are committed. The assumptions of such researchers challenge the notion of causation (whether social or individual) and instead assume that it is important to look at the interplay between the individual and society in order to assess the weight that should be given to each before attempting to change policy or suggest 'treatment'. That is, such researchers try not to fall into the trap of operating with the assumption that individuals are either completely determined by their biology or by the social order but they see the merit in using quantitative methods that are associated with natural science.

Researchers operating within the positivist theory of knowledge usually start out by examining the relationship between two variables – a '**bivariate relationship**' (e.g. poverty and crime; intelligence and crime) – and to do this they need to think about which variable is dependent upon the other. In these examples crime is the **dependent variable** but sometimes it might be hard to know which variable is the dependent one, for example, with the variables illegal drugs and crime does illegal drug use necessarily lead to crime? Can involvement with other crimes actually be a factor that leads to drug use? It is important to think about these issues in order for the research to be fair as well as to think about other possible variables that might challenge the relationship we have found (this moves us on to 'multivariate analysis', as in Durkheim's study of suicide). As we saw in Chapter 4 there are several variables that might be related to crime. Furthermore we saw that we need to be quite clear about the sorts of crimes we are talking about in our studies. An individual researcher will not be able to test out all possible variables alone but s/he will be able to look at other studies in order to see what has been suggested already. S/he will also be able to decide whether a relationship is **spurious** (leading us up the garden path, as it were) or not. So, for example, claims that there is a relationship between low intelligence and crime can be challenged by a shift in focus onto crimes such as corporate crime or crimes that take place in the private sphere. Even when there is evidence that might be quite convincing it is important that researchers specify the circumstances in which their theories hold true. For example, if poverty is found to be an indicator of certain types of crime does this relationship hold true in all circumstances? We might want to compare rural areas with urban areas, for example, to decide whether we need to qualify the conditions in which poverty is a significant factor. Furthermore, we might identify other **independent variables** that are equally significant and each of these might suggest different types of policy response. Researchers using positivist assumptions will always need to discuss their samples (see Chapter 10) in order to demonstrate that they have done everything possible to avoid sample bias. They must also show understanding of 'sampling error', which can always occur simply because criminological researchers cannot ever study the whole population of those involved in particular types of crimes. This is why it is important to carry out tests of statistical significance (see Chapter 9).

It is important that criminological researchers today continue to look for **correlations** between variables but we suggest that it is equally important to challenge the assumptions of early positivists who, in our view, mistakenly conflated causes and correlations. We believe that it is because of this conflation that extreme determinism was a feature of early positivistic research which, in turn, made it possible to justify some of the most worrying measures to prevent crime that we have discussed above. We need to be alert to the ways in which some researchers today may use what we believe are outmoded assumptions about science in general and causation in particular to try to implement policies that go beyond the findings of their research.

INTERPRETIVISM: WHERE SOCIOLOGY AND SOCIAL PSYCHOLOGY COLLIDE

As we pointed out at the beginning of this book, crime is a socially constructed concept and crimes take place in different social contexts. To understand crime more completely, therefore, it is also important to carry out research in a way that takes account of people's subjective accounts of their motivations. Theories within this perspective challenge the idea that people can be treated as if they are 'things' and instead focus upon the ways in which people come to understand themselves in relation to others. One perspective within the interpretivist theory of knowledge, interactionism, developed from the work of the sociologist George Simmel (1908) and the social psychologist George Herbert Mead (1934). Mead's work influenced the symbolic interactionist perspective, which was concerned with social processes. In criminology the concern with the social processes that lead to the status of criminal is usually referred to as the labelling perspective. The impact of labelling has been a key idea in the study of crime because, as Kitsuse (1962) noted in his discussion of deviance, it is only at the point where a person places a label on another that behaviour comes to be seen as problematic. In other words it is the social reaction to an act that is significant rather than the act itself. The ways in which others react to our behaviour shape our sense of who we are – a 'kind' person, a 'happy' person, an 'eccentric' person ... a 'criminal'. Labels of any kind are likely to affect the ways in which people subsequently perceive themselves and act so this suggests that studying the interaction between individuals and others in the wider society might expand our understanding of crime. This said it is important to be mindful that people react to labels in different ways therefore it might be important to work out when and in which circumstances a negative label might produce a positive response.

The person who influenced criminological thinking most with regard to labelling was Howard Becker. In his book *Outsiders* (1963), one issue he examined was the way in which the development of laws in relation to the use of marijuana in 1930s America created a climate in which the young people who used this drug came to be perceived as a risk to society. Once this process has taken place those labelled become outsiders and – so the theory goes – develop their own cultural norms, which they see as being counter to the general culture of society. Young (1971), in a similar vein, discussed the way in which the police reaction to the use of marijuana in Britain gave rise to what he called a 'fantasy crime wave' which served to amplify this form of 'deviance' as the drug users lived up to the stereotypes that were a feature of newspaper reports. The media outrage created political pressures, which in turn gave rise to heavier policing and harsher sentences. As Valier (2002: 93) states there was a tendency for policy makers to

> ## BOX 6.5 THE ASSUMPTIONS OF THE LABELLING PERSPECTIVE
>
> Plot the position of labelling theorists on the matrix in Figure 6.1. Think about the following questions before you decide upon their position on the matrix:
>
> - What would be the attitude of labelling theorists to official crime statistics?
> - What does this perspective assume about human nature and the social structure?
> - What questions do you think criminologists who are influenced by this perspective are likely to ask?
> - What methods are most appropriate to this perspective?

mistake the changes which were caused, in Young's view, by the social reaction as further evidence of the problematic nature of *all* drug users.

THE THRILL OF CRIME

Many explanations of crime have tended to overpredict crime amongst the working class. This is partly because, in general, criminologists have focused less on the crimes of the powerful than they have on the crimes of those with least power. However, we know that some conventional crimes, for example shoplifting, are not solely committed by the poor therefore this knowledge leads to the questioning of explanations that link shoplifting to determining variables, such as the boring jobs that were carried out by the working classes or their basic need for more resources in order to live. As O'Malley (2010) has pointed out, this was a point that was made by Jack Katz in his book *Seductions of Crime* (1988). Katz therefore shifted his attention to the lived experiences of those committing crimes and identified the thrill associated with the risk as a reason for crimes. This shift of focus can explain why those who are *not* poor might engage in shoplifting, indeed it was theorised that the thrill might be greater the more a person had to lose. The only way we can find out whether this theory might be important is to talk to criminals or to enter their worlds through participant observational studies. O'Malley (2010: 9) refers to the ways in which cultural theorists pointed to the normality of thrill and risk in the modern culture of the consumer society where 'the boundary between legitimate and illegitimate is becoming more volatile and ambiguous'. Cultural criminology acknowledges that whilst some criminals may be rational calculators of risk and reward there are also other constructions of risk that might be relevant to our understanding of crime precisely because they reject this calculating form of rationality. This means that the role of emotion becomes an important element in the search to widen knowledge of criminal behaviour. There is also a sense in which recent developments in cultural theory fit with the **dialectical** (see below) analysis that is associated with critical criminology. You should have deduced that here the assumption of free will is central to the way in which research within this perspective is carried out.

MARXIST THEORIES AND CRIMINOLOGY

In general Marxist criminologists were critical of attempts to see the causes of crime as evidence of individual pathology and they maintained that this was a way of perpetuating the idea that criminals can be distinguished from non-criminals. These conflict theorists argued that the conventional study of crime was tied to the capitalist economic system and indeed that the laws supported that system in so far as they were developed in the interests of capital. A key moment for criminology was the publication of a book called *The New Criminology* (Taylor *et al.,* 1973) in which a thorough critique of existing criminological theories was presented. Some of the main issues to which they pointed were: the failure of criminologists to ask questions about control as well as about crime; the over-determinism of some explanations (this critique also included those Marxist theories that implied the capitalist system would have to be overthrown in order to solve the problem of crime) at the expense of recognising the purposive actions of human beings; the inadequacy of some theories of knowledge. Indeed, Muncie (1998) stated that this book transformed criminology from a science of social control to a struggle for social justice. The book also led to a focus on the crimes of the powerful. In a sense conflict theorists assumed that the law produced criminals (see Lilly *et al.,* 2011) because in their view laws served to conceal the crimes of those who had the most power. These ideas challenged the value-neutrality that (supposedly) was a feature of positivism and the assumption that society was characterised by consensus, which was an assumption of mainstream criminology, as in Durkheim's view. However, *The New Criminology* (1973) was an important book not because it provided a 'blueprint' for research but more because the huge intra-left debates and divisions between idealists and realists to which it gave rise, as well as the critiques from the opposite ('right') end of the political spectrum which were sparked by this book, were significant to the task of doing research as they signalled the need to be ever-mindful of the assumptions all researchers make as well as of the strengths and limitations of their evidence.

BOX 6.6 RESEARCHING THE CRIMES OF THE POWERFUL

Corporate crimes have been explained in various ways using the insights of many of the theorists to whom we have referred. Imagine that having done some reading about corporate crime you have become interested in the relationship of this type of crime to the political economy and that you want to do some research that utilises this knowledge. Try to do the following:

- Outline your philosophical assumptions.
- Define the type of corporate crime upon which you will focus your study.
- Outline the main aim/s of your research.
- Construct a research question that relates to your aims.
- Identify the most appropriate method/s.
- Suggest some outcomes.

MAINTAINING THE LEGITIMACY OF THE STATE

Hall *et al.*'s (1978) *Policing the Crisis* provides us with a good example of a study that attempted to explain a panic about street crimes (referred to in the press as 'muggings') in Britain. You will find accounts of this study in several texts (e.g. Downes and Rock, 2007; Valier, 2002). Briefly this study challenged the notion that there was a new crime (mugging) by providing historical evidence of the existence of similar street crimes across several time periods. The researchers spent 13 months trawling through the press coverage of 'mugging' and they demonstrated that several types of street crime were conflated under this heading thereby giving rise to fear and moral panic. Their research into the incidences of street crimes, as revealed through official statistical records, suggested that the social reaction was out of proportion.

This led the researchers to ask how this came about. They explained how the media and judiciary interacted in such a way as to present a (false/exaggerated) picture of the increasingly unsafe British streets that were supposedly becoming like their US counterparts. Crucially attention was drawn to the way in which the term mugging was used to refer to incidences of crimes that involved black perpetrators and white victims. Hall *et al.* developed a theoretical explanation of the panic surrounding mugging, which was grounded in their analysis of the social and economic changes that were challenging the prosperity and full employment of the working classes for the first time since World War II. Their analysis suggested that black youth became a scapegoat, the means by which attention was deflected from the crisis that challenged the legitimacy of the state and united the public against the perceived threat of black youth. This process divided the white and black working classes by constructing the 'enemies' as youth, crime and 'race' (see Downes and Rock, 2007) and facilitated the practice of 'stop and search', which in turn gave rise to the amplification of street crimes perpetrated by young black males. The point made by Hall *et al.* (1978) is that this whole process takes place *without* coercion. They use Gramsci's (an early Italian Marxist) concept of **hegemony** to provide understanding of the ways in which states in crisis need to unite their citizens, without coercion, against a common 'threat' in order to legitimate and sustain their control.

BOX 6.7 POLICING THE CRISIS

Plot the different assumptions underpinning the study by Hall *et al.* on the matrix in Figure 6.1.

- Can you discern what this study assumed about regulation?
- How do you think the authors thought about the issue of objectivity?
- What methods were used in this study? And what was their attitude to official crime statistics?
- Now, look up left realism. How do you think left realists might respond to Hall *et al.*?

To avoid confusion between what we have called a critical epistemology and Marxism in general we think that it is important to remind you that *critical criminological research* refers to a theory of knowledge that is characterised by an effort to overcome some of the binary oppositions to which we have referred in this chapter. Whilst much of radical criminology is influenced by the ideas of Marx it is the **dialectical** elements of Marx's work that underpin the theory of knowledge which we refer to as critical criminology. Harvey *et al.* (2000: 85) define **dialectical analysis** as 'a process of locating events or actions in a wider social and historical context and involves conceptually moving backwards and forwards between the specific part and the whole'.

ANTI-DISCRIMINATION

In recent years criminologists have been concerned with the ways in which concepts such as gender, ethnicity and sexuality might be relevant to our study of crime, especially those crimes that appear to be motivated by hatred. However, as a discipline, criminology has been particularly slow to confront feminist insights in research. In general, debates within feminism have informed research that has been concerned with both sexism and racism, but as Heidensohn (1985: 162) argued it was necessary to 'step outside the confines of criminological theory altogether and seek models from other sources in order to achieve a better understanding of women and crime'. This said, the influence of black feminist thought on criminology at that time was 'almost nil' (Daly and Stephens, 1995). What is of interest here, given that the focus of our discussion is the relationship between theories and methods in the research process, is that criminology has been for the most part dominated by white males. For many years male criminologists made unproblematic generalisations about *all* criminals, which were based on a male 'norm'. Furthermore, despite men's use of methods, such as in-depth ethnographic interviews (see Chapter 8), that have in more recent years come to be associated with 'feminist' research, the gaze of the (predominantly male) criminologist has been on criminal men's crimes against other men.

It was feminists who raised the question of violence against women and children in the private sphere and black men and women who identified the need to question, amongst other issues, why more black people in general were policed and incarcerated than white people; why racist violence was overlooked. Feminists who were concerned with the victimisation of women (as opposed to women's lawbreaking) led the way in terms of advocating methods that involved the subjects of research in research design. Any criminological research that is concerned with the unequal treatment of victims is likely to utilise a variety of methods such as in-depth ethnographic interviews and participant observation as a way of 'telling it like it is' from the perspective of those who have found it hard to obtain justice. Such studies are often criticised because they are small in scale and therefore generalisations cannot be made. However, it is important for researchers to be mindful of the fact that the purpose of such studies is *not* to make generalisations but rather to gain in-depth knowledge and understanding of an issue from the perspective of those who are affected by it. For those feminists who were concerned with women's lawbreaking the focus of study was often centred on the ways in which assumptions about 'proper' gender roles, especially as represented in the press, impacted upon the processes of sentencing (see for example Lloyd, 1995; Jewkes, 2011) or on the different conditions of existence in which women carried out crimes (Carlen, 1992). Feminist debates in turn led to gender research carried out by men, which was concerned with explaining the different ways in which men come to understand their masculinity. Such research suggested that many violent crimes, but especially those against women, can be linked to the perpetrators' understandings of their gender roles.

The new millennium has been characterised by increasing worries about crimes that are motivated by fear – or more accurately – hatred of lesbian and gay people, bisexual or trans-sexual (LGBT) people who do not fit into the so-called heterosexual norm. These concerns suggested that research into crime needed also to examine the victims of crime. Questions concerning when, where and on whom the status of victim is conferred became important to those who wished to change the ways in which we think not only about criminals but also about victims. Research in this area has led to improvements in policing, for example see Herek *et al.* (2003).

The main value underpinning critical criminological research is the need to overcome oppressive practices that serve to maintain unequal relationships. Hence critical criminology is open about its value positions and is quite eclectic in its choice of methods. Anti-sexist and anti-racist perspectives as well as those that take account of social class and the diversity of culture will all therefore come under this heading. As we saw in Chapter 2 critical criminology does not just seek to find causes of crime, nor does it simply attempt to reveal the ways in which those committing crimes interpret and account for their own actions, rather critical criminology attempts to provide theoretical understanding of specific crimes as well as of the response to those crimes. In order to do this critical criminological researchers, whether they call themselves Marxists or not, will be concerned to follow Marx's example of attempting to 'dig below the surface' in order to challenge everyday perceptions. It is through this process that they are able to go beyond causation and beyond interpretation in order to provide analyses of the many ways in which the law might be seen to operate in the interests of those with the most wealth and power.

Instructor PPoint Slides

Epistemologies and real life reasearch

BOX 6.8 USING MIXED METHODS TO INFLUENCE POLICY: KELLY *ET AL.* (1999)

Liz Kelly's Home Office Study *Domestic Violence Matters* was, on her own admission, very complex (see Darlington and Scott, 2002). The aims of this study were:

1   to provide crisis intervention follow-up to police responses to domestic violence calls;
2   to develop stronger commitment locally to a law enforcement response;
3   to encourage more consistent and coordinated responses.

The fulfilment of each aim was gained through the use of multiple methods that were both qualitative and qualitative.

In relation to the first aim the quantitative data came from a database filled out by workers. This revealed the numbers of women who received a response within the required time limit; the other agencies to which they were referred; the number of times they contacted the domestic violence project subsequently.

- List some reasons why you think the researchers thought that the collection of quantitative data was insufficient to the task of fulfilling aim 1.
- Which other methods might be helpful? Give reasons for your choices.
- In what circumstances do you think that quantitative and qualitative methods can be mixed?

Liz Kelly told Yvonne Darlington (2002: 132) that the research team had:

never hidden the fact that we are feminists, but I think that does mean that you are held to account and accusations of bias in a way that people who pretend a neutral position are not, so one of the ways we have responded to this is to never publish anything where we weren't really certain that it was actually in the data, so that we can defend the position from the research material and not an ideological position.

Would you say that this is good advice for all researchers? Why/why not?

DISCUSSION

Our brief examination of some of the key theories of crime with which you will be gaining familiarity demonstrates that the history of criminological debates remains relevant to research in the present. As we saw in Chapter 4 it is most important that we define our terms as clearly as possible. Early theorists tried to come up with general theories of crime but a shift in focus onto the issue of definitions helped criminologists to explain the incidences of particular types of crime in specific settings. We have seen that some critics of positivism were unhappy with its assumption of determinism and some even saw the studies as futile (see Tierney, 2010). However, we do not believe that they were futile, rather we see research as a holistic process through which different academics and practitioners share their knowledge. For example, if we take the social issues of poverty and unemployment, which have been identified by some as *causes* of crime, we can see that despite refutations of such a causal relationship the original theories have given rise to important debates that have shown the *relevance* of these issues to the incidences of some crimes. For example, Nicholas *et al.* (2007) found that those living in areas of high deprivation are most likely to suffer from burglary and that the perpetrators are likely to come from the same area, a view expressed generally by left realists. Whilst left idealists criticised left realists for reproducing what we might call stereotypical ideas about working-class crime – a criticism levelled at Merton's strain theory you may remember – Tierney (2010) defends left realists for their acknowledgement and explanations of intra-class crime.

The intra-left debates highlighted the ways in which research assumptions can have the effect of polarising the key concepts of regulation and change. Left realists' concern with the experiences of working-class victims of crime was an important aspect of their research, but their work also led to more and more regulation of the working class without a concomitant concern for addressing some of the conditions in which crimes perpetrated by and against the working classes are committed. As Carlen (1992: 58, cited by Tierney, 2010: 295) pointed out, the problem with left realists was that, unlike the earlier scientific realism of Durkheim and of the philosopher of science Karl Popper, they neglected to subvert **common sense** and instead fed into common-sense ideas about 'the' problem of crime. The constant process of critique should help researchers to increase the strength of their arguments by sensitising them to the ways in which it is possible to overcome the oppositional forms of thinking that have often been a feature of the different dimensions of research – as outlined at the beginning of this chapter. We hope that the mapping exercises demonstrate that the nearer a theory is to the centre of the subjective/objective continuum the more likely it is that the researcher has taken account of the interplay between individual criminals and the social world in which their crimes are committed and of the difficulties involved in treating the social world in exactly the same way as the inanimate world of science. The nearer the theories about crime and how we should respond to it are to the centre of the regulation/change continuum the more likely it is that the researchers will be inclined to examine the relationship between power and control in society and to point out *who* has the power to bring about policy changes and *who* is being regulated.

Neo-conservatives such as Herrnstein and Murray (1994) explained the crimes of those living in areas of deprivation in terms of cognitive disadvantage rather than economic disadvantage. In their view economic disadvantage was a function of poor cognitive skills. They put forward the already discredited argument that low intelligence was more likely amongst the black population without providing convincing evidence for this reassertion and, as we hope you have discovered as a result of reading this chapter and looking at the online resources, critics argued that their study was poorly executed because it displayed confusion between correlation and causality. As researchers you should become aware of the ways in which the language of science can be invoked to support spurious evidence. You should also become aware of the ways in which politicians and reporters repeatedly draw upon old ideas that have been shown to be problematic by the academic peer review process. For example, debates about the UK riots in 2011 drew upon Charles Murray's ideas, even if not in an explicit way (see Burnett, 2011).

Herrnstein and Murray's study (1994) demonstrates the importance of knowing the difference between a well-executed scientific study of crime and one that claims to follow the rules of science yet fails to conform to them. When carrying out or critiquing research within one of the other two theories of knowledge we have identified here it is very important to avoid the trap of assessing it in terms of positivist criteria as these will not be appropriate. You will need therefore to examine the claims made for each piece of research. As a general rule any studies that are carried out within the interpretivist theory of knowledge will explicitly reject the search for causal relationships in favour of providing detailed descriptions of a particular social phenomenon from the perspective of those who are the subjects of research. There is much to be gained from obtaining a level of understanding of how people make sense of their own worlds. Straight away this should tell you that interpretivists do not assume that they can know exactly what it is they wish to find out before they have begun the process of exploration, although they will undoubtedly operate with some domain assumptions that they may or may not make explicit through the process of research.

We hope that it has become clear through the exercises above that interpretivists make the assumption that human beings have free will therefore they assume that people can act upon their world. However, as we have hoped to convey, the free will/determinist opposition can be misleading as it does not adequately reflect reality and it is for this reason that many researchers attempt to show through their studies that in real life experiences we are neither totally constrained nor totally free. The constraints upon us all vary from person to person. Just as some structural approaches can be criticised for reducing human beings' experiences to social structures (determinism) so some humanist and interpretivist approaches can be criticised for reducing all experiences to individual consciousness. This is something that labelling theorists were aware of when they pointed to the need to focus upon *interaction*. The labelling perspective also gave rise to debates about the nature of crime itself. As such it was a very important development that drew attention to the ways in which crime in society is constructed at any given time. There was thus a shift of focus from criminals to those who made and upheld the law as well as to the processes that were involved in the construction of criminal identities. This led to debates about the extent to which official crime statistics can be said to reflect the reality of crime, as we saw in Chapter 2 and as the exercise relating to the study of suicide in this chapter should have demonstrated.

Once crime statistics are understood as a **social construction** (rather than 'facts') further questions can be raised about the assumed linkages between variables that are taken for granted in some studies. Such questioning requires different methods of research that enable researchers to observe decision-making processes, such as when or in what circumstances people report crimes; when or in what circumstances the police take action; how decisions are made in court. However, as critical criminologists acknowledge, official statistics are real in their effects therefore some researchers may wish to explore how they serve to create fear of specific groups or neighbourhoods and thereby legitimate constraints. One important theme in research by black feminist scholars, for example, has been the distorted view of black crime (see Daly and Stephens, 1995; May, 2001) that is gained from treating criminal statistics as 'facts'. We hope that you were able to identify the way in which Hall *et al.*'s work (1978) was also concerned to challenge the statistical 'facts' that were used to justify the overly heavy policing of black youth. Those researching in the critical criminological research theory of knowledge assume that people do have free will but that there are often constraints that potentially can determine their future. However, through dialectic analysis the possibility of change is always envisaged, which points to the need to be cautious about responses to crime that involve more and more regulations.

Some criminological researchers carry out in-depth studies of particular groups of criminals, victims or 'settings' in which crimes take place. Their purpose should not be to make generalisations but rather to develop theory (remember that it would be justifiable to criticise a small-scale study if generalisations *were* made but not if the researcher makes no such attempt). However, when several researchers carry out similar small-scale studies the confidence in the theories being developed increases and it is at this stage researchers might decide that they have sufficient evidence to make some limited generalisations. It is not helpful to think of these studies as less important or as inferior to larger-scale studies but rather it is best to think of them as having a different, but as important purpose. When critical criminologists use these in-depth (or ethnographic) methods their purpose will go beyond description and the development of theories in order to offer an explanation of how the social conditions within which criminal actions take place might affect the way we think about the crimes, how we respond to them and how we treat the victims. Thus again it is possible to see that their major concern is more likely to be about the need to consider change rather than regulation.

CONCLUSION

It is important to have a general overview of the history of criminological theorising because it is through the processes of peer review that our knowledge and understanding grow. It is also through the process of moving from one theory of knowledge to another that researchers are able to gain a more thorough understanding of crime in society and of the strengths and limitations of each perspective. In reality, criminologists need to explain the circumstances that are most likely to lead to specific types of crimes; to question the definitions of crime that hold sway at any given time; to understand the different reasons why people turn to specific types of crime; to reveal the processes through which some crimes stay off the political agenda, despite the seriousness of their effects and through which some (oftentimes lesser) crimes create moral concerns that result in the acceptance of harsher punishments. All of these issues should be important to criminologists in order to guard against the dangers of policies that appeal to a misguided 'common-sense' approach to crime that fails to take account of the complexity of our lives. To admit that there are no definitive 'right' answers to the problem of crime should not prevent us from looking for the best answers we can find. If we forget what has been said before then we might fail to challenge the reproduction of ideas that have been refuted.

✳ KEY LEARNING POINTS

- The big question for researchers, if we wish to be taken seriously, is 'How can we make sure that our work is as convincing as possible?'
- We need to demonstrate that we are aware of the assumptions that we have made in our research by providing an explanation not only of what we did but *why* we did it.
- We need to show awareness of the ways in which theories imply methods.
- Whether we choose a 'scientific' approach or not should not really be the important issue, rather the key issue should be how well our research questions are answered.
- We need to remember the lessons learnt from the processes of critique – for example, despite powerful critiques of biological determinism it continues to rear its head in political debates about 'the crime problem' as well as serving, as Lilly *et al.* (2011: 210) note, to maintain the invisibility of many forms of victimisation. Knowledge and understanding of the strengths and limitations of previous research is the hallmark of a good study.
- If we provide insufficient detail of our research we fail to allow others to understand how and why we have made our judgements.
- If we stay stuck with an attitude that science is either the best or conversely the most inappropriate way to do criminological research we will close our minds to many important questions that fall between these extremes. Furthermore, such polarised positions can lead to the sorts of conclusions to which administrative criminologists came when they abandoned the search for explanations of crime altogether in favour of the more limited concern of reducing the opportunities for crime.
- Administrative criminology concentrated on manipulating the social environment rather than the social conditions of existence. The role of theory in such research is minimised as the assumption that we all know what it means to act rationally reduces the research enterprise to the need to measure the impact of any given crime prevention strategy.

Student video

Part 3 – students talking about their own research

Chapter 7

Preparing for the practical challenges of 'real-world' crime research

GOALS OF THIS CHAPTER

At the end of reading this chapter and by completing the online resources that accompany it, you will be able to:

1   make an informed decision about whether 'real-world' research is appropriate for your research topic;
2   consider the range of places and types of participants that can be involved in 'real-world' criminological research;
3   understand the importance of good research design and pilot studies in 'real-world' criminological research;
4   appreciate the significance of researcher safety in 'real-world' criminological research;
5   demonstrate an awareness of some of the practical issues faced in 'real-world' criminological research, and how to overcome these.

Instructor PPoint Slides

Preparing for the practical challenges of 'real-world' crime research

OVERVIEW

*   'Real-world' criminological research typically involves participants with real experiences of crime and the criminal justice system.
*   Criminologists conduct research with prisoners, ex-prisoners, the public, and staff and volunteers working within the criminal justice system or relevant third-sector organisations, including victim charities.
*   Conducting criminological research in the real world can be challenging and time-consuming, but highly rewarding if there are likely to be significant benefits for practice and understanding within the criminal justice system and/or relevant third-sector organisations.

- Good research design is important in any research, but perhaps even more so when conducting research within the criminal justice system. Often researchers will be dealing with an inherently vulnerable group of individuals and because access to prisons and other agencies in the criminal justice system for research is notoriously difficult, once access is gained things must be done right as it is often impossible to return to the research site(s).
- For the above reasons, piloting research should be the first stage of any data gathering in order to overcome any potential problems before taking the research large-scale.
- Once you have recruited participants, it is important to manage your relationship with them carefully, as drop-out rates can be high.
- Ensuring the safety of both researchers and research participants is paramount. Issues of researcher safety should be taken very seriously and thoroughly considered with your research supervisor and your university ethics committee.
- It is important to fully consider the practical issues that can affect real-world criminological research. Potential issues can be varied and numerous, but by learning from more experienced researchers it is possible to overcome some of the common pitfalls.
- Some of the lessons from this chapter apply to all research, not just 'real-world' criminological research. For example, the ability to successfully manage your participants is a skill all researchers need to develop.

INTRODUCTION

We preface this chapter by noting that it is simply not practical for most undergraduate students to conduct research with agencies of the criminal justice system, and the issues around this are discussed throughout this chapter. However, this chapter offers many lessons that are applicable to all criminological research and will also provide you with a greater depth of understanding of the practical challenges involved in much of the research you read about as a student of criminology. This will provide you with further knowledge and understanding that will allow you to develop your ability to think critically about the research you read about elsewhere in your studies.

Unlike the other chapters in this book, this chapter has been developed around particular case studies of research in prisons, which we hope will provide you with interesting insights into the practice and challenges of conducting research in criminal justice settings. The prison-based research examples are supplemented with examples of research in other criminological areas that are broadly applicable to criminological research. While, as noted above, this type of research is typically not practical for students, for those who may progress to postgraduate and professional research careers, we encourage you to return to the guidance in this chapter again in the future. We hope that this chapter may also help inspire some readers to pursue this type of research in the future.

SHOULD I DO 'REAL-WORLD' RESEARCH?

As a student of criminology, your research focus might include either victims or perpetrators of crime or those working within the criminal justice system. It may be that secondary research or research on student populations can tell you what you need to know for your research, and this is explored elsewhere in this book, but you could consider the benefits of 'real-world' research. We use the term 'real world' here to refer to research outside of the university setting, involving people with real experiences of crime and criminal justice.

The answer to whether you should do real-world research depends on a few things. Ask yourself the following questions:

- Would I be able to answer my research questions better by conducting 'real-world' research or through secondary or student-participant based research? Refer to Chapter 10 of this book for further information that will help you answer this question.
- Would any research I conduct in the real world be beneficial both to academic knowledge and practice?
- Do I work/volunteer in an organisation where I could easily and ethically access a group of participants?
- Do I have contacts, or do my lecturers have contacts, in relevant organisations where I could easily and ethically access a group of participants?

If you can answer yes to questions 1 and 2, and either question 3 or 4, then you could consider conducting research in the real world. Whatever your decision, you should thoroughly discuss this with your supervisor and gain their approval before beginning any research.

Remember, a key principle in conducting real-world research is not how useful will this be for your research project or dissertation, but whether the research is relevant to the needs of that particular group of individuals or organisation. Keeping this in mind is fundamental to ensuring all research participants are treated with respect. Many excellent research studies that fully address clearly defined research questions are conducted using secondary data sources – see Chapter 10 for more on this.

WHERE DO CRIMINOLOGISTS DO 'REAL-WORLD' RESEARCH?

Criminological research can take place in any number of settings and research populations. These range from victims of crime, to people in prison and on probation, to ex-offenders, and to the role and experiences of those working within the criminal justice system or relevant third-sector organisations. The authors of this book primarily conduct research with offenders in prison, with ex-offenders, and with victims of crime.

The key point to note for student researchers is the time it can take to get research access agreed, particularly in agencies of the criminal justice system. If you already work within the criminal justice system or have contacts, the process may be quicker, but you are still expected to follow formal research application procedures, even if you have had your research agreed informally.

Crighton (2006) outlines what the prison service looks at when assessing research applications; these points are broadly relevant to other agencies of the criminal justice system:

'Applications are assessed against a number of key criteria.

- The research must be ethically sound.
- The research must be methodologically sound.
- The research must be of potential value to the prison service or Home Office National Offender Management Service' (Crighton, 2006: 19).

At present, when aiming to do research within agencies of the criminal justice system, you should apply through the Integrated Research Application System (IRAS: https://www.myresearchproject.org.uk/). However, it is wise to have had prior contact with the organisation you aim to work with so they know to expect the formal research application. Also note that you are typically expected to have gained ethics approval for your research from your university prior to making a formal IRAS application. The main aims of the application process are to protect individuals and ensure resources are used effectively.

Other researchers work with the police, offenders in the community, victims of crime, the courts, the probation service, the NHS, and more. The NHS research application and ethics procedures are particularly complex and lengthy, and so we advise you to avoid embarking on this route unless you have a great deal of time available. Other organisations where you might access a sample, such as community and voluntary groups, have no formal application processes and so the time between first making contact and conducting your research can be short.

RESEARCH DESIGN

Good research design is important in all research, but this is even more apparent when aiming to conduct research with offenders, ex-offenders or victims. Carlen and Worrall (2004) document two main reasons for this: first, because researchers will be dealing with an inherently vulnerable group of individuals; and second, because access to prisons and other agencies of the criminal justice system for research is notoriously difficult; once access is gained things must be done right as it is often impossible to return to the research site(s). Doing research in prisons, for example, is qualitatively different from other forms of research, often related to the safety and security concerns of the institution (Crighton, 2006). However, 'a good research design outside a prison will often be a good research design within a prison' (Crighton, 2006: 8).

Over four decades ago, in 1970, Matza highlighted that research into crime had become too far removed from the key players: the offenders themselves. Despite this acknowledgement many researchers in the area often rely solely on impersonal statistical data. While there are many cases where this is appropriate to address specific research questions, it is clear that those directly involved and responsible for criminal activity can tell us much about their own lives and the crimes they have committed, just as those who have been the victims of crime or who work with these groups can do. We cannot expect to obtain a full picture of the thoughts, experiences, development and needs of any group of people without speaking with them directly. As Nee (2004: 4) states: 'If we can show that we can research offenders' understandings of their own behaviour reliably ... then surely a grounded approach to research, using the offender as expert, is a method we ignore at our peril.' When done well, the information gleaned from interviews with those involved in the criminal justice system can provide us with a wealth of information that is simply not available through official records. Indeed, Sapsford and Jupp (1996) suggest that self-report methods provide researchers the opportunity to collect information free from the restrictions of official data (both practical and political) – as discussed in Chapters 1 and 6. However, it is important to note that there are numerous reasons why self-report data from interviews may not be entirely accurate. The reliability of self-report data relies on the honesty of respondents' accounts, and there is always a risk that these accounts will provide 'an imaginative organization of experiences that imposes a distortion of truth ... a mixture of fiction and non-fiction

BOX 7.1 KEY TERM EXPLAINED: OFFENDER ASSESSMENT SYSTEM

The Offender Assessment System (OASys) was developed by the probation service and prison service in England and Wales as a standardised measure to provide a consistent and in-depth assessment measure of areas of need for individual offenders, and to provide a risk of reconviction score. The OASys was piloted three times from 1999, and in 2001 the decision was made to implement the assessment throughout England and Wales' prison and probation services. The OASys consists of 13 sections that assess offenders' criminogenic needs, risk of harm, and likelihood of reconviction based on areas covered in the widely used Level of Service Inventory-Revised (LSI-R: Andrews and Bonta, 1995). The first 12 sections relate to risk of reconviction, while section 13 is used when considering suitability of interventions. Assessment is carried out at the beginning, end, and throughout the sentence and has been designed to highlight areas of risk and need, to trigger further assessments, as the basis for sentence planning, and to measure change. In order to predict the likelihood of reconviction, sections 1 to 12 of the OASys examine offending history and current offence, social and economic factors, and personal factors. From 2003 implementation of the OASys in electronic format (e-OASys) began and this format is now used throughout England and Wales. Data is collected from a range of sources, including the probation service, courts, and prison service. From a research perspective, the measure provides a useful tool from which to obtain demographic data collected about offenders and cross-check sections of interview data.

... about life and particular lived experiences' (Denzin, 1989: 24). When interviewing offenders, Nee (2004: 19) notes that these issues may be even greater, with 'self-protection; overconfidence; and inaccuracies of memory to name just a few'. In an attempt to combat this, a 'triangulation' of data has typically been found to be the best approach to increase validity. While all information should be taken seriously, researchers should check stories wherever possible.

Official records held by HM Prison Service and the probation service, such as Offender Assessment System (OASys) records, can be used to cross-check some of the information provided by offenders and allows the likely accuracy of the self-report data to be assessed.

The use of such records also allows for the collection of demographic and other data that does not require explanation by the offenders. This then allows more time for discussion of more pertinent issues during contact with participants. Given the time pressures faced by researchers in prison settings in particular, the ability to save time in this way during an interview is invaluable. While a typical rule of thumb is to begin with records before moving on to data collection with the offender (King, 2000), the rights of informed consent and privacy of offenders must be adhered to, meaning that it may not be possible to review records prior to interviews as interviewees should give written permission for the researcher to view their individual documents.

Remember, even if you gain access to conduct research with offenders in prison or the community, there is no obligation for the criminal justice system or an individual offender to let you see their records.

DATA COLLECTION METHODS: CONSIDERATIONS WHEN INTERVIEWING VULNERABLE GROUPS

While a full discussion of interviews as a method of data collection can be found in Chapter 8 of this book, there are a number of specific issues relevant to conducting interviews with vulnerable groups that warrant discussion in this current chapter.

Prison staff in particular often note the problems experienced when researchers have attempted to use questionnaires with offenders. Issues with literacy and the length and complexity of some questionnaires often result in prison staff being needed to help offenders work through questionnaires. This has obvious time and resource implications and removes anonymity from participants. Staff report being much happier having prisoners interviewed by researchers to avoid the above issues. Outside of prison settings, researchers must also be mindful of potential issues with literacy and ensure the language used in data-collection tools is appropriate. Experienced researchers will tell you that a great deal of sensitivity is needed in offering to read questions to someone you suspect may have literacy problems. Aside from such practical issues, the benefits of interviews have been espoused by many, being one of the most widely used **qualitative research** methods, as discussed in Chapter 8 of this book. There is the opportunity for researchers to increase rapport with interviewees, thereby hopefully increasing openness. As King and Wincup (2008) note, establishing rapport with research participants is one of the keys to successful interviewing in prisons.

BOX 7.2 RESEARCH IN ACTION: PILOTING RESEARCH WITH EX-OFFENDERS

Background

We suggest that the first stage of any data gathering should involve a pilot study in order to overcome any potential problems before taking the research full-scale. This is particularly important in prison research – such as that described below – where once access to prisons has been granted it is important to get things right. However, you should note that the pilot study described below is taken from a piece of postgraduate study and thus is larger than would be expected from undergraduate researchers. Nonetheless, there are important lessons to be taken from this real example.

Between 2007 and 2011 one of the authors of this book conducted a study across three women's prisons in England (see Caulfield, 2012). Prior to conducting semi-structured interviews with incarcerated women, a small number of pilot interviews were conducted with a sample of women ex-offenders. Whilst the pilot sample differed from the main research sample in terms of their status as ex-offenders, their status as women UK citizens who had been in prison meant that they had been through similar experiences and understood the relevant issues. It is however vital to be aware that the differences between actually living in prison and in the community are significant and so will have had some impact upon the interviews. Nonetheless, this stage formed an important part of the research development.

Pilot interviews are also useful to ensure appropriate language and terms of reference are being used within the research. Within Caulfield's study the purpose of the interviews was primarily to assess the appropriateness of the questions being asked in the interview, and also in part as a 'practice run' to iron out any problems and to enhance familiarity with the interview schedule. The pilot also acted as a forum to check the language used in the consent form and participant information form. In an ideal world these pilot interviews would have been best conducted in a prison with current inmates to allow the pilot to be as similar to the 'real' situation as possible. However, given the difficulties of accessing a prison sample, interviewing ex-offenders provided a suitable pilot sample.

Prison Link

The pilot sample was recruited from a charity organisation 'Prison Link'. Prison Link was a Birmingham-based charity, run primarily by volunteers, which worked with prisoners and their families. Prison Link assisted members of the community in maintaining family ties through assisted visits and a family support network. They also offered one-to-one support and befriending to members of the black community in Birmingham who were serving a custodial sentence. Prison Link 'aims to empower and support prisoners and ex-offenders and their families and children by offering a range of services designed to maintain family links and stability and encourage positive change' (Prison Link, 2007).

The researcher contacted Prison Link and discussed the aims of the research with them. Prison Link felt the research was likely to be of benefit in understanding the needs of offenders and so agreed to help recruit participants for the pilot study. Volunteer staff within Prison Link liaised with women ex-offenders who were in contact with the charity to recruit a pilot sample for this research. Four women were identified and all agreed to take part. Their experiences of imprisonment ranged from five to twenty years ago, with three women having been in prison in the past ten years. While being in prison such a considerable time ago made this sample different to the main target sample for this research, the pilot interviews were useful in testing the interview schedule. The researcher conducted interviews at the Prison Link premises. Participants were offered payment of 20 pounds sterling for their time (see the discussion of whether or not you should pay your participants later in this chapter).

Findings from the pilot study

One of the interviews from the pilot exercise was transcribed in order to test out the transcription process. Rather than analyse the specific content of the interviews that took place, the aim of the pilot interviews was to practise interview techniques and the interview schedule, and to get feedback on the experience from participants. It is always surprising how different conducting a real interview is to reading the interview questions at home beforehand. As discussed in chapter 8 of this book, you may need more prompts than you think and some questions may feel difficult to ask. This is particularly the case if the research topic is of a sensitive nature.

The interviews included questions about participants' past experiences. All four women spoke at length about their past experiences. While the structure of the interview schedule flowed well — beginning with broad background questions before approaching any questions of a sensitive nature — when probed, feedback from three participants was that the interviewer could be more direct with some sensitive topics. This feedback was useful in developing a balance between trying to avoid offending participants with very personal questions, and also encouraging them to speak about their experiences in these areas. An example of this is questions about childhood experiences, where initially the researcher was reluctant to ask outright about negative childhood experiences. However, the interviewees felt that as long as interviewees did not feel pressured to respond, the interviewer could be more direct with such lines of questioning.

After completing the interview, interviewees were asked to discuss their experience of the interview, and specifically how they felt about the questions they were asked. All four women reported feeling at ease during the interview, and three reported enjoying the opportunity to express their experiences and how they had rebuilt their lives after prison. Of note, was that two of the women felt that the time taken to discuss the research prior to the interview had been important in helping them understand why their part in the research was important. It is possible that because of this they were more open and willing to discuss their past experiences.

Overall, the pilot interview process significantly increased the researcher's familiarity and confidence with the interview schedule. While these interviews were not able to prepare the interviewer fully for the experience of interviewing women in prison, they were vital in developing appropriate language and confidence for the main study.

Those with experience interviewing vulnerable groups have also commented that it is preferable, wherever possible, to use individual rather than group interviews (Nee, 2004). As with many other types of research, group interviews or focus groups can be useful in the initial stages 'in order to identify salient issues, tighten research questions and clarify terminology' (Nee, 2004: 11) but issues such as poor literacy, communication and social skills can result in some participants failing to express themselves and thus limiting the validity of the data collected. In an individual interview, the interviewer is more able to work around literacy problems and, as above, build a rapport with the interviewee, in an attempt to overcome communication issues.

Asking research participants to talk openly about their life experiences will undoubtedly result in sensitive issues being broached. As mentioned earlier, building a rapport with research participants is vital, particularly when seeking openness about sensitive topics. Additionally, Harvey (2008) reports that in a low-trust environment such as a prison, emphasising independence and social remoteness from the prison establishment encourages the disclosure of information.

RECRUITING A SAMPLE

Recruiting organisations

If you work within an agency of the criminal justice system or voluntary organisation, or have good contacts, it is usually best to informally discuss your research initially. If you don't have such contacts, you may also find that an initial informal approach works best. First, try making contact via phone call, and once contact has been established and some discussion had concerning the research, you should send a letter and/or email outlining the research. At the phone call stage it will probably be clear that some organisations are not able or willing to participate. This may be due to limited time to help with research, or perhaps feeling that the research would not be beneficial to them. It is also worthy of note that some organisations prefer to work only with postgraduate and professional researchers.

A key element of research recruitment is benefit selling, whether this is to the organisation as a whole, staff who you wish to help in identifying participants, or participants themselves, and it is important to ensure that the particular benefit to each group is made clear. Staff within an organisation may be the gatekeepers to your research participants, or indeed the participants themselves, and so it is vital you try to engage them with your research. In order to protect and inform colleagues, all those either involved with the research or likely to be asked about the research should be informed of the nature of the study and given the opportunity to discuss this with you. This might be through a formal presentation you give to staff where they are able to ask questions and discuss the research, or it might be that you provide relevant staff with non-technical written materials explaining the research, and give them the opportunity to discuss the study with you on an informal basis.

Participant recruitment

Once access has been granted from the organisations, you may need to develop a range of participant recruitment activities to get a suitable sample. These will depend on the type of organisation, but below we suggest some tried and tested approaches. As noted previously, ensuring potential participants are aware of the benefits of the research is essential.

Table 7.1 Participant recruitment strategies

Strategy	Pros	Cons
Posters	Easy to produce Good to raise awareness of the research Does not take much staff time	Does not result in high recruitment Other strategies needed Need to be highly visible to the target population
Letters/emails	Easy to produce Personal so better response rate A tear-off slip and return envelope help increase responses to letters	Relies on having contact details/staff may be needed to deliver them in some settings May be ethical concerns – discuss with your supervisor and ethics committee
Media (for example, an interview or advert in the organisation's newsletter, a prison TV station interview)	If targeted well, can be high impact Good if followed up with a letter	Not always possible
Staff directly approach potential participants (including colleagues, victims, prisoners, and so on)	They can 'sell' the benefits on your behalf Results in high recruitment	Staff need to fully understand the benefit of the research and be engaged Potential for misunderstandings to be communicated Staff may be too busy to do this
Through a community group meeting	You can 'sell' the benefits of the research Potential participants can ask questions Results in high recruitment You may be able to arrange data collection straight away	None in our experience

MANAGING YOUR PARTICIPANTS

Recruiting participants is only half of the challenge. Any experienced researcher will tell you that drop-out rates are often high between contacting participants and collecting the data. Once you get to the point of meeting with participants for data collection drop-out rates are very low, so it is what you do between first contacting a participant and meeting them to collect data that is often important.

Our keys tips are:

- 'Strike while the iron's hot!': the sooner you can conduct your data collection the better. You must ensure that potential participants have time to consider taking part, but the sooner you can collect data the less time you have to lose track of participants.
- Keep track of them: if you are going to be conducting research with people in the community, but won't be collecting the data immediately, phone your participants to check they are still happy to take part on the date you agreed.
- Re-confirm visits close to the time: the time and travel involved in real-world research is wasted if you turn up to a research visit but your participant does not. This has happened to most researchers, but you can minimise this risk by calling participants the day before or on the day to re-confirm your meeting.

RESEARCHER SAFETY

Ensuring your own safety, and the safety of anyone else involved in your research, is paramount. Issues of researcher safety should be taken very seriously and thoroughly considered with your research supervisor and your university ethics committee. Below we discuss some issues to consider and provide some tips on ensuring researcher safety.

As a researcher you should think very carefully about where you meet research participants to collect data. If you have gained access to your participants through the probation service or a charity or community group, see if they can provide a space for you to meet with participants. If that is not practical, arrange to meet participants in a public area such as a coffee shop. You should avoid meeting research participants in their home if possible. Wherever data is being collected, many researchers use what we term a 'call-in system' when conducting research in the community. Our advice is to go out to conduct research in pairs where this is appropriate, but at the very least make use of the call-in system.

If you find yourself in a position where you are conducting research in prisons, there are other safety issues to consider. Fundamentally, prisons are places concerned with security, and so the likelihood is that your safety as a researcher will have been considered. However, you should not take this for granted, and if you feel concerned or uncomfortable in any way you should alert your research contact in the prison.

If you are discussing sensitive issues with offenders in prison it may be important to have somewhere private within each establishment to conduct your research. In closed prisons in particular this may pose an issue concerning researcher safety. It is perfectly

BOX 7.3 **KEY TERM EXPLAINED: THE 'CALL-IN SYSTEM'**

The 'call-in system' is an approach to researcher safety used by many researchers who conduct research in the community. This system is not only to be used when working with offenders and ex-offenders, but when working with all participants in the community. The basic principle is this: that a nominated 'research buddy' knows where you are at all times during data collection, and that your research buddy knows what to do if they cannot contact you.

A step-by-step guide to the call-in system

1   Nominate a 'research buddy' – this can be any responsible adult, just make sure it is someone you can rely on.
2   Let your research buddy know the time you have agreed to meet the research participant, exact details of where you are meeting, and how long you expect the data collection to take.
3   Call your research buddy when you arrive at the research destination and then call them again when you leave.
4   If you do not call your research buddy within the time discussed, they should try to call you. If you do not answer they should continue to try.
5   If your research buddy cannot contact you within ten minutes they should call the police.

Thankfully, most research experiences are positive and safe ones, and we have never been in a situation where we have needed to use point 5 of the call-in system. However, using this system helps ensure that you are protected and safe.

acceptable for you to ask your research contact at the prison, or another member of prison staff, about the psychological and behavioural state of the offenders you will be in contact with. While prison staff may not anticipate any problems, it is good practice to either conduct the interview in a room with a safety alarm or provide researchers with a personal attack alarm. It is unwise to take any unnecessary risks and it is important to always respect any safety concerns of prisons staff.

PRACTICAL ISSUES

It is important to fully consider the practical issues that can affect 'real-world' criminological research. Potential issues can be varied and numerous, but by learning from more experienced researchers it is possible to avoid some of the common pitfalls. We consider some of these issues below. While you can consider many issues in detail prior to beginning the research, you should also be prepared to be flexible in your approach and able to respond to issues as they arise.

Accessing official reports

You may encounter particular issues if you plan to access official reports as part of your research, particularly those that may be held by the criminal justice system about individuals. Access to large group data sets, such as the Crime Survey for England and Wales, is covered in Chapters 9 and 10. The benefits of accessing individual data – such as OASys records – was discussed earlier in this chapter. You must first ensure that each organisation involved in your research has given permission to access records for each participant, provided that the individual participant concerned gives consent. In every instance individual participants should also give their consent and it must be very clear why gathering individual data is important to the research. The principles of informed consent apply equally to all participants and 'there are no grounds for not addressing issues of consent from prisoners' (Crighton, 2006: 11) or others involved in the criminal justice system.

Given the importance of security and anonymity, issues may occur when attempting to transfer information from official documents into Word, Excel or SPSS. The prison and probation services in particular have high levels of IT security, meaning information cannot be saved and taken outside of the prison. In our experience, the best course of action is to print paper copies of each record and anonymise these prior to leaving the prison, probation, charity or other offices. Alternatively, if you only need part of the information stored in official records, it may better to copy information into a notebook. You can then manually transfer the data into an Excel or SPSS file at a later date. Two things are important here: first, ensure you discuss your wish to access official data early on in your discussions about possible research access; second, carry a black marker pen with you for anonymising records.

Should you hold keys if you are conducting research in prisons?

Few student researchers will be faced with this question, as typically prison staff escort researchers around the prison. However, when conducting larger pieces of research in prison during postgraduate research we have been offered keys, and so it is worth considering this issue.

Many researchers have discussed the issue of researchers holding keys within prison (Genders and Player, 1995; King, 2000; King and Leibling, 2008; Leibling, 1992; Mills, 2004; Sparks et al., 1996). King (2000), for example, argues that researchers should not hold keys to the prison as in the eyes of the offenders this puts researchers too close to the position of staff and thus decreases trust, while Mills (2004) discusses issues of personal safety, particularly for female researchers holding keys. While some have commented that 'if the prison want you to do the research, then it is their responsibility to ensure your safety, and to escort you around the prison' (Cowburn, 2004), the issue is rarely this straightforward. Often the prison may simply be kind enough to *let* you do the research, rather than actively *want* you to do the research, and this distinction is very important. What always remains is that gaining access to prisons is never guaranteed and researchers must be flexible and willing to work around the prison staff and prison regimes. An important factor is that holding keys considerably limits the burden on prison staff, primarily by drastically reducing the need for escorts. Pragmatically, the only sensible decision seems to be to do what each individual establishment suggests: if they wish researchers to hold keys, then researchers should hold keys. Holding keys has the added benefit of increasing researchers' sense of independence within the prison and ability to control their own time to some extent.

Working around the organisation of prisons

If you are conducting research in prisons a member of staff may be identified as your 'research liaison officer'. This may be a prison officer or prison psychologist appointed by the governor to take overall responsibility for recruiting participants, ensuring suitable space is available for data collection, and generally ensuring the research runs smoothly. This can help significantly with participant recruitment and arranging interview times. However, be aware that participants will not always be available when they are called up. This clearly highlights some of the challenges faced when conducting research within the prison service. Not only is it difficult to gain initial access, but researchers must be constantly aware of the regimes within prison that dictate when inmates are available. This is both a practical consideration, but also an important point to highlight when applying to conduct prison research as a willingness to be flexible and the ability to work around the demands of the prison should be made clear right from the initial application.

An awareness of the practical issues of prison research and planning around the prison day is vital. Carlen and Worrall (2004: 185) highlight the importance of working to suit the prison, noting that prison staff can often be 'wary of researchers, especially of any who fail to show their appreciation of prison staff priorities or institutional concerns'. Furthermore, while most prisoners who have agreed to participate in research will find it a welcome change, and therefore the imposition is minimal, there are likely to be greater time consequences for staff who are already very busy.

Involvement with research participants

While the majority of research relationships are uncomplicated, on occasion researchers can find themselves very involved with participants, and it is wise for all researchers to be aware of this, particularly when undertaking research of a sensitive or emotional nature. In such situations it is easy to see how researchers can find it difficult to walk away from participants and their problems at the end of the research. It is hard not to be affected emotionally by participants who open up to you as a researcher (Smith and Wincup, 2000), and this has certainly been the case on a number of occasions during our research over the years. This highlights how important it is for researchers investigating sensitive issues to ensure they have some kind of debriefing process in place. Whether this is formalised with your supervisor, or an informal arrangement with a partner or close friend, it is good practice to have some system in place to deal with these emotional issues. Remember, while you may suggest further sources of support for participants in your participant information form, it is not appropriate for you to attempt to provide either subsequent support or friendship.

Payment, payback and feedback

There is considerable debate concerning the payment of research participants, with some suggesting that payment is potentially coercive (McNeil, 1997). Much of the debate around this issue stems from the medical sciences, where ethical debate centres on the capability of participants to assess risk accurately when financial incentives are offered. While these issues also apply to the social sciences, where considerations of risk to participants are paramount in assessing the ethical nature of research, many social scientists argue that participants should be adequately and appropriately reimbursed for their time (cf. Carlen and Worrall, 2004). We agree with this view, and furthermore, many charity and community organisations expect this (for example, see Box 7.2).

Within prison establishments it is in no way appropriate to provide offenders who participate in research with rewards for their participation, be this monetary or affecting standards of care, privileges or parole. It is though often the case that research

Table 7.2 Research in action: a summary of the research process in three English women's prisons (Caulfield, 2012)

1. Ethics and approval	Ethics approval was granted by the university ethics committee and approval to access women's prisons in England and Wales granted by HM Prison Service National Research Committee.
2. Pilot interviews conducted	A small sample of women ex-offenders in the local community were identified through a charity organisation. The pilot interviews were useful in highlighting a number of small issues, but overall the semi-structured interviews worked well and the structure and content remained the same for the main study.
3. Participating establishments identified	Three women's prisons in England agreed to participate: one open prison, one semi-open prison and one closed prison.
4. Participants recruited	Different strategies for recruitment were implemented at each establishment. In total 45 women were recruited and interviewed.
5. Obtaining consent	A participant information sheet was used to explain the research and a consent form was used to obtain consent to interview and access individual OASys records.
6. Interviews	Semi-structured interviews were conducted, lasting an average of 53 minutes. Interviews were recorded using a digital voice recorder and each participant was interviewed only once.
7. Files	Once consent had been given, information from OASys reports was printed for the researcher by prison staff. The researcher removed all identifying data from the paper records before leaving each prison. Relevant information was later transferred into an SPSS database.
8. Anonymity	Each participant was allocated a unique research reference number to ensure that it was not possible to identify any of the participants. The unique research reference number given to each participant was placed on all information related to them, including the anonymised print-outs of their OASys reports.
9. Data analysis	Interview recordings were transcribed and this data was managed and coded using the software package NVIVO 8. Other data was analysed using the software package SPSS.

participation can be a welcome break for prisoners and so the most a researcher can do, other than verbally thank individuals for their participation, is to make the process as comfortable as possible and be considerate to any needs the offender may have as a result of participation. While it is typically not viable or advisable to provide participants with individual feedback, you may wish to advise participants that they can receive general feedback from the researcher via the contact details provided in the participant information form. Remember to only give out your university contact details, not your personal ones.

You should also consider the role of the people who have helped you identify research participants or helped facilitate your research visits. In addition to being respectful, polite and courteous, you could consider sending 'thank you' cards for their help and support. It is often a good idea to send organisations an overview of the research findings.

Table 7.2 provides an example of a large piece of research undertaken in prisons by one of the authors of this book. Note that this was a postgraduate (PhD, to be exact) piece of research and so larger and more involved than undergraduate research. However, this provides an example of the stages involved in the research process.

BOX 7.4 CRITICAL ACTIVITY

Think about a piece of real-world criminological research you would like to conduct. First, work through this chapter and list any practical considerations and issues that might be faced with your chosen topic. Second, next to each consideration or issue, identify at least one way in which you could overcome this. If you are planning your final-year research project or dissertation in a 'real-world' setting, this will go a long way towards the smooth running of your research. We encourage you to show your supervisor and ethics committee that you have considered these factors.

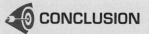 CONCLUSION

This chapter has outlined some of the benefits and challenges of conducting what we have referred to as 'real-world' research. While most undergraduate researchers will conduct research using secondary data sources, or with student/public samples, many of the lessons involved in conducting research involving agencies of the criminal justice system apply to all criminological research. Whatever type of 'real-world' research is being conducted, the research should be relevant to the needs of that particular group of individuals or organisation. Keep in mind that it may well be possible to address your research questions using secondary data sources.

✦ KEY LEARNING POINTS

- After considering the range of factors presented in this chapter, you should now be in a position to make an informed decision about whether real-world research is right for you and the type of research you would like to conduct.
- It is important to note how vital good research design is in conducting criminological research in the real world.
- There are numerous considerations when conducting research with offenders in prison in particular that make the use of a research pilot study an important consideration.
- Numerous tried and tested strategies exist for recruiting a research sample. There are pros and cons of most methods, so researchers should decide what is appropriate for their particular research.
- Following the guidance in this chapter on researcher safety, and discussing these issues with your research supervisor and ethics committee, will go a long way to ensuring you are kept safe throughout the entire research process.

PART 3

Doing criminological research: data collection

Chapter 8

Ethnographic approaches to research

GOALS OF THIS CHAPTER

At the end of reading this chapter and by completing the online resources that accompany it, you will be able to:

1   identify the settings in which in-depth interviews are appropriate;
2   explain the differences between the various forms of in-depth interview;
3   choose appropriate techniques and interviewer 'roles';
4   carry out in-depth interviews;
5   identify the settings in which the collection of observational data is appropriate;
6   understand the different philosophical underpinnings of observational studies;
7   justify your chosen method and technique.

OVERVIEW

- An ethnographic approach to criminological research involves in-depth detailed descriptions of criminal behaviour and lifestyles as well as of the processes involved in responding to crime.
- Detailed description is obtained via in-depth qualitative interviews and/or observational techniques.
- There are several ways in which qualitative interviews may be carried out.
- Your chosen technique should reflect the philosophical assumptions that underpin your research and be appropriate to the questions you wish to answer.
- Similarly, observational studies can be carried out in different ways depending upon the philosophical assumptions you make.
- You should always be able to discuss the relationship between your choice of method and your research question/s.

IN-DEPTH INTERVIEWS

Types of in-depth/ethnographic interviews

There are two main types of in-depth or 'ethnographic' interview: guided (sometimes called semi-structured) and unstructured. Guided interviews reflect the fact that researchers usually have an idea of the topics they would like to explore with the research participants in advance of carrying out the interviews. They are easier to manage than the more conversational unstructured form, however the unstructured approach is particularly useful when carrying out life histories or case studies (Kirby *et al.*, 2006). It is important to be clear about the aims of your research as these will enable you to make clear decisions about the most appropriate form of interview. The data should be as relevant as possible to the desired aims and outcomes of the research, otherwise the task of analysing the data will become very daunting because of the large quantities of data that will be generated.

**Student
guide to
...**

Moder-
ating focus
groups

Some researchers make use of focus group interviews, an interviewing method that has its origins in market research. These too can vary in terms of how far they are guided by the issues which the researcher seeks to explore. When there is a semi-structured approach it is usual for a facilitator to identify some key topics for participants to consider. Participants will often be divided into several, quite small groups. They may be asked to jot down their individual thoughts on each topic before sharing their thoughts within their group. The next stage would be for the groups to summarise their views before sharing with the other groups present. Focus groups can be used in a less structured way too. In these cases they are often a precursor to quantitative data-gathering processes. As Pole and Lampard (2002) have noted they can provide a degree of synthesis between quantitative and qualitative approaches.

Focus groups are particularly useful following individual in-depth interviews when researchers may want to explore the ways in which participants' views, as expressed in individual interviews, may change in the context of the focus group interview. Here the task of the researcher is to assess whether these changes are the result of group pressure, which might serve to create a false consensus (see Somekh and Lewin, 2009: 43), or whether in fact, especially in cases where the participants have similar experiences, they are the result of an individual participant's ability to force a meaningful discussion that leads to greater honesty. In the process of carrying out research for a PhD on inter-agency cooperation in child protection work, for example, one of us (Hill, 1999) used a focus group interview following in-depth interviews with social work professionals in order to explore the differences between what participants were prepared to say when alone and when in a group. The field work was carried out at a time when there was great anxiety amongst professionals responding to child abuse therefore professionals were, at least at first, often at pains to state their knowledge of statutory guidelines and their unfailing adherence to them. It was during a focus group interview that one participant expressed some of his worries about aspects of the procedural response and this enabled the other professionals to speak more honestly about some of their own concerns.

Life history interviews (note life histories may also involve participants *writing* autobiographical accounts) also may be either guided or unstructured. The decision about the style of interview depends upon whether the researcher simply wishes to access in-depth knowledge about a life/lives in order to show what that life was like or whether the researcher is trying to do more than this by developing theories about the relationship between individual acts and the society in which people live their lives. A life history approach may simply serve to present a detailed narrative that does no more than present one person's 'story'. However, a researcher may also use narratives in order to attempt an explanation of why something may have happened. A guided approach to life history interviews will be more likely to be underpinned by a particular theoretical perspective. For example, one of us (Hill, 2007) in a study of young black people's reflections on their offending used a life history approach to interviewing in order to explore the conditions in which the young offenders had lived their lives prior to and during custody in order to make sense of their post-custody decisions and attitudes.

BOX 8.1 STUDENT ACTIVITY: CRITICAL ETHNOGRAPHY

Read Hill, J. (2007) 'Daring to Dream: Towards an Understanding of Young Black People's Reflections Post-Custody', *Youth Justice*, 7(1): 37–51.

- How far do you think that the type of interview used in this study exposed the interplay between a) the conditions in which offences were committed and responded to; and b) the meanings that the young offenders gave to their actions?
- How far do you think that such an analysis can be useful?

Tierney (1999: 309) states that the challenge for researchers is 'not to make the individual into a cohesive self, but instead to create methodological and narrative strategies that will do justice to . . . multiple identities'.

- How far do you think that Hill's study does this? Give reasons for your answers.
- Do you think that your own identity has influenced your answer to this question?
- If so, how important do you think it is for a researcher to discuss her/his identity?

Prepare to carry out a life history interview with young, black offenders who have been released from custody. Decide whether you want to take a guided approach or not and give reasons for your decision.

- List the issues you think you will need to consider before you begin the interviews.

When to use in-depth interviews

Many methodology texts provide students with a simple 'advantages/disadvantages' table which compares structured (quantitative) approaches to semi- or unstructured (qualitative) approaches to interviewing. We do not intend to begin in this way as we do not think that it is helpful to compare techniques that have different purposes. For example, the fact that it is possible to generalise from a large-scale survey but not from 20 in-depth interviews is not relevant to a discussion of an in-depth study that does not claim to make any generalisations. Indeed, to list this as a disadvantage of **qualitative research** is quite meaningless, just as it would be meaningless to say that a disadvantage of a structured survey is the failure to gain in-depth detail. If a researcher chooses an in-depth method of interviewing it should be because this fits with the purposes of the research.

If you take time to look at research reports you will soon get the hang of identifying the key words that imply the use of ethnographic methods of data gathering. Perhaps what is more difficult is being clear about the criteria by which this kind of research should be evaluated since, as we have seen, it is often the case that ethnographic research can be viewed as inferior to, rather than simply different from, **quantitative research**.

BOX 8.2 STUDENT ACTIVITY: WHEN SHOULD I USE IN-DEPTH INTERVIEWING METHODS?

Which of the following research aims indicate the use of in-depth interviews? Give reasons for your answers.

- To explore the conditions in which women are engaged in prostitution (see Phoenix, 2000).
- To investigate the extent of gang membership in the United Kingdom (see Bennett and Holloway, 2004).
- To measure the relationship between lack of street lighting and incidences of violent crime.
- To explore the issues that women face when they end a violent relationship (see Humphreys and Thiara, 2003).
- To study the personal relationship between female offenders and their co-defendants (see Jones, 2008).
- To identify the trends in violent crime across England and Wales.
- To understand the processes through which criminal careers are developed.
- To test for a relationship between alcohol use and aggression (see Newberry et al., 2013).
- To explore the experiences of female staff working in a male prison (see Kumari et al., 2012).

Table 8.1 Data gathering via in-depth 'ethnographic' interviews

Type of interview	Reasons for choice	Issues to consider
Unstructured	To allow the participants to reveal the meaning of their actions or the reasons for their attitudes in their own terms.	How can you gain the trust of the participants in your research? Have you considered the power relationships within the interview process and the role you will assume? (Note that you will need to be reflexive throughout the whole process of research.) How far will you divulge your aims? How can you ensure that when you do ask questions they are clear? Have you identified some possible probes? How can you ensure the validity of the data? How will you record the data? (Don't forget to gain permission). How will you maintain confidentiality Will the location of the interview be safe for the participants and researcher?
Guided (semi-structured)	Usually when the researcher has identified specific areas that s/he wishes to explore in order to develop a particular theory.	As above plus: Do the topics you have identified help you to answer the research questions? Have you allowed the participants sufficient flexibility to raise issues that you may have omitted?
Focus group	Can be a way of collecting qualitative data from a large number when resources are short. Allows differences of view and contradictions to emerge.	As 1 and 2 above plus: How will you deal with group dynamics? What are the specific problems relating to data recording focus group interviews?
Life history (guided, unstructured)	In situations where the researcher wishes to explore the relationship of key points in an individual's life to particular social norms and events; where the researcher seeks to identify the life events that brought about specific actions or changes to behaviour and/or attitudes; where thick description helps others to understand what it is like to be in a particular situation. Some researchers may wish to check accounts against historical 'facts'.	As 1 and 2 above plus: Consider the role of chronology – is it the most important thing or is it the significance of events that is important?

Doing in-depth (ethnographic) interviews

Our own experiences as researchers, as well as our experiences as teachers of research, have demonstrated to us that carrying out interviews is often considered to be an easy task by beginners to research. This is largely because interviews are seen as an extension of what we do in our everyday conversations as we go about our daily lives. The reality of doing in-depth interviews is quite different to our first expectations precisely because interviews are *not* the same as conversations. This said it is actually quite important to try to reproduce the conditions of a 'natural' conversation when carrying out an in-depth interview so it is really important that researchers prepare carefully before carrying out any kind of interview. You should refer back to Chapters 1, 3 and 4 in order to refresh your memory about gaining access, ethical considerations and how to review literature and translate your ideas into questions. There are also some practical decisions that must be considered, such as whether or not to carry out the interview face to face or via a telephone or computer, which involves, in turn, consideration of whether the setting of the interview is appropriate and safe; the type and reliability of the recording instrument; whether or not to use a note taker in a face-to-face interview in order to record facial reactions/gestures (this means that the interviewer can avoid the distraction of note-taking); how to deal with a participant who is distressed.

In addition to these practical issues researchers must consider their own social location in society in relation to their interviewees (research participants) in order to take account of the impact this may have on the data collected. For example, Hill (2007), a white, late middle-aged woman, interviewed young black people who had been in custody and therefore it was vital that she considered the impact her own characteristics might have upon the research participants prior to the interviews. In particular she needed to think of ways in which she could gain the trust of the young people she was to interview. It is always a good idea, especially when the research topic is sensitive, to ask some very general questions that put the participants at their ease and which allow them to develop rapport with you.

PAUSE TO THINK . . .

- Try to list your ideas about the ways in which you think interviewers should conduct themselves. Give reasons for your answer.
- How might a researcher's philosophical assumptions influence her/his interview style and her/his stance on the relevance of interviewer/interviewee 'matching'?
- Can you think of some examples of research that we have discussed already in this book that might help you to justify your own future decisions about the roles you might choose to take during the interview process?

Research beginners will often grasp the different purposes of qualitative research as compared to the purposes of quantitative research yet when it comes to their thoughts about the *process* of in-depth interviewing they may hold on to the positivist idea of value neutrality. It is likely that many of you will have suggested that interviewers should remain remote from the research participants and that they should not offer their own views or discuss any aspect of their own personal biography to a research participant. We hope that your reading of this text so far has enabled you to think about the ways in which different research contexts might suggest different interviewing styles. For example, in situations where criminological researchers are concerned with sensitive issues, such as rape, it will be wholly appropriate to put the participant at ease and to express some views that may increase their trust in you as a researcher. The existing literature indicates that assumptions are made about the sexuality of men who are raped and that this makes it difficult for male victims to speak out, especially if they are gay (for a good review of some of the recent literature see Rumney, 2008). This suggests that if male survivors of rape consent to be interviewed in-depth then researchers would not only need to show sensitivity and compassion but that it would also be appropriate for them to comment from time to time. For example, if a male rape victim spoke about the difficulties involved in getting people to believe him it would be important for the interviewer to allude to her/his wider knowledge of other men *and* women who have had the same experience. Indeed, Berg, (2004: 99) mentions the fact that some researchers share their own experiences within the interview setting, for example Patricia Gagne talked of her own experiences of domestic violence when carrying out a study with Tewksbury (Tewksbury and Gagne 1997) which concerned Appalachian women's experiences of domestic violence. Feminist researchers have called this type of exchange within interviews a *dialogic* approach. It is a style of interviewing that many feminists use as it challenges the 'scientific' impersonal approach advocated by those who assume the possibility of complete value neutrality. This also challenges standard views of the interviewer/interviewee relationship where one person gathers information from another and treats the subject more like an object.

PAUSE TO THINK . . .

- Does a **dialogic interview** style increase or decrease the validity of the interview data? Give reasons for your answer.
- How might the validity of qualitative data in general be improved?
- Hint: Refer to Chapter 2 if you have forgotten what validity means in the context of qualitative research.

Whilst we want readers to see the benefits of interviews in which researchers make an 'active contribution' (see Enosh and Buchbinder, 2005) it is not always appropriate to assume such an interviewer role. For example, let's say you had gained permission to interview criminals convicted of violent crimes. It is likely that you would want to get at the participants' 'subjective' truths as opposed to the actual truth of the criminal act. If we wish to further our knowledge of why criminals act in particular ways then interviewers will need to allow the participants to speak in their own terms in order to further understanding of the ways in which they are able to justify their actions to themselves,

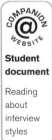

Student document

Reading about interview styles

as this reveals something about the conditions in which people will break the law. Researchers may find this difficult at times as they may have to listen to things which they find abhorrent without showing their feelings. This does not mean that they need to rid themselves of their own value position, but rather that they should act in a way that maximises their participants' ability to speak openly. We can sum this up by stating that some researchers will focus on achieving authenticity whilst others will try to explain why and how participants make sense of things in particular ways.

BOX 8.3 POWER AND THE INTERVIEW PROCESS

Take another look at Malcolm Cowburn's reflections on his interview of 'Martin' in the article to which we referred in Chapter 2. Now read Enosh, G. and Buchbinder, E. (2005) 'The Interactive Construction of Narrative Styles in Sensitive Interviews: The Case of Domestic Violence Research', *Qualitative Inquiry,* 11: 588–617.

- Does the article by Enosh and Buchbinder help you to understand what happened in Cowburn's interview with Martin?
- Do you think that a struggle within an interview might sometimes elicit information that is useful to a criminologist? Give reasons for your answer.
- What did the article by Enosh and Buchbinder teach you about qualitative interviewing skills in general?
- What did you learn about the interviewing skills that are needed when the research topic is sensitive?

Whilst interviews are an exciting part of research that new researchers are usually keen to carry out it requires skill and practice to become an effective interviewer. Our own early experiences as interviewers as well as our knowledge of our students' first attempts at interviewing have taught us that in practice it is important to try out interviewing skills on some willing 'guinea pigs' before embarking upon the real thing. The most common problem is that participants' answers will be too brief if an interviewer does not think in advance of some ways to draw out more in-depth responses. The most important task for an interviewer is to put the participant at ease by establishing rapport at the beginning of an interview. You might tell the participant about something funny that happened on your way to meet them, or perhaps mention and discuss a topical news event as a way of breaking the ice. It is especially important to make participants feel comfortable with you when the research topic is sensitive so it is a good idea to leave the most sensitive questions until towards the end of your interviews. We can liken this process to dipping your toes in a bath tub to ensure that the water is not too hot before jumping in. It is often useful to use **vignettes** in circumstances where your research aims to access participants' attitudes toward sensitive issues. A vignette is a short summary of a scenario that is designed in such a way as to invite comment. Vignettes are often followed by some questions that are designed to draw out the participants' views. Here is an example:

Jackson was raped at the age of 18. He told his friend, Jake, whose response suggested to Jackson that Jake did not believe it was rape. Jake said that because Jackson was gay he must have wanted sex. Jackson failed to report the offence to the police for fear that they would not believe him.

- What do you think about Jake's response to Jackson?
- What would your advice have been?
- What would your advice have been if the victim was heterosexual?

In general, do remember to keep professional 'jargon' to a minimum, unless of course you are interviewing professionals who will understand it. It is most important that the participants in your research do not feel intimidated by the language you use so try to make sure that you speak in plain English. Furthermore, you should ensure that you do not upset participants by using language that may be offensive, therefore you will need to make sure that you are culturally sensitive. Table 8.1 provides you with a quick checklist of things to consider before making your final choice about your choice of interview.

OBSERVATION

Ethnography is usually the term used to describe complete participant observation in which the researcher takes on a covert role. For this reason this type of observational research is relatively rare within criminology owing to the ethical issues to which it gives rise (see Chapter 3). However, as Yates (2004) has stated, it has made a considerable contribution to our criminological understanding and for this reason it is important for new researchers to have knowledge of observational methods and to understand the assumptions that underpin them. Yates (2004) also admits that it is important to note that most observational research within the field of criminology has been focused on those with least power in society, therefore it is incumbent upon researchers to be clear about the reasons for their study and we would add that it is important to ensure that stereotypical representations are not reproduced in such research.

New researchers in criminology are unlikely to be guided towards research that involves complete participant observation and so the section below on doing observational studies will be less detailed in this regard.

Types of observation

Pole and Lampard (2002: 71) characterise observation as 'the first-hand involvement of the researcher(s) with the social action as it occurs', which describes all forms of observation whether that be the complete immersion of a researcher within a particular setting over a protracted period or not. Whilst the term ethnography is often restricted to complete participant observation we do not believe that this is a particularly useful distinction, especially when observation is used in conjunction with ethnographic interviewing. Observation may be overt or covert. Overt observation gives rise to fewer ethical concerns, although there is perhaps more chance that the observer will have an impact on the data collected than in covert studies. Many methodology texts also speak of participant or non-participant (sometimes referred to as simple) observation (see for example Matthews and Ross, 2010; Flick, 2009). Gold (1958) is frequently cited in general social science methodology texts which discuss different types of observational data collection. He spoke of four key roles that researchers may choose to take in the process of carrying out observational studies, which are defined by the degree of detachment or involvement a researcher has with the subjects of the research. We can represent this as a continuum:

Complete participant; Participant as observer; Observer as participant; Participant as detached observer

Subjective ◄──► Objective

Figure 8.1 Researcher roles in observation studies

Given that we have tried to challenge oppositional modes of thinking in this text it will come as no surprise to discover that in reality we do not think it is helpful to think of these researcher roles as discrete or ideal types. Researchers may move in and out of the first three roles during the process of research, although we think that it is unlikely that criminological researchers would be able to carry out a complete and by implication, covert, observer role as this suggests the treatment of human beings as if they are inanimate objects. Toward the objective end of the continuum it is likely that observations will be more structured. Structured observations may be used in combination with in-depth interviews and non-structured observations, especially by critical criminologists who might wish to use quantitative strategies as a way of explaining the relationship between structure and meaning.

When to use observational methods

In simple terms criminological researchers should choose observational methods when they wish to gain insider understanding of people involved in criminal activities or indeed of those who are involved in responding to criminal activities. For example, it is possible to use observation from the perspective of an **ethnomethodologist** (a researcher who tries to identify people's methods of making sense of situations). In such research decision-making processes, such as jury decisions, will be the focus of the observation and the researcher/s will try to identify what assumptions underpin people's decisions. Whilst observational studies are most often described as qualitative, observational methods can be used in a quantitative way too. As May (2001: 151) says, 'there is a central ethnographic component to successful survey work, while numbers may equally appear in the representation of ethnographic studies'. This means that it may sometimes be appropriate to count the number of times a particular decision is made and to record the details. For example if there was a concern about bias in sentencing, an observation schedule would be appropriate to record such things as the age, gender and ethnicity of the offender. As in all decisions about methods, researchers need to ensure that their choice of observational method is suited to the aims of their study. As we indicated in Chapter 3 however, we suggest that caution is needed when assuming a complete participant researcher role because of the special ethical concerns to which it gives rise. This said, if you can justify your ethical decisions and it seems highly unlikely that it would be possible to gain important data in any other way then we are certainly not against this method, but we would suggest that it requires a higher level of expertise than other forms of observation.

PAUSE TO THINK . . .

Refer back to Box 8.2 and think about whether any of the listed research aims might also indicate the use of observational methods.

BOX 8.4 OBSERVATION AND THEORIES OF KNOWLEDGE

Consider the following:

Conventional ethnography

A research team decides to observe groups that define themselves as a gang in several different areas. The researchers gained access to the gangs through trusted local individuals. They produced detailed descriptions of what they saw in as neutral a way as possible and compared what they had recorded. As a result of this process they developed a **hypothesis**: 'the sense of belonging of which gang members speak is more tenuous for male gang members than for female members', which they tested out by further observations of the gangs.

- What role did theory play in the first set of observations?
- What theory of knowledge does the development of a hypothesis usually imply?
- What is the role of theory in the subsequent observations in this study?
- How can the concept of belonging be made measurable?
- How could researchers be sure that the key **dependent variable** is gender?
- How is this similar to and different from **positivism**?

Interpretivist ethnography

A research team aims to observe young people in an area designated as 'high risk' in terms of crime. The researchers wish to access what life is like in this area from the perspectives of the young people who live there. Two members of the team have become involved with a voluntary organisation working with young people in the

Instructor
activity

Workshop
– ethno-
graphic
research
on gangs

Student
web links

Responses
to crime

Student
activity

Getting
started
with
ethno-
graphic
research

community who have been in trouble with the police. They move into the community and through their voluntary work they have an opportunity to get to know the young people and to observe them in their everyday lives. They are participant observers who choose to be covert about the fact that they are recording their observations for the purposes of research. They wished to provide insights into what these young people thought they were doing and why they are doing it. In other words they were trying to uncover the meanings that actions had for the young people in order to widen understanding of their risk-taking behaviours.

- What role does theory play in the data-collection process?
- What do you think are the strengths and limitations of this approach for criminologists?
- Would the results have been better had the researchers chosen to be overt about their observation?

Critical ethnography

A research team aims to observe young people in an area designated as 'high risk' in terms of crime. The researchers wish to access what life is like in this area from the perspectives of the young people who live there. Two members of the team have become involved with a voluntary organisation working with young people in the community who have been in trouble with the police. They move into the community and through their voluntary work they have an opportunity to get to know the young people and to observe them in their everyday lives. They are in effect participant observers whilst being covert about the fact that they are recording their observations for the purposes of research. However, these two members of the research team are able to introduce the other members of their team to some key young people in the area. They explain to the young people that their 'friends' (i.e. the other members of the research team) would like them to help them with some research they are doing in areas of high deprivation. They ask the young people whether they would be willing to be trained in videoing skills so that they could make a film depicting everyday life in their neighbourhood. The plan is to show the films in several key places in order to raise awareness of the social conditions in which some young people are identified as a problem to society and to facilitate discussions through which understanding of the relationship between meaning and structure is exposed. In this way the researchers are demonstrating that the meanings the young people give to their actions are not the whole of the story because their actions take place within a particular social context. This social context interacts with the meanings that the young people give to their actions and therefore these meanings cannot be understood in isolation from it.

- What role does theory play in the data-collection process?
- Do you think that relations of power shape meanings in people's lives? Give reasons for your answer.
- Do you think that there could be a role for hypothesis testing in this type of ethnography? Give reasons for your answer.

As Box 8.4 indicates the theoretical assumptions that underpin the choice of observational methods will vary in the same way that our choice of interviewing method and the researcher role will vary. As we have stressed throughout the book it is important that you are clear about your own assumptions and that you are consistent. This said, some researchers do attempt 'theoretical' (as opposed to method) triangulation. This is where researchers try to analyse an issue from different standpoints, such as an interpretivist account of why a crime is committed compared to a structuralist Marxist approach, for example. This kind of analysis actually takes place within a literature review but it is more usual to use the review to justify why one position is deemed more appropriate than the others that are being discussed. We think that theoretical triangulation is quite complex for beginners and indeed we are uncertain as to the merits of such triangulation as it assumes that it is possible to arbitrate between competing accounts. So theoretical triangulation rather goes against the position we have taken throughout this text because we have tried to convey the ways in which different theories of knowledge provide us with different types of knowledge that are all important if we wish to have a more rounded understanding of a social phenomenon such as crime.

Ethnographic researchers will often use a combination of in-depth interviews and observation. Overt observation might be used in situations where a researcher has already had access to a setting, say in order to carry out interviews. Having gained trust the researcher may subsequently obtain permission to observe an important meeting, for example a case conference. However, it may be that a researcher will gain permission to observe a particular setting in advance of interviewing as a way of identifying some key topics for interviews. Covert observation, as we suggested in Chapter 3, is best used when the data cannot be generated via any other method.

Doing observation

Like interviewing, observation is often thought to be an easy option when in fact this is far from the case. Apart from the fact that observation is a very time-consuming activity it can also be quite a risky activity. Criminological researchers who choose to become complete participants must consider their personal safety, the safety of those they are researching, what they will do if they witness a crime and the reputation of the research institution (refer back to Chapter 3). They will also need to think about the best way to record their data. When researchers are completely immersed in the research setting it is often hard to know what to record at first. It is often also practically difficult to make notes without blowing one's cover so researchers will need to develop strategies that enable them to 'jog' their memories at a later time, such as making brief, covert notes from time to time whilst still 'in the field'. The detailed notes should be made as soon as possible and should include detailed descriptions as well as reflexive comments about the researcher's own reactions to what has been seen and heard. It can take some considerable time for the main focus of the research to emerge from the large amounts of data. This means that the process is largely inductive (although as we have suggested throughout this text no observation can be completely free from theory). In reality, as beginners in research, most of you will be unlikely to be thinking about this type of observation as yet.

Where the researcher's role is overt the researcher must consider how s/he may put the people being observed at their ease in the same way that this issue must be considered within an interview. After the observation has taken place the researcher will need to think carefully about his/her impact upon the behaviour of those being observed. As Pole and Lampard (2002) suggest, researchers may actually be directly responsible for some of the things being observed. Where the researcher is already a part of and therefore accepted in the research setting the impact of the researcher may be less than when s/he is an outsider.

It is increasingly likely that researchers will choose to make audio and or visual recordings in order to have an accurate record of their observations. However, this may well impact negatively upon the data that is gathered and be overly intrusive. Consequently some researchers may involve the participants in their research in recording their own activities, which might overcome the problem of the researcher having too great an impact on the data.

Overt observation may be structured or unstructured (or somewhere in between). If a structured approach is chosen then theory will inform the process from the start. It might be the case that an unstructured approach is followed up by structured observation once certain kinds of behaviour have emerged from the initial unstructured process. In reality researchers will be influenced by their review of existing knowledge but the 'thick'

Table 8.2 Data gathering via observation

Type of observation	Reason for choice	Issues to consider
Complete participant (covert)	To get an insider view that it would be impossible to gain in any other way – the setting is not artificial.	What are the ethical problems associated with covert research? (See Chapter 3.) How will you reflect upon your own role? How will you record your data? Can you counter criticisms such as 'researcher lack of objectivity'? How will you leave the field sensitively?
Participant as observer (overt)	To study in detail a setting in which you are already a member. Your role as a researcher is known to those in this setting, so you will not be running the risk of being morally compromised.	You may need to consider how much detail about your research you will reveal. How will you reflect upon the impact of your own role?
Observer as participant (overt)	To gain legitimate access to a specific setting whilst maintaining an element of detachment.	How will you make your presence as unobtrusive as possible? How can you be sure that your presence has not affected the data? Will your observations be structured?
Complete observer (covert)	This is not really appropriate in criminological research as it suggests a 'social experiment'.	

data gained through observation may cause them to reconsider their initial focus. This is why research journals recording when, where, why and how a research aim was modified are of utmost importance when writing up one's methodology.

CONCLUSION

Ethnographic research is concerned with gaining 'thick' description of aspects of the social world. In criminology knowledge about the lives of those involved in crime has been important to the task of understanding criminal behaviour and challenging some of the social conditions that might contribute to that behaviour. We have noted, however, that in criminology much of the ethnographic research has been aimed at the most powerless members of society. This means that researchers need to present their data in ways that challenge stereotypical representations of 'criminal types'. It is important to be mindful of both the practical and philosophical issues that will necessarily impinge upon the process of data gathering. In this way you will be able to justify your research decisions and maintain consistency.

KEY LEARNING POINTS

* Ethnographic methods require careful preparation in order to elicit the depth of data needed to access the meanings participants give to their lived experiences. You should familiarise yourself with the practical skills that will enable you to carry out effective interviews and observations.
* You should apply your knowledge and understanding of the philosophical assumptions that underpin different research traditions to your discussion of your choice of interviewing and observation methods. You should also apply this knowledge to your discussion of your chosen researcher role.
* Ethnography is concerned with meanings that are normally associated with an interpretivist theory of knowledge.
* The data you collect should be relevant to your research aims. Note that critical social research will attempt to explain the relationship between meaning and structure and may therefore use a variety of methods in order to fulfil the research aims.

Chapter 9

Questionnaires and surveys

GOALS OF THIS CHAPTER

At the end of reading this chapter and by completing the online resources that accompany it, you will be able to:

1 demonstrate an understanding of the advantages and disadvantages of using questionnaires in criminological research;
2 appreciate the importance of selecting appropriate samples;
3 design questionnaires using robust and appropriate question structures;
4 appreciate the importance of sensitivity when using questionnaires.

OVERVIEW

- Questionnaires are widely used in criminological research and when designed well they can provide a useful tool for collecting data on large samples using a standard set of questions.
- One of the best known questionnaire/survey methods in criminological research is the Crime Survey for England and Wales (formerly known as the British Crime Survey).
- As with all methods of data collection, there are advantages and disadvantages to questionnaires. In addition, there are a number of different methods of collecting questionnaire data – in person, by telephone, web-based surveys, and postal surveys – and the merits of each method should be considered by researchers.
- The structure and wording of questions within a questionnaire are extremely important to get right and this chapter provides guidance on this.
- Criminological research often addresses sensitive topics, therefore it is essential to consider sensitivity in using questionnaires in any criminological research.

WHAT ARE QUESTIONNAIRES AND SURVEYS?

The use of questionnaires and surveys is widespread in criminological research and while the terms are often used interchangeably, there are some differences in meaning. While the content may be similar, surveys are sometimes longer and often used on a larger scale as we will discuss in more detail later. For ease, we'll primarily refer to the term questionnaire throughout this chapter.

When designed well, questionnaires provide a useful way of answering research questions or addressing hypotheses. Their purpose includes: gaining factual demographic data on specific groups of people or population samples; obtaining general information relevant to specific issues in order to understand or examine what is not currently known; gaining a range of insights on specific issues and experiences.

Questionnaires are used at all levels of criminological research, from undergraduate research projects to national crime surveys such as the Crime Survey for England and Wales (discussed later in this chapter and in Chapter 10). They comprise sets of questions that when answered will enable the researcher to address her or his research questions and/or hypotheses, typically through statistical analysis. We'll examine the types of questions that can make up a questionnaire later in this chapter, but most questionnaires consist of **closed questions** where respondents must choose from one of a pre-defined set of answers. This enables statistical comparison of the answers of large numbers of respondents. However, some questionnaires include one or more **open questions** in addition to closed questions so that participants can provide some individual responses. Unlike interviews or focus groups, questionnaires typically exist in a standard and non-variable format so that all respondents are asked exactly the same questions in exactly the same order.

As all respondents are presented with a standard questionnaire, typically a list of questions, it is vital to ensure that the questionnaire is well designed. A badly designed questionnaire is likely to result in useless data that cannot answer the research questions and so you need to ensure that your questionnaire measures the concepts that you have set out to measure. Piloting your questionnaire on a small sample can help in testing this. Good design also includes appropriate consideration of your intended participants and how the questionnaire will be completed: participant self-completion; face-to-face with a researcher; or by telephone. For these reasons you should pay particularly close attention to the section on questionnaire design later in this chapter.

HOW ARE QUESTIONNAIRES AND SURVEYS USED IN CRIMINOLOGICAL RESEARCH?

First used in 1982, the Crime Survey for England and Wales (known until 2012 as the British Crime Survey) is the largest-scale example of criminological survey research in England and Wales. The survey aims to provide information representative of the entire population of England and Wales about their experiences of crime (including crime not reported to the police). As the survey is not reliant on official statistics, it is regarded by some as a good indicator of the real extent of crime in England and Wales. For a discussion of the potential problems with official statistics, see Chapter 1. However, as discussed in Chapter 7, it is also important to be aware of potential issues with self-report data.

The Crime Survey for England and Wales includes anonymised data from approximately 40,000 people aged 16 and over living in England and Wales. The survey needs to be large scale to better ensure the data collected can be generalised to the whole population. However, if the respondents were 40,000 students or 40,000 people living in rural areas, for example, then the data could not be said to be representative of the broader population. This is a good example of why choosing your sample appropriately is vital and you can find more information about this in the 'Selecting participants' section below. The survey is administered face-to-face by interviewers who ask questions about experiences of crime and views on government crime policy, who then enter each answer into a laptop computer. The only exception to this is a self-completion part of the survey that respondents are asked to complete individually about their own behaviour. This section includes potentially sensitive topics such as personal drug and alcohol use where respondents may be more likely to be honest than if reporting the answers to these questions to the interviewer.

You can find information and data on the Crime Survey for England and Wales here: http://www.crimesurvey.co.uk/index.html

Questionnaires are not only useful for such large-scale data collection but are often used for much smaller-scale research. For instance, using postal questionnaires one of our own undergraduate dissertation students, Hannah, conducted a successful investigation of the experiences of prison mental healthcare staff. Hannah designed a short questionnaire that sought to understand how such staff have dealt with changes to policy and practice in prison mental healthcare (for more information on Hannah's work see Caulfield and Twort, 2012). Another student, Nikki, used a mix of question-naires and pre-existing scales to measure the relationship between women's alcohol consumption in licensed premises and self-reported aggression (for more information on Nikki's work see Chapters 11 and 14 of this book, and Newberry et al., 2013).

Both of these students designed highly focused questionnaires that directly addressed their research questions. They also chose samples appropriate to their research question. Both of these facts were important in that they contributed to the high grades which these two students achieved for their dissertation projects and to the resulting peer-reviewed journal publications. You should note that while it is unusual for undergraduate dissertation projects to reach publication standard it is not impossible to achieve, as Nikki and Hannah have shown.

ADVANTAGES AND DISADVANTAGES OF QUESTIONNAIRES AND SURVEYS

As discussed earlier in this book, the area you are investigating should inform the methods used and not vice versa. Once you have decided what to investigate and discussed this with your lecturer or supervisor, one of the most important next steps to consider is what the appropriate methods are to best investigate your research questions. The overview here of the advantages and disadvantages of using questionnaires and surveys should help you in the process of making this decision and also in justifying the decision you make.

There are also advantages and disadvantages to specific types of questionnaires. Questionnaires conducted face-to-face allow the researcher to establish a rapport with

Table 9.1 Advantages and disadvantages of questionnaires and surveys

Advantages	Disadvantages
Allows each respondent to be asked a standard set of questions.	Does not allow for a high level of individual responses.
Provides data suitable for quantitative analysis.	Does not allow a depth of data to be collected.
Useful for gathering information from large numbers of people.	More effective with a large sample.
Allows for collection of anonymous data on sensitive issues (e.g. illegal activity).	Does not allow for an exploration of the factors underlying responses.

respondents and to observe body language. However, they can be highly time-consuming and may also be expensive in financial terms, particularly if the researcher has to travel to administer the questionnaires. An alternative is phone interviews. While it is more difficult to establish a rapport, both face-to-face and phone interview methods allow respondents to seek clarification on any questions they do not understand.

Conversely, postal questionnaires are much more cost effective in terms of time and often money. However, postal questionnaires are unlikely to elicit a response rate of more than 25 per cent so keep this in mind when thinking about sample size. Of course, you can post follow-up letters to try to increase the response rate, but you should be wary of harassing people. Postal methods can also be lengthy and you may need to wait some time for responses. Factor this into your planning.

Web-based questionnaires, using sites like SurveyMonkey or Bristol Online Surveys (which your university might have a subscription for), can be useful and very cost effective. They can also be a very quick way of collecting data from large numbers of people and people may be more likely to be open and honest about sensitive topics than when answering questions in person. However, when using web methods you should consider how you will manage the sample and respondents to ensure that your target group and not others complete the questionnaire.

SELECTING PARTICIPANTS

Questionnaires are normally used with a sample of a larger population. Often, researchers seek what is known as a **random sample** in an attempt to gain an accurate representation of the population. Random samples are explained further in Box 9.1, and at a basic level a random sample means that every person in the population being studied has an equal chance of being selected. When seeking a random sample consideration must be given to the size of the population the sample is taken from. For example, recruiting a sample of 25 people will not enable a researcher to make generalisations about the entire UK population. When using random sampling, it is also vital to ensure that all groups within the broader population are sufficiently represented and this may mean the sample needs to be larger. By population, we mean all those who form part of specific groups. For example, 'the population of the UK' would mean everyone living in the UK, and the 'English prison population' would mean everyone incarcerated in prisons in England.

Random sampling is not the only sampling technique used by researchers. Researchers may use what is known as convenience (or opportunistic) sampling where participants are chosen due to their availability and therefore the broader population is not included as potential participants. In terms of ease and accessibility this type of sample has merit, although researchers using this method of sampling are typically unable to generalise their findings. That said, this is a method often adopted by students

---

BOX 9.1　TYPES OF RANDOM SAMPLES

Simple random samples

A random number table or computer is used to generate a sample at random from the population under investigation, where every member of the population has been assigned a number.

Systematic sampling

As the name implies, this is a systematic process of choosing say, every seventh student on a list or whatever number works to obtain the sample size needed. For example, if you were investigating your fellow students (of whom we'll say there are 700 across all years) and you are seeking a sample of 10 per cent, you would choose every seventh student. Typically you would begin with any number between 1 and 7 and then sample every seventh student after that.

Stratified sampling

This takes data from different strata − or layers − of the population, for example, by selecting samples from different age groups or prison categories. The sample size from each layer is proportional to the size of that layer. For example, if we were seeking a sample of 10 per cent of the prison population, we might split this up and sample 10 per cent of those in category A prisons, 10 per cent in category B prisons, and so on.

Cluster (multi-stage) sampling

This is a more complex method where multi-stage sampling is used, in which clusters are randomly sampled, then a random sample of elements is taken from sampled clusters. For example, imagine you are investigating the effects of a programme aimed at reducing aggressive behaviours in pupils at schools across the West Midlands. Three schools are chosen to investigate, 33 pupils are randomly selected from each school, 11 pupils from each of the school years taking part.

because it may sometimes be the only practical way of obtaining a sample. Provided you acknowledge the limitations of this method – primarily in terms of lack of generalisability – this is unlikely to be problematic for research at undergraduate level.

Certain types of research benefit from contacting participants through network (or snowballing) sampling, based on pre-existing connections. For example, if a researcher was seeking to investigate a particular sub-group in society, they may not have ready access to all those in the sub-group so may use initial contacts to contact others. Other researchers use purposive (sometimes known as judgemental) sampling, where the researcher chooses participants subjectively and tries to include a range of participants between extremes. Others may take a more systematic approach, although less so than true random sampling: quota sampling. Using this method researchers choose participants in pre-set categories that are characteristics of the broader population under investigation, for example, 20 women and 20 men, 30 undergraduate students and 30 postgraduate students, and so on.

As a general rule of thumb, your sample is likely to be more representative of the broader population you are investigating if: the sample is large proportionate to the population; there is little diversity in the population under investigation and your sample; and if you keep in mind that the smaller the population, the bigger the sampling ratio must be for an accurate sample. For example, if you applied a 10 per cent sampling ratio to the UK prison population of approximately 84,000 when this text was written, you would have a sample of 8400. However, if you applied a 10 per cent sampling ratio to the population of your undergraduate seminar class of 20, your sample would be a mere two and would not therefore be appropriate.

DESIGNING QUESTIONNAIRES AND SURVEYS

This section covers the practicalities of questionnaire design: it takes you through the types of questions that can be used in a questionnaire, what other sorts of information you might wish to collect, and how the order in which questions are presented can have an impact on responses. It is vital that you pay close attention to the guidance provided here as designing your questionnaire is an extremely important part of the research process. Once you have designed your questionnaire you have set the questions and so, to some extent, also set the answers that respondents can give. You will not be able to go back and collect more information from respondents so it is vital to ensure that the questions you ask clearly address your research questions and will enable you to collect the data you need. It is worth a reminder here of the difference between research questions and questions you ask in a survey/questionnaire. The former refers to the over-arching focus of your research, while the latter refers to the detailed questions you ask in attempting to address your main research question(s).

While it is important to ensure you use appropriate question formats (information on which you can find below), there are a few things that you should think about before designing the questions themselves. The first is to ensure you begin with a clear and concise introduction or welcome message so that respondents know: who you are; the purpose of the research; who they can contact for more information (you may want to provide either your university email address or the email address of your supervisor). Second, remember to KISS (Keep It Short and Simple). Imagine that you are given a questionnaire that is very long. How likely are you to fill it out? The more concise you can keep your questionnaire the better, so keep this in mind when designing the questions – this goes for the number and length of questions, but you should also pay close attention to the formatting of your questionnaire as this can affect the overall length too. For example, Qureshi and Farrell (2006) give a useful example of a concisely formatted survey they designed for police officers, which resulted in a 100 per cent response rate (although note that the 100 per cent response rate was not due solely to the formatting of the questionnaire).

There are also a number of other things to think about:

- font – ensure the text is clearly readable;
- language – is the language suitable for the audience? In general, avoid jargon and ensure the language is as straightforward as possible;
- ensure there is always a 'don't know' or 'not applicable' or 'other' option;
- ask for only one piece of information at a time;
- be precise with your questions and ensure they are relevant to your research questions;
- ensure there are clear instructions on how to complete the questionnaire.

Types of question

Now you should be ready to compose your questions. There are two main categories of questions you can use: closed and open-ended. We'll look at each of these individually.

Table 9.2 Advantages and disadvantages of closed and open-ended questions

Closed questions		Open-ended questions	
Advantages	Disadvantages	Advantages	Disadvantages
Relatively quick for respondents to answer	Options are limited, so conclusions may not truly represent the thoughts and opinions of respondents	Respondents can more fully express their thoughts and opinions	Coding answers for analysis is time-consuming compared with closed questions
Easy to code for analysis	Respondents cannot explain their choice or why this might depend on circumstances	Results may more fully represent the thoughts and opinions of respondents	Answers can be misclassified if misinterpreted by the researcher
Respondents' level of skill in reporting their thoughts and opinions does not matter	Respondents cannot explain that they do not understand a question, particularly in web/email/postal surveys	Respondents can explain their answer	Where respondents write answers by hand, illegible handwriting can be problematic

Closed questions can include simple *multiple-choice questions* where respondents should tick the box next to the answer they choose:

How many crimes do you think were reported to the police in England and Wales in the 1990s?	3 million ☐ 5 million ☐ 7 million ☐ 8 million ☐

Or *yes/no* answer questions:

Have you consumed any alcohol in the last 24 hours?	Yes ☐ No ☐ Don't know ☐

When collecting information on demographic details, such as age or educational attainment, questions with a number of closed categories are often used:

Are you (please tick as appropriate):

☐ Under 18
☐ 19 to 34
☐ 35 to 44
☐ 45 to 54
☐ 55 to 64
☐ 65 or over
☐ Prefer not to say

Note that a common error is to duplicate ages. For example, 19–35, 35–45. In this example, if you were 35, which box would you tick? This is why each option must be distinct.

Researchers also use *rating scales*:

How would you rate the decision to replace Ken Clarke with Chris Grayling as Justice Secretary?	An excellent decision ☐ A good decision ☐ Neither a good or bad decision ☐ A bad decision ☐ A terrible decision ☐ Don't know ☐

Rating scales can also ask respondents to rate something on a scale of one to ten.

You might also see *agreement scales* used in questionnaires:

How far do you agree with the following statements?	Strongly agree	Agree	Don't know	Disagree	Strongly disagree
'It is important for me to learn more about why I do the things I do.'					
'It is important for me to grow and learn new things.'					

The type of scale above is known as a **Likert scale**. There are two widely used versions of the Likert scale: a five-point scale and a seven-point scale. While the five-point version is often used, it is worth noting that a seven-point scale is likely to be more reliable and may avoid respondents being overly neutral in their response choice (Colman *et al.,* 1997). These scales allow for degrees of opinion, or even no opinion at all, and so can be more useful than yes/no questions where appropriate.

All of the above were closed questions. Open-ended questions might include numeric open-ended questions:

How old are you?	_____ years

While other questions might be open-ended text questions:

You answered 'yes' to Question 17. How has your knowledge of the 2007 Lord Bradley review impacted your current working practices? Please write your answer in the space below.

It is good practice to end a questionnaire with an open question asking for anything respondents wish to say/add about the topic. It is usual to provide a couple of line spaces for this, but no more, in order to avoid large amounts of textual data. Even where this information is not useful to the research, it allows respondents to know that their opinion is being heard and thus they may feel more engaged and satisfied with the research process.

Some questions might be closed but have an 'other' option where an open-ended text line also appears.

It may be useful to route certain questions as you may design a questionnaire where not all questions are relevant to every respondent, depending on their answers. These are sometimes known as filter questions. For example:

Question 5. Are you employed directly by the probation service?

Yes   ☐   Go to question 6

No   ☐   Go to question 9

You must ensure that each question only asks one thing. For example, what is wrong with the following question?

'Women make better prison officers but men make better therapy staff.'   ☐   Agree
☐   Disagree

This question asks two things and so respondents cannot be clear whether they are being asked to answer a question about women as prison officers or men as therapy staff. It is surprising how often questions like this are included in questionnaires.

You must also ensure you avoid leading questions. A leading question is a question that subtly – or not so subtly – prompts respondents to respond in a particular way. For example, let's imagine your research involved asking members of staff working for a voluntary agency dealing with victims to complete a questionnaire about their relationship with the police:

'Do you have any problems in your meetings with police officers?'

or

'Briefly describe your meetings with police officers.'

While the differences in the questions in the above example are relatively minor, the first is a leading question and in a fairly subtle way raises the possibility that there are problems. The result of asking questions in a leading way may be that the answers you gain are unreliable. We have seen our own students write leading questions in their own questionnaires and surveys as, without due consideration, it is an easy trap to fall into but one that must be avoided.

When asking for any information you must think very carefully about whether you need it and why you need it. Even though assurances should have been made in writing about confidentiality, respondents may feel concerned about why you wish to know certain things about them, so really make sure you need the data you ask for. For example, do you need to know the educational level or ethnic background of your respondents? When you have decided which information you need you must also think carefully about what categories you might include. Above we gave an example of age categories, but you might find for your research that it is more useful to ask for each respondent's exact age. Rather than design your own categories for collecting information on things like ethnic group, education and employment, we advise using existing categories such as those used in the 2011 census:

http://www.ons.gov.uk/ons/guide-method/census/2011

You should also carefully consider how the questions you ask and the words you use in your questions might affect the responses you receive. For example, if you ask questions about 'fear of crime' might you find that some individuals are reluctant to tick a box that means admitting they are afraid? Similarly, the way we ask about sensitive issues, such as Intimate Partner Violence (IPV – the formal term sometimes used for domestic violence), can significantly affect responses. Caulfield and Wilkinson (2014: 177–8) explain how changes in screening questions used in crime surveys have affected responses:

> Researchers have sought to investigate IPV in a number of ways. Official crime statistics have been reviewed over the past 30 years to look at changes in reported incidences of IPV. Notably, the British Crime Survey (renamed the Crime Survey for England and Wales in 2012) in both 1982 and 1985 found that all victims of IPV (or Domestic Violence as it was referred to) were women. Similarly, official statistics collected in Canada at around the same time (1981) found that between 80 and 90% of victims were women. In contrast, in later years official statistics in both Britain and Canada reported equal numbers of men and women were victims of IPV.
>
> *Why might this be the case? Was there a particular occurrence in Western society during the 1980s and 1990s that prompted women to become the perpetrators of IPV?*
>
> Actually, the explanation is a much more straightforward one. All of the 1981, 1982, and 1985 official surveys discussed above included screening questions that made it very clear that respondents were being asked about 'domestic violence'. Men often do not believe that this term applies to them, even when they have experienced physical, psychological, or other forms of abuse. When no screening question was used, the 1996 British Crime Survey found that 4.2% of men and 4.2% reported being a victim of IPV.

Arranging the questions

The order that the questions are presented in is also important. Some general tips are that you should:

- Begin with general questions before more focused and/or difficult questions. This allows respondents to think about the topic.
- Do not begin with sensitive, or potentially sensitive, questions.
- Begin with closed questions, for much the same reason as above.
- Where possible, leave asking demographic and personal questions until the end of the questionnaire. Beginning with these questions may make some respondents less likely to complete your questionnaire. Exceptions to this rule are any demographic questions that qualify someone to be included in the survey. For example, many researchers limit some surveys to people in certain age groups and therefore these questions must come near the beginning.
- Group similar questions together.

BOX 9.2 SPOT THE DELIBERATE MISTAKES

The questionnaire below includes several mistakes. Can you spot them all? Check your answers on the companion website.

Have you ever engaged in criminal activity?   Yes ☐

                                                            No   ☐

What is your ethnic group? _____

How old are you?   Under 18
                   18–30
                   30–45
                   Over 45

Have you ever worked in the criminal justice system?   Yes ☐

                                                            No   ☐

What was your job title? _____

'P.O.V. crime has increased in urban areas.'

Strongly agree   Agree   Disagree   Strongly disagree

Do you agree that violent crime has become more
of a problem in Birmingham recently?   Yes ☐

                                                           No   ☐

What do you think about Birmingham? _____

Do you currently have double glazing in your main residence?_____

Please return this questionnaire to your lecturer.

Instructor exercise

Spot the mistakes

SENSITIVITY IN USING QUESTIONNAIRES AND SURVEYS

Criminological research often addresses sensitive topics. This may, for example, include topics such as people's experiences of victimisation, investigations of deviant behaviour, or research with vulnerable groups. Some of the questions to be asked as part of the research may potentially cause distress. While these issues will have been given thorough consideration prior to applying for ethical approval for the research (see Chapter 3) and the decision may have been made to utilise another data collection method, is it possible to appropriately investigate sensitive topics using questionnaires? The Crime Survey for England and Wales includes questions on sensitive and difficult topics such as sexual assault and domestic violence. We suggest you look at some of the questions asked in the survey by visiting the link given earlier in this chapter. You will note that the explanations for all of these sensitive questions are carefully written and thoroughly explained. Importantly, respondents are always given the option not to answer these questions. These are vital lessons in designing sensitive questionnaires. However, before getting to this stage it is important to consider whether questions on sensitive topics or of a sensitive nature are fully justified, i.e. can the potential emotional cost of including these questions (to both the research participants and the researcher) be justified compared to the potential benefits of the research? If yes, we strongly recommend piloting the questionnaire on a small scale before conducting the main study.

In research where participants are asked to report highly personal experiences, there are also other issues to consider. Under-reporting has been noted as a serious concern (American Correctional Association, 1990; Leigey and Reed, 2010; Williams, 1994). Where possible, researchers should spend time talking with participants to establish rapport and put them at ease before they complete the questionnaire. However, this is not always possible and thus it may be the case that questionnaire data collection methods may not be the right method for very sensitive topics. You should always discuss this with your supervisor. Even where rapport building is possible, 'shame, stigma, and social desirability' (Jansson et al., 2008: 6) may play a part in under-reporting of certain events.

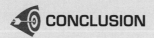

CONCLUSION

Questionnaires and surveys form an important part of the data that exists about crime, victims and the criminal justice system. Large-scale crime surveys are well established and, while subject to some criticism, can provide a useful source of data. In designing your own questionnaires and surveys, you must ensure that what you produce clearly addresses your research questions and that what you ask is appropriate. Understanding what questionnaires and surveys can and can't do – their strengths and limitations – is vital in deciding how far they are appropriate to your own research, and we advise thorough consideration of this before beginning.

One of the most important parts of using questionnaires and surveys is having a clear understanding of methods of sampling and how to ensure your sample is appropriate to your research. Finally, we cannot emphasise enough the importance of sensitivity in using these methods in criminological research – from the questions you ask to the people you approach. You may be dealing with potentially vulnerable people or asking questions about sensitive and/or upsetting issues and you must take care to protect the people in your research from any insensitivity and consequent upset or concern.

 KEY LEARNING POINTS

- Questionnaires can be a useful tool in criminological research provided they are well designed with questions that directly address the overarching research questions/**hypothesis** of the investigation.
- All methods of data collection have advantages and disadvantages and it is important to consider these thoroughly to ensure you can justify the approach you take in your own research.
- One of the most important parts of questionnaire-based research is appropriate sample selection. Even if the questionnaire is very well designed, choosing an inappropriate and/or unrepresentative sample may make your research little more than worthless.
- Good questionnaire design follows a number of rules and guidelines for the composition of questions and questionnaire structure.
- It is possible to address sensitive topics using questionnaires, but significant thought should be given to whether questionnaires are the most appropriate way of investigating sensitive topics or for collecting data with vulnerable groups.

Chapter 10

Using documentary and secondary data sources

GOALS OF THIS CHAPTER

At the end of reading this chapter and by completing the online resources that accompany it, you will be able to:

1   demonstrate a critical understanding of the benefits and limitations of using existing data in research;
2   appreciate the range of sources that exist and how these might be used in criminological research;
3   understand the difference between existing sources of data and existing data sets that have already been analysed;
4   begin to ask appropriate questions of existing data sources.

OVERVIEW

- The world around us is awash with data. If we know where to look, what we are looking for, and what questions to ask of existing data, we can use this to produce both robust and insightful research.
- Research that makes use of existing data by no means needs to be inferior to empirical research. There is little use in spending time and resources collecting new data when data may already exist that can address your research questions, perhaps in a more useful way than any data you could collect yourself.
- Existing data is all around us as sources that are yet to be analysed.
- Existing data sets that have been collected and already analysed are available to us as criminological researchers to conduct secondary analysis upon.
- There are a number of points of caution that researchers must be aware of when using secondary sources. Asking critical questions of the data is vital in understanding the context of, and limitations to, the data.

WHY USE EXISTING DATA SOURCES?

It is common, particularly at undergraduate level, for students to undertake non-empirical research using **secondary data** sources. However, this does not mean this is inferior to empirical research: there is much secondary data in existence that, through analysis and re-analysis, can provide important insight into criminological phenomena. Indeed, even where the research may include an empirical element, many researchers make use of secondary data sources as a part of their research. As gathering empirical data is such an ingrained part of the research process, we sometimes fail to explore whether the data we need may already exist. In some cases it makes little sense to collect our own data; particularly where the data that already exists may have been collected by researchers and organisations that have far greater resources than we have. While there is a disadvantage in that you have had no control over the way the data was collected, if you use existing data in the 'right' way and ask the 'right' questions about the data (see Chapter 13), you can reveal much.

There is a distinction here between secondary data that has been collected by researchers and analysed, and documents that exist not necessarily for research purposes but may be useful sources for researchers. We consider secondary data and **documentary data** separately below.

This chapter discusses the types of data that criminological researchers may benefit from accessing, exploring the strengths and limitations of particular data sources. Part 4 of this book looks at data analysis: Chapter 13 focuses on analysing documents and text-based data; while the data analysis techniques discussed in Chapters 11 and 12 can also be applied to secondary data sources. You will also find some information on analysing secondary data later in this chapter.

DOCUMENTARY DATA SOURCES

Documentation about our lives and the world around us is everywhere. From newspaper reports and news websites, television programmes, books and social media, information about the social world is there for us to absorb, review and analyse. Events are reported, photographed, tweeted and blogged, emails are written and life is recorded. As social scientists, we see all of this as potential sources of data. As criminological researchers we are acutely aware of what all of these existing sources of data can tell us about attitudes towards crime, sentencing and punishment, the experiences of victims and criminals and so much more. The world is rich with data and in the technological world in which we live, much of this is readily available. It is clear to see that collecting new data is not always the best course of action when what we are looking for might already be out there.

When writing the previous paragraph we felt the sense of excitement we often feel when thinking about opportunities for research. However, we must signal a note of caution. It is all too easy to run away with an idea, but we must think carefully about the sources we use in our research, their credibility, reliability, representativeness and ethics. Can they be trusted? We must also think carefully about where to look for data and what we might be able to do with it. Once we know where the data can be located we need to consider whether special access is needed. Make these checks early and ensure you have a contingency plan in case you cannot use the data you wanted.

Remember: You should begin with your research question and then seek out data that might help you address that question. Don't choose sources at random – you should employ the same level of thorough and critical thinking as you would when devising an interview schedule or questionnaire.

What types of data sources exist?

O'Leary (2010) provides a comprehensive list of potential documentary data sources (see Table 10.1).

For criminological researchers, there are some existing sources of data that may be particularly interesting in addressing our research questions. *Life histories and autobiographical* accounts of ex-prisoners, and prison staff can provide a wealth of information. For example, Wilson (2010) analyses prison officer autobiographies in order to draw together the information presented by current and former prison officers. This is against an existing, if fairly limited, background of research on prisoners' autobiographies. While there has often been hostility towards both prisoner and prison officer accounts of prison, they provide a rich source of data (Morgan, 1999).

PAUSE TO THINK . . .

How far are diaries and autobiographies likely to present a full view of prisons? Does this matter, or is the reality experienced and presented by that individual more important?

One of our current dissertation students (let's call him Sayid – not his real name) is conducting an in-depth analysis of materials written by two perpetrators of mass school shootings in the United States. These materials are *diary entries* that describe what might be termed 'manifestos' and they already exist in the public domain. Done well, using robust methods and ensuring consideration of the cultural context of the materials, Sayid could produce a very good piece of work. We will be advising him to think carefully about his methodology and methods, starting with reading this book.

With both of the above types of data, there is work for the researcher to do in seeking out relevant and appropriate sources.

There are some criminological researchers who make excellent use of *newspapers and other mass media* to interpret and understand criminological issues. Using methods of analysis, such as qualitative content analysis (discussed in Chapter 13), researchers are able to examine how particular criminological phenomena are presented in the media. Mawby and Gisby (2009), for example, examined how newspapers covered crime risks associated with gaining European Union membership in two Eastern European countries.

Table 10.1 Broad-ranging texts

Type of text	Examples
Official data and records	While you may have to work at getting access, it may be worth exploring: • *international data* held by organisations such as the United Nations, World Bank or World Health Organization; • *national data* held by many federal or national governments and government departments, e.g. national census data; • *local government data* such as state of environment reports, community surveys, water quality data, land registry information etc.; • *non-governmental organisation data* collected through commissioned or self-conducted research studies; • *university data*, which is abundant and covers just about every research problem ever studied; • *archival data* such as records of births, deaths, marriages, etc.
Organisational communication, documents and records	Generally official communication that includes, but is not limited to: • websites; • press releases; • catalogues, pamphlets and brochures; • meeting agendas and minutes; • inter- and intra-office memos; • safety records; • sales figures; • human resource records; • client records (these might be students, patients, constituents, etc. depending on organisation type).
Personal communication, documents and records	Personal and often private communication, which includes but is not limited to: • letters and emails; • journals, diaries and memoirs; • Facebook/MySpace sites; • blogs; • mobile phone texts; • sketches and drawings; • poetry and stories; • photographs and videos; • medical records, • educational records; • household records, e.g. cheque book stubs, bills, insurance documents etc.
The media/ contemporary entertainment	Data here is often examined in relation to questions of content or portrayal, e.g. the content of personal ads, how often male characters are shown crying, or how often sexual assault has made the news over the past two years. Data can come from: • websites; • newspaper or magazine columns/articles/advertisements; • YouTube content; • news programmes and current affairs shows; • TV dramas, sitcoms and reality shows; • commercials; • music videos; • biographies and autobiographies.

continued . . .

Table 10.1 *Continued*

Type of text	Examples
The arts	The arts have captured and recorded the human spirit and condition over the ages in every corner of the globe, making them perfect for comparing across both culture and time. Societal attitudes are well captured in: • paintings, drawings and sketches; • photography; • music; • plays and films.
Social artefacts	These include any product of social beings. Examples of social products or social traces are extremely broad-ranging and can include things like: • garbage; • graffiti; • children's games; • rites and rituals; • jokes; • t-shirt slogans; • tools; • crafts; • videos (YouTube has created a huge and accessible database here).

Reproduced from O'Leary 2010, with permission.

What is important to note with their work is that they did not fall into the trap of only seeking out articles available on the internet, but used a specific newspaper article search tool available in most university libraries. If you have not come across LexisNexis, ask your librarian to give you an overview of the best way to use this database.

Wilson *et al.*'s (2013) analysis of a range of sources of information on 'family annihilators' is a fascinating example of research that employs both qualitative and quantitative methods of analysis on mass media sources to provide an account of a particular type of offending and offender. We also recommend noting how useful using both qualitative and quantitative methods can be, to provide both a breadth and depth of information.

Caulfield and Twort (2012) provide an example of how *official documents* can be reviewed as the first stage of research, in order to inform later empirical stages of research. In their paper they review a series of government reports relevant to mental healthcare in prisons, and use this as a basis for developing a questionnaire for prison staff. Of course, official reports do not need to be used only as a basis for empirical work. For example, documents from the Ministry of Justice and other government departments can form a basis for numerous criminological and social research studies. Official documents are of great interest and great potential significance to criminological researchers. If we view the state as holding power within society, the information it produces is clearly of significance. This can range from Acts of Parliament, transcripts of political debates, policy documents, transcripts of expert testimonies, state-funded research reports, state-produced research reports and more. We discuss the use of official state-produced data later in this chapter.

The types of data used by social researchers tend to be categorised as personal, official or media documents. All of these may include text-based documents as well as visual and virtual data. There is also a distinction between documents that are in the public domain and those that are private. Criminological researchers may be able – with consent – to access some of these private documents, including court files, police records, probation and prison reports (for example, see the discussion of Offender Assessment System records outlined in Chapter 7). Indeed, one of the authors of this book made use of the Offender Assessment System records of 43 women in prison and analysed these alongside in-depth qualitative interview data from each of these women (Caulfield, 2012). Note that she was given informed consent from both HM Prison Service and each individual woman involved in the research. Students working in criminal justice agencies may be able to access useful data, but if you are in this position you must consider whether this is appropriate, necessary and ethical. For example, you must fully consider how you use and present this data to ensure the anonymity of individuals. The work by Caulfield (2012) is an example of how quantitative data taken from official records can be successfully used in combination with qualitative methods, in this case in-depth semi-structured interviews.

Advantages and disadvantages of using existing data sources

Accessing the data sources you need in order to address your research questions can be time-consuming, but ultimately well worth it. Existing data:

- already exists, so you don't need to recollect it;
- may represent the 'real' world rather than a convenience research sample;
- can provide a depth and breadth of data;
- can reduce costs – both financial and time;
- avoids many of the pitfalls of collecting new data outlined in Chapter 7 of this book.

While using existing sources of data can provide rich, detailed insights into the phenomena we are researching, there are some downsides. By being aware of these you may be able to minimise some of them. Existing data:

- was not generated specifically for the purposes of your research and so may be harder to work with;
- may be value-laden in ways that are, or are not, immediately obvious.

The student activity in Chapter 13, 'Recognising the role of underlying values', addresses this issue, and that of your own potential biases. Much of the credibility of your research with existing data sources comes from the ability to recognise your own subjectivities and analyse the data in an appropriately robust way. Whichever data sources you choose to use in your research, we advise you to be mindful not to take them at face value. There is a stream of thought that suggests that all documents present something about the reality of organisations/groups of people/individuals. However, most documents are written for a particular audience and in the knowledge that they may be public. Consequently, all documents and data sources have a specific ontological status and the 'reality' that is presented may therefore not be wholly transparent.

When identifying and working with existing sources of data, we suggest you ask yourself the following questions and ensure you could write about the answers to these in the methods section of any research report or dissertation you may write:

- Are the sources you have used relevant and appropriate to your research questions?
- What methods did you use to ensure a broad and encompassing search strategy (i.e. that you didn't miss any key relevant data sources)?
- What selection methods have you employed in deciding which sources to use? Did you put particular parameters or selection criteria in place?
- Have you taken account of the standpoint and values of the author? Have they been selective in what they present?

All of the authors we discussed earlier in this chapter made use of data sources that are available in the public domain and therefore easily accessible. When done well, this type of research can offer important insights into, and deeper understanding of, the lives of individuals and functioning of organisations.

SECONDARY DATA SOURCES

There is a wealth of data out there that is available to us if we know where to look. From large-scale surveys, to census data, to transcripts, data sets exist that may hold the answers to our research questions. Using existing data sets can allow us to focus on the analysis of the data and removes many of the constraints associated with empirical data collection. Often existing data sets are far larger than we could ever hope to obtain as individual or small groups of researchers. Often they have employed robust sampling techniques and may provide both a breadth and depth of data. However, we must be rigorous in assessing the assumptions underlying the data, the data collection techniques used and the sampling techniques used – we have no control over these factors yet must fully understand them to judge whether the data is likely to be credible, reliable and valid.

You should also be mindful of the ethicality of existing data sources. When considering the ethical issues around using secondary data sources – for example, web forums and networking sites – revisit Chapter 2 of this book and also discuss ethical concerns with your lecturers and supervisors.

Secondary analysis of existing data sets is most often done by researchers who had no involvement in the collection of the original data, and typically the secondary analysis seeks to answer questions that the data may not have been originally, or at least directly, designed to answer. The data sets can be either qualitative or quantitative. As highlighted in Box 10.2 later in this chapter, you need to know what you are looking for, and where. To answer your research questions you may need to access and conduct a secondary analysis of either data collected by other researchers or data collected by organisations.

Advantages and disadvantages of secondary analysis

In many circumstances, secondary analysis should be considered as an alternative to collecting new data for numerous reasons. Several of the observations about existing documents are also relevant here – 'Existing data: already exists, so you don't need to recollect it; can provide a depth and breadth of data; can reduce costs – both financial and time; avoids many of the pitfalls of collecting new data outlined in Chapter 7 of this book'. The secondary analysis of existing data sets allows researchers more time to focus on the analysis of often large amounts of data. For example, you may be able to conduct research on nationally **representative samples**; something that is otherwise unlikely to be possible for student researchers.

However, despite the many advantages of this type of research, there are some issues that you must be aware of. Aside from the lack of control over the data, mentioned above, you may find that the data sets are highly complex. This may in part be due to their size and the number of variables they include. The only way to deal with this is to spend time working with the data. Get used to it. Find out what the data set contains. You may find that you are not able to ask some questions of the data that you would like to have addressed, but familiarity with the data set may mean that you can find alternative ways of answering your questions through analysing different variables.

There are some specific issues associated with accessing statistical data sets that have been produced by and for governmental and other organisations. The concepts and methods of data collection are often designed to serve the functions of the organisation and so it is crucial for researchers to engage in robust critical thinking when considering such data sources. Related to this, Box 10.2 below suggests some questions you may wish to ask of the data sets you access. Being aware of the boundaries and limitations of the data you perform secondary analysis of is absolutely vital.

Think back to Chapter 1 where we examined the role official statistics play in our thinking about crime. Among other things, we asked you to answer the following questions:

* How far do you think that official crime statistics tell us the 'truth' about crime?
* Are all crimes reported'?
* Do all reported crimes become official statistics?
* Are all crimes recorded in the same way?

Overall, we believe that the advantages of conducting secondary analysis of existing data sets can outweigh the disadvantages for student and professional researchers alike.

Which data sets might be readily available?

As criminological researchers, we have a wealth of data available to us for secondary analysis as crime is of particular interest to government bodies and wider society.

Data from other researchers – if your supervisors and/or lecturers have conducted research in an area that interests you, you may wish to discuss with them the possibility of having access to their data sets.

For the most part however, the data sets you access will be large organisational data sets. Below are two examples that are of particular interest to criminological researchers:

The UK Data Archive – This is an excellent source of quantitative and qualitative data available for secondary analysis. It includes many large-scale, and some smaller-scale, data sets. As a university student it is likely that any data you request from this source will be free to access, although you may be required to sign a document stating that you will adhere to the conditions of use. It is worth spending some time exploring the data archive website (www.data-archive.ac.uk) to get a sense of the data available. You may wish to speak to your librarian for advice on making the best of keyword searches. For example, simply searching the archive for the word 'crime' elicits 5805 results so you will need to be a little more specific! You can also search the archive thematically, and, for example, look at the theme called 'crime'.

The Crime Survey for England and Wales – Formerly known as the British Crime Survey, and in existence since 1982, this is the largest-scale example of criminological survey research in England and Wales. The survey aims to provide information representative of the entire population of England and Wales about their experiences of crime (including crime not reported to the police). As the survey is not reliant on official statistics, it is regarded by some as a good indicator of the real extent of crime in England and Wales. Earlier in this chapter we asked you to revisit the discussion from Chapter 1 of the potential problems with official statistics. At this point we recommend that you also revisit the discussion in Chapter 7 of potential issues with self-report data. Chapter 9 provides a more detailed description of the Crime Survey for England and Wales, its purpose and the data it includes. You can access the Crime Survey for England and Wales here: http://www.crimesurvey.co.uk/index.html

Student web links

Social data sources

There are a range of other data sources available to both researchers and the general public. You may wish to investigate these and consider whether the available data might be useful in answering your own research questions. The companion website to this book lists up-to-date web links to a variety of social data sources.

An interesting recent example of the quantitative analysis of secondary data is provided by Lankford (2013). Using data from a 2010 New York Police Department report, Lankford undertook a sophisticated statistical analysis of 185 mass shooters in an attempt to identify any differences between attackers who live and attackers who die.

BOX 10.1 STUDENT ACTIVITY

Read Lankford (2013) and refer back to Chapter 6 where we discuss choosing appropriate methods.

- What did the author seek to find out and/or demonstrate from the data?
- Why was existing data used, rather than collecting new data?
- Was the method they chose appropriate? Why?
- What did the author do to ensure the analysis was robust? Could he have done more?

SECONDARY DATA ANALYSIS

Many researchers, including students at all levels, conduct research based on critical examination of existing data. You can find detailed information on data analysis techniques in Part 4 of this book. However, when analysing secondary data there are some specific points to consider in addition to the information provided later in this book. Box 10.2 gives you some questions to consider when analysing secondary data.

BOX 10.2 ANALYSING SECONDARY DATA

Ask yourself these questions:

1   What are you looking for?

   a   Ensure you have a clear research question. This is as important as it would be with an empirical piece of research.

2   Where might relevant data be available?

   a   The internet can be a valuable tool in seeking out relevant data. However, don't rely solely on this. The keywords you use (or don't use) influence what you find. Ask a librarian to help you with your key word searches.

   b   Speak with your research supervisor(s) and lecturers, who may be able to suggest relevant sources.

3   What are you looking for within the data you have located?

   a   As with your overarching research question, ensure the questions you wish to ask of the data you have located are clear.

   b   Clear questions will help you decide upon the methods of analysis you use to analyse the data.

   c   Clear questions will help you thoroughly understand the relevance of the data.

4   Is the data credible?

   a   To some extent this question is fairly subjective. You may wish to review the guidance on document analysis in Chapter 13 to help you think about assumptions underpinning the data.

   b   Consider how clear and transparent the methodology is. Is this consistent with similar types of data from other sources?

   c   Are the researchers credible? Here you may want to consider things like who funded the research.

5   How will you analyse the data?

   a   The information throughout this book on appropriate analysis applies equally here. This may well involve some of the statistical techniques in Chapter 11.

BOX 10.3 STUDENT ACTIVITY: PUBLIC AND PRIVATE PRISONS

Imagine a piece of research has examined the ability of public prisons to effectively reduce reoffending rates. The research was funded by an organisation that runs a number of private prisons.

*   Would you have any concerns about the credibility of this research?

You request, and are given access to, the quantitative data set underpinning the research. You re-run their analyses and produce the same results.

*   Now how do you feel about the research? Are you convinced that the research is credible?

PAUSE TO THINK . . .

When answering the questions in Box 10.3, refer back to our discussions of power and knowledge in Chapter 1.

CONCLUSION

There is no doubt that existing data can be highly useful to researchers. Whether this is existing documents that researchers may search for and analyse, or data that has been collected by other researchers and agencies and already analysed. A researcher looking at an existing data source may be able to ask different questions and glean new things from the data. While we would always advise student researchers to fully consider both the advantages and disadvantages of using existing data sources, we contend that research using secondary data sources can be just as useful as research based on new empirical work. However, as some of the examples in this chapter highlight, combining existing data and new data can work particularly well.

Conducting a strong piece of research using existing sources requires a robust approach. By ensuring you answer some of the questions posed in this chapter we hope this will aid your critical thinking about the data. Remember that all data sources are value-laden in some way and that all research requires consideration of ethical issues. Researchers must always ensure the source of their data is clear and acknowledged, both as an ethical point and as a way of aiding others in judging the reliability of your research.

 **KEY LEARNING POINTS**

- When thinking about your own research interests and ideas, consider whether data already exists that might help you address these. If so, is it useful for you to expend time and energy collecting new data that might be much more limited in scope than this existing data?
- While using existing sources can save you time, energy and cost, you must ensure that you employ the same level of thorough and critical thinking as you would when devising any empirical data collection strategy.
- The data available to you is wide-ranging. It is your duty as a criminological researcher to critically consider the credibility, context, reliability and limitations of the data you access.
- While large governmental data sets can provide a wealth of data, when considering how best to use these in your own research you should be mindful of the lessons introduced throughout this book concerning power and knowledge.
- Being aware of the limitations of existing data and asking the 'right' questions of the data, can result in research that is insightful and in no way inferior to empirical research projects.

PART 4

Doing criminological research: analysis and writing-up

Chapter 11

Analysing the data

Quantitative analysis

GOALS OF THIS CHAPTER

At the end of reading this chapter and by completing the online resources that accompany it, you will be able to:

1   understand basic statistical concepts and terminology;
2   enter data into SPSS;
3   understand the basics of choosing appropriate statistical tests;
4   produce descriptive statistics from your data;
5   conduct *t*-tests and Chi-square tests.

OVERVIEW

*   Statistical analysis allows researchers to say with confidence whether patterns in their data or changes over time exist in their data, whether these are significant or whether they are likely to be due to chance. This can provide more robust evidence than simply presenting data from questionnaires in percentage terms or in graphs.
*   The thought of conducting statistical analysis can be daunting. However, understanding the basics can be relatively straightforward and, contrary to popular opinion, does not require any particular competency with maths. This is largely because of computer programs like SPSS. Providing the researcher is able to choose an appropriate test for their data, follow instructions on running this in SPSS, and follow instructions on correctly interpreting the output, the task is much less scary than students often assume.
*   Before being able to perform statistical tests it is important to understand some basic statistical concepts. Understanding things like the type of data you have and the types of test available equips you with the knowledge to decide which statistical tests are the most appropriate to run on your data.
*   There are many statistical tests available, some used more commonly than others, and some more complex than others. This chapter focuses on two of the more basic

and commonly used statistical tests. These tests are useful, telling you much about your data, and providing a good introduction to running and interpreting statistical tests. However, they are not appropriate in all circumstances and so you may need to use other tests when you come to work with your own data.

INTRODUCTION

You may be a little relieved to read that this book does not seek to make statisticians of its readers. Instead, it seeks to ensure that students understand key concepts in statistical analysis and have the knowledge and skills to analyse the data they collect. Too often criminology students are wary of statistical analysis, so with this in mind this chapter provides a step-by-step guide to basic quantitative analysis. The chapter focuses on fundamental processes such as descriptive statistics, *t*-tests and Chi-square tests, and provides a guide to inputting data into SPSS, choosing and running the appropriate tests and interpreting the output. However, we encourage you to consider whether the data you have would really benefit from quantitative analysis and we hope that by reading this chapter you will be more equipped to answer this question. It may be that you simply require straightforward graphical representations of your data, and this can be done quite easily in programs such as Excel.

Even if you do very little statistical analysis in your degree course and decide to conduct qualitative research for your dissertation, understanding the basics of statistical analysis is still a vital skill to have. For example, think back to Chapter 5 and the focus on critiquing the literature. In order to understand and critique research papers that use quantitative techniques you must be able to understand what the researchers have done and why they have done this. These skills are important to your development as a criminological researcher and indeed as a criminologist.

The aim of this chapter is to equip you with a guide to conducting basic statistical analysis of questionnaire data. However, keep in mind that the types of analysis discussed in this chapter may not enable you to analyse your data in the way you want and so, once you have understood the basics by reading this chapter, you may wish to read one of the range of books that are dedicated to statistical analysis. We recommend some of our favourites at the end of this chapter.

Remember – you DO NOT need to be good at maths to be proficient in quantitative data analysis!

BASIC STATISTICAL CONCEPTS

At this point we should make it clear that we will not be looking at how to conduct statistical analyses by hand. Later in the chapter we will introduce you to the most popular statistics computer program used in the social sciences. Before thinking about, let alone attempting to conduct, any analysis of your quantitative data it is vital to understand some basic statistical terms and concepts. Let's begin with the basics:

Variables

A variable is anything that varies and can be measured. For example, in Nikki's research mentioned in Chapter 9, she wished to measure the relationship between women's alcohol consumption in licensed premises and self-reported aggression. In this case the variables are 'amount of alcohol consumption in licensed premises' and 'self-reported aggression'. Often it is sensible to categorise variables. For example, when collecting data using a questionnaire we may wish to know things like the age of participants. Rather than asking each person to write a number, we may have age groups, as discussed in Chapter 9. For ease of use with SPSS, we may reduce some terms to numbers. For example, if we have collected information on participants' educational background, we may label 'No qualifications' as '0', 'GCSE/O-level' as '1', 'vocational/professional' as '2' and so on. We'll come back to this point later in the chapter.

It is important to identify which variables are independent and which are dependent – or put another way, to understand which variable(s) we expect to have an effect on which other variable(s). The **independent variable** influences the **dependent variable**. For example, if we want to explore the relationship between age and criminality, we might look at different age groups and how many criminal convictions each age group has on average. In this situation age is the independent variable and number of criminal convictions is the dependent variable as we are seeking to understand what effect age has on crime. Researchers may manipulate the independent variable(s) to see what effect this has on the dependent variable. The **dependent variable** is not something controlled or manipulated, but is what is being measured. Let's take a closer look at Nikki's work (see Box 11.1).

Later in this chapter you'll find examples where we ask you to use your knowledge of variables to work out which are the independent and dependent variables.

Types of data: nominal, ordinal, interval and ratio

All data is not the same. In order to work out which is the most appropriate test for the data you collect you need to understand what type of data you have.

Nominal refers to categories that are separate to others, such as name of your university, the gender of your participants, the name of a research methods book or hair colour. You can remember this easily as nominal sounds like name (both words have the same Latin root).

Ordinal is numerical data, usually quantities that have a natural order. The easiest example of this is the place runners finish in a race: first, second, third and so on. The most usual type of **ordinal data** we deal with in criminological research is choices on a Likert scale. Think back to the examples in Chapter 9. With ordinal data the intervals, or differences, between each value are not equal. You can remember ordinal as it sounds like order.

Interval data is like ordinal except the intervals between each value are equal. For example, the temperature difference between 29 and 30 degrees Centigrade is the same size as the difference between 4 and 5 degrees Centigrade. While data from attitudinal scales and Likert scales are typically ordinal, they are often treated like interval

BOX 11.1 CAUSE AND EFFECT IN AGGRESSION AND ALCOHOL: DEPENDENT AND INDEPENDENT VARIABLES

Nikki is interested in researching the relationship between alcohol consumption and aggressive behaviour in undergraduate students. Her review of the literature suggests that there might be a relationship between the amount of time women spend in bars, pubs and clubs and their likelihood of behaving aggressively. She designs a questionnaire to collect data on the amount and type of alcohol participants consume, how much time they spend on average in a variety of establishments where alcohol is sold and their self-reported involvement in a range of aggressive incidents.

In this research, the dependent variable is the aggressive incidents and the independent variable is the amount of time spent in places where alcohol is sold. However, Nikki has also included another variable that might have an effect on aggression: the type and amount of alcohol participants consume. So in this research there are two independent variables.

We might hypothesise that an independent variable is the cause, and the dependent variable is the effect. However, we need to conduct a statistical analysis to start to investigate whether our **hypothesis** might be correct. Keep in mind that even if we find a statistically significant relationship between two variables, it does not prove that one causes the other. This is an important point to keep in mind as it may well be that some other, untested variable is actually influencing both variables. In this example Nikki needs to test whether alcohol consumption and/or time in licensed premises has a statistically significant effect on aggression. If she finds a statistically significant relationship between these variables that might indicate that alcohol consumption and/or time in licensed premises have an effect on aggression, but it does not prove this. We can show a relationship, but cannot prove cause and effect.

data in statistical analysis. There is no simple way to explain why this is the case, but you can find an example in Box 11.3.

Ratio data has all the properties of interval data, except that there is a clear zero value. For example, height or weight – something cannot be less than zero centimetres tall or weigh less than zero kilograms. To help you work out if your data is ratio, consider the ratio of the measurements. For example, a weight of 2 kilograms is twice as much as 1 kilogram. However, a temperature of 60 degrees Celsius is not twice as hot as 30 degrees Celsius as temperature measured in this way is not a ratio variable.

At this point you might be asking 'why does it matter what type of data I have?' The reason we need to understand what type of data we have is to help us decide what type of statistical test to use. See Table 11.1 below for more information.

Types of statistical test: parametric and non-parametric

The main distinction between parametric and **non-parametric tests** it that **parametric tests** are more powerful and allow us to have more confidence in our statistical analysis. Therefore, wherever possible it makes sense to use parametric tests. However, our data has to fulfil certain criteria in order to be suitable for analysis using parametric tests.

Normal distribution: to use a parametric test your data must be from a population that has a normal distribution. This means that most scores or cases cluster around the average (mean) and that as you move further away from this average there are fewer and fewer cases. If your data is not from a normally distributed population, parametric tests could give you incorrect answers. One way of understanding this is to visualise what your data might look like. If we were to plot the data from our entire sample on a graph, a normal distribution would give us a bell-shaped curve, like these:

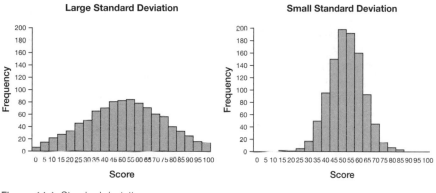

Figure 11.1 Standard deviation

The graphs in Figure 11.1 also refer to **standard deviation** (often reported simply as S.D.). This is how much dispersion exists from the average (mean). Later in this chapter we look at how to report descriptive statistics and you'll notice that the standard deviation is always reported. This is so those reading about your data can understand how close to the mean the majority of your data falls. For example, if the mean age of your sample is 20.2 years and the standard deviation is 3.4, we know that the majority of your sample is close in age to 20.2 years. Put simply, standard deviation refers to how spread out the numbers are.

Homogeneity of variance: this only refers to times when you are comparing groups – for example, if you were investigating whether undergraduate criminology students have different views about the treatment of sex offenders than undergraduate chemistry students. Homogeneity of variance means that the different samples you are comparing must have similar variance, so with the example above the variance in factors like age is likely to be similar. However, if you were comparing the views of undergraduate criminology students with the general population, you would expect the general population to have a much wider variance of age, and therefore a parametric test might not be appropriate.

Statistical significance

Significance is a statistical term that tells you how sure you can be that a difference or relationship exists. For example, in Nikki's research discussed in Box 11.1, her hypothesis stated that 'Women who spend a lot of time in licenced premises will report more involvement in aggressive incidents than women who spend little time in licenced premises'. In order to ascertain whether this hypothesis should be accepted or rejected, Nikki needed to measure the statistical significance of the relationship between time in licensed premises and aggression. Statistical significance shows that the relationship between the variables is probably not due to mere chance and that a real relationship most likely exists between the two variables. There are a number of different ways of measuring statistical significance. The type of statistical test used depends largely upon the type of research design that was used and the type of data you have collected.

P-values

You will often see statistical significance represented like this: $p < .05$. This is known as the p-value. A p-value of less than .05 indicates that the possibility that the results are due merely to chance is less than 5 per cent (or 1/20). If the p-value is less than .05 this means the hypothesis can be accepted. If the p-value is greater than .05 this means the hypothesis should be rejected as there is no statistical significance and any relationship is likely to be due to chance.

There are three levels of significance ($p < .05$, $p < .01$, $p < .001$). It is relatively unusual to see authors refer to anything other than $p < .05$ and so for the purposes of this basic introductory chapter we will refer to $p < .05$ in order to ascertain if a statistically significant relationship exists between the variables we test in the examples below.

THE BASICS OF SPSS

The Statistical Package for the Social Sciences, known as SPSS, has been used in its various formats by researchers for the last 45 years. SPSS provides a highly useful tool for analysing data in ways that would be very complex were they to be attempted by hand or using a calculator. The package we use today looks very different to the product that was first conceived in 1968. Thankfully the most current version at the time of writing – IBM SPSS Statistics 22 – is very user friendly. Your university may be running a slightly older version of SPSS and so you should note that this may look different from the screenshots included in this chapter. However, the basic guidance applies to older versions of the package.

On the website that accompanies this book, you can find an SPSS data file for you to practise the skills learnt later in this chapter. In order to open the file you must be using a computer with SPSS installed and your university should be able provide guidance on how students can install this on their personal computers. We recommend having SPSS installed on your home computer so that you can work through this chapter in your own time. The website provides guidance that should help you familiarise yourself with navigating SPSS and how to calculate simple statistics, such as the average (mean).

DATA ENTRY

There are two view tabs in SPSS: Variable View and Data View. Variable View is where you label your variables and Data View is where you enter your data. For example, in Variable View you may decide to add the label 'age' first and then switch to Data View (using the tabs at the bottom of the page) to enter the age (or age group) of each of your participants.

Variable View looks like this (Figure 11.2):

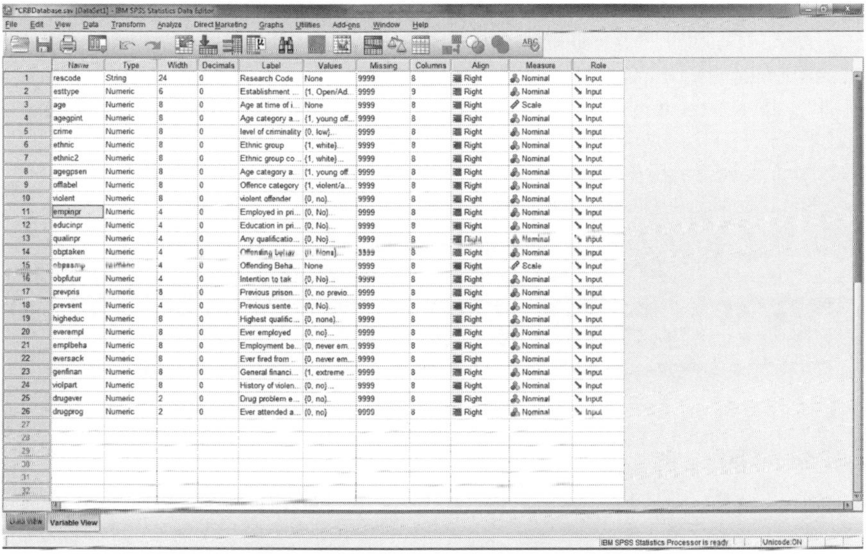

	Name	Type	Width	Decimals	Label	Values	Missing	Columns	Align	Measure	Role
1	rescode	String	24	0	Research Code	None	9999	8	Right	Nominal	Input
2	esttype	Numeric	6	0	Establishment ...	{1, Open/Ad...	9999	9	Right	Nominal	Input
3	age	Numeric	8	0	Age at time of i...	None	9999	8	Right	Scale	Input
4	agegpint	Numeric	8	0	Age category a...	{1, young off...	9999	8	Right	Nominal	Input
5	crime	Numeric	8	0	level of criminality	{0, low}...	9999	8	Right	Nominal	Input
6	ethnic	Numeric	8	0	Ethnic group	{1, white}...	9999	8	Right	Nominal	Input
7	ethnic2	Numeric	8	0	Ethnic group co...	{1, white}...	9999	8	Right	Nominal	Input
8	agegpsen	Numeric	8	0	Age category a...	{1, young off...	9999	8	Right	Nominal	Input
9	offlabel	Numeric	8	0	Offence category	{1, violent/a...	9999	8	Right	Nominal	Input
10	violent	Numeric	8	0	violent offender	{0, no}...	9999	8	Right	Nominal	Input
11	empinpr	Numeric	4	0	Employed in pri...	{0, No}...	9999	8	Right	Nominal	Input
12	educinpr	Numeric	4	0	Education in pri...	{0, No}...	9999	8	Right	Nominal	Input
13	qualinpr	Numeric	4	0	Any qualificatio...	{0, No}...	9999	8	Right	Nominal	Input
14	obptaken	Numeric	4	0	Offending behav	{0, None}...	9999	8	Right	Nominal	Input
15	obpsamp	Numeric	4	0	Offending Beha...	None	9999	8	Right	Scale	Input
16	obpfutur	Numeric	4	0	Intention to tak	{0, No}...	9999	8	Right	Nominal	Input
17	prevpris	Numeric	8	0	Previous prison...	{0, no previo...	9999	8	Right	Nominal	Input
18	prevsent	Numeric	4	0	Previous sente...	{0, No}...	9999	8	Right	Nominal	Input
19	higheduc	Numeric	8	0	Highest qualific...	{0, none}...	9999	8	Right	Nominal	Input
20	everempl	Numeric	8	0	Ever employed	{0, no}...	9999	8	Right	Nominal	Input
21	emplbeha	Numeric	8	0	Employment be...	{0, never em...	9999	8	Right	Nominal	Input
22	eversack	Numeric	8	0	Ever fired from ...	{0, never em...	9999	8	Right	Nominal	Input
23	genfinan	Numeric	8	0	General financi...	{1, extreme ...	9999	8	Right	Nominal	Input
24	violpart	Numeric	8	0	History of violen...	{0, no}...	9999	8	Right	Nominal	Input
25	drugever	Numeric	2	0	Drug problem e...	{0, no}...	9999	8	Right	Nominal	Input
26	drugprog	Numeric	2	0	Ever attended a...	{0, no}	9999	8	Right	Nominal	Input
27											
28											
29											
30											
31											
32											

Figure 11.2

You can see that in this example there were 28 variables: including 'research code', 'age at time of interview', 'offence category', 'drug problem ever' and 24 other variables.

To add a variable, simply highlight a cell under 'Name' and type in a name that describes the variable. For example, 'Age', 'Gender', 'Offence Type'. Note that each variable must have a distinct name. All of the columns can be changed. For instance, under 'Label' you may wish to add a fuller description of that variable.

The value column is particularly important. Earlier in this chapter we talked about how it can be useful to reduce some terms to numbers for ease of use in SPSS

> ### TIP
>
> When entering data from a questionnaire or other source, it is not unusual to find that you have some missing data, perhaps where someone has omitted to complete one of the questions. It is important that you do not leave any blank cells in your Data View, so we suggest replacing any missing data with the numbers 9999. To ensure that SPSS recognises this as missing data and so does not try to analyse this, ensure that in the 'Missing' column in Variable View, 9999 is inserted in each row.

– we call this 'coding' our data (not to be confused with the use of the word coding with qualitative analysis). For example, if we have collected information on participants' educational qualifications, as in the example database used here, we may label 'None' as '0', 'GCSE level/equivalent' as '1', 'A-level/equivalent' as '2' and so on. The numbers are the codes – a shorthand way of presenting our data, a method that allows us to transform nominal data into other types of data that can be more readily used with statistical tests. The value column allows us to label values so that in the data view, rather than type 'GCSE level/equivalent' and so on many times, we can simply add the appropriate number. We recommend that all **nominal data** is given a value as entering the data in this way also helps SPSS in conducting any statistical analysis you perform.

When you click on a cell under 'Values' a box appears where you should add the value (number) and the label: in the example above, you would begin with '0' and 'No qualifications'. You then click 'Add' before moving on to add the next value and label ('1' and 'GCSE level/equivalent') and so on until you have added them all for this variable. Once you have finished simply click 'OK'.

Data View looks like this (Figure 11.3):

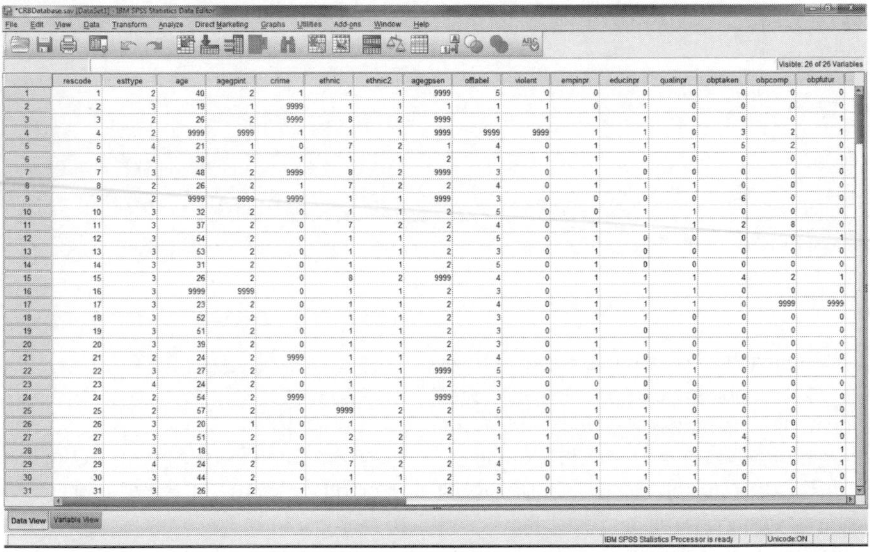

	rescode	esttype	age	agegpint	crime	ethnic	ethnic2	agegpsen	offlabel	violent	empinpr	educinpr	qualinpr	obptaken	obpcomp	obpfutur
1	1	2	40	2	1	1	1	9999	5	0	0	0	0	0	0	0
2	2	3	19	1	9999	1	1	1	1	1	0	1	0	0	0	0
3	3	2	26	2	9999	8	2	9999	1	1	1	1	0	0	0	1
4	4	2	9999	9999	1	1	1	9999	9999	9999	1	1	0	3	2	1
5	5	4	21	1	0	7	2	1	4	0	1	1	1	5	2	0
6	6	4	38	2	1	1	1	2	1	1	1	0	0	0	0	1
7	7	3	48	2	9999	8	2	9999	3	0	1	0	0	0	0	0
8	8	2	26	2	1	7	2	2	4	0	1	1	1	0	0	0
9	9	2	9999	9999	9999	1	1	9999	3	0	0	0	0	6	0	0
10	10	3	32	2	0	1	1	2	5	0	0	1	1	0	0	0
11	11	3	37	2	0	7	2	2	4	0	1	1	1	2	8	0
12	12	3	54	2	0	1	1	2	5	0	1	0	0	0	0	1
13	13	3	53	2	0	1	1	2	3	0	1	0	0	0	0	0
14	14	3	31	2	0	1	1	2	5	0	1	0	0	0	0	0
15	15	3	26	2	0	8	2	9999	4	0	1	1	1	4	2	1
16	16	3	9999	9999	0	1	1	2	3	0	1	1	1	0	0	0
17	17	3	23	2	0	1	1	2	4	0	1	1	1	0	9999	9999
18	18	3	52	2	0	1	1	2	3	0	1	1	0	0	0	0
19	19	3	51	2	0	1	1	2	3	0	1	0	0	0	0	0
20	20	3	39	2	0	1	1	2	3	0	1	1	0	0	0	0
21	21	2	24	2	9999	1	1	2	4	0	1	0	0	0	0	0
22	22	3	27	2	0	1	1	9999	5	0	1	1	1	0	0	1
23	23	4	24	2	0	1	1	2	3	0	0	0	0	0	0	0
24	24	2	54	2	9999	1	1	9999	3	0	1	0	0	0	0	0
25	25	2	57	2	0	9999	2	2	5	0	1	1	0	0	0	0
26	26	3	20	1	0	1	1	1	1	1	0	1	1	0	0	1
27	27	3	51	2	0	2	2	2	1	1	0	1	1	4	0	0
28	28	3	18	1	0	3	2	1	1	1	1	1	0	1	3	1
29	29	4	24	2	0	7	2	2	4	0	1	1	1	0	0	1
30	30	3	44	2	0	1	1	2	3	0	1	1	1	0	0	0
31	31	3	26	2	1	1	1	2	3	0	1	0	0	0	0	0

Figure 11.3

As you will see in the full data set on the companion website, this was a very large piece of research including 200 participants, but there is no limit that researchers are likely to reach on how many participants can be included in an SPSS database.

In Data View the top of each column shows the name you assigned each variable in the Variable View. You begin entering your data by simply highlighting a cell, entering the number or word and then pressing return. You will then be in the cell below.

WHICH TEST SHOULD I USE?

Now that you have read about the basic statistical concepts discussed above, you are in a much better position to work out which statistical test is appropriate for your data.

In addition to understanding what type of data you have, you should also ask yourself what it is you want to do with your data. For example:

- Do you want to see if there are differences between two sets of scores? For example, you might be interested in whether a 'prison awareness' course has had any effect on young people's attitudes towards crime, as measured on a pre-existing attitudinal scale before and after taking part in the course. Or, you might want to see whether undergraduate and postgraduate students at your university score differently on a questionnaire looking at knowledge about the criminal justice system. These are looking for differences in the data.
- Are you trying to determine if one variable predicts a particular outcome over and above other variables? For example, if you were seeking to find out what affects increases in self-reported alcohol consumption, you might consider a number of potential factors such as: stress levels; boredom; unemployment; major televised sporting events; and any other factors the literature suggests might be relevant. Certain statistical analyses, when conducted on appropriate data, could suggest which factors are more strongly related to increases in alcohol consumption, for example. This is looking for predictors.

Below we explain the three statistical tests highlighted in italics in Table 11.1. This chapter focuses on understanding descriptive statistics and basic tests of 'differences' in the data as these are commonly used, relatively straightforward to perform in SPSS, and therefore a good introduction to statistical methods.

Note that there are other tests that also fulfil the purposes outlined above but in different ways. As highlighted earlier in this chapter, if you wish to read more about these we have listed some of our favourite SPSS/statistics books at the end of the chapter.

Table 11.1 Common types of study and statistical analyses

Purpose	Suggested statistical test	Types of data it can be used with
All **quantitative research**	Descriptive statistics	All
Comparing two sets of scores for differences	Unrelated t-test or Related t-test	Ratio, Interval
Comparing nominal data (looking for a relationship/ correlation)	Chi-square	Ordinal
Comparing the means of two or more sets of scores	Unrelated ANOVA (Analysis of Variance) or related ANOVA	Interval
Finding predictors	Regression	Dependent on the type of regression analyses

If you want to check which tests might be most appropriate for your data, we highly recommended www.whichtest.info

DESCRIPTIVE STATISTICS

There are two main types of statistics: descriptive statistics and inferential statistics. What we have discussed thus far in this chapter primarily relates to inferential statistics. Inferential statistics are those that tell us whether there is statistical significance and this branch of statistics aims to infer from samples to populations, i.e. we use inferential statistics when we are trying to reach conclusions that extend beyond the data in our sample. This is why sample size is so important as we need to be able to make inferences from our sample so the sample must be suitably large. Descriptive statistics on the other hand are used to describe the main characteristics of our sample or variables and are needed for all types of study. For example, when writing up quantitative research it is usual to present information on the age and gender of participants, and other factors that might be relevant depending on your research, such as occupation or criminal history. This information is often presented in the methodology section, with inferential statistics forming the results section.

Running descriptive statistics

Using the SPSS data set on the companion website, follow the instructions on the SPSS screenshots below to run descriptive statistics for the age of the sample. The information we need is the mean, range, maximum, minimum and Standard Deviation.

Student document

Database: SPSS dataset

1   Go to the 'Analyse' tab. In the drop-down menu go to 'Descriptive Statistics' and then 'Descriptives' (Figure 11.4).
2   Next, click on the variable 'age at time of interview' to select it and click the arrow to move this variable to the 'Variables' box. Click 'OK' (Figure 11.5).

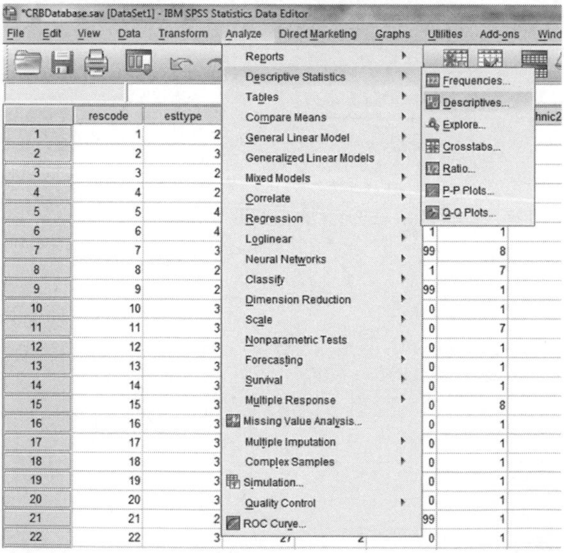

Figure 11.4

3   SPSS output will appear on your screen giving you the statistics you requested (Figure 11.6). You should see that there are 178 participants in the sample whose age at interview was known, the youngest of whom is 16 and the oldest 60. The mean age of the sample is 30.15 years with a standard deviation of 9.76.

To write this up you would say, 'The mean age of the sample was 30.15 years (min. 16 years, max. 60 years, S.D. 9.76)'. Note that SPSS tables and output should never be included in the write-up of your research but may, if you wish, be included in any appendices.

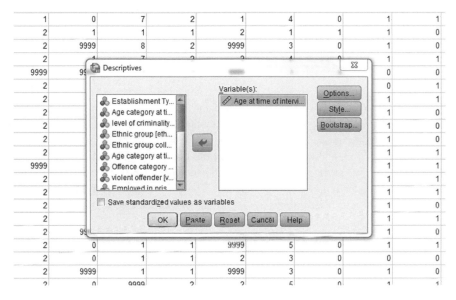

Figure 11.5

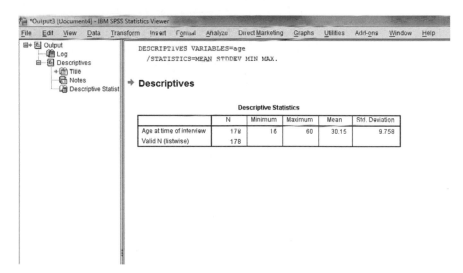

Figure 11.6

You can find other information, such as the gender breakdown of a sample, by choosing 'Frequencies' instead of 'Descriptives' at stage 1.

We strongly recommend that you spend some time looking at your data with the aid of descriptive statistics. This will help you understand much more about your data and will also help you work out which statistical tests you might use later in your analysis of your data. For example, if in your data you have two age groups, and the descriptive statistics highlight that only 10 of your sample fall into one age group while 120 fall into the other age groups, you could be certain that running parametric tests using age as a variable would not be suitable.

SIGNIFICANCE TESTING: THE *T*-TEST (COMPARING SCORES TO TEST FOR DIFFERENCES)

A *t*-test is typically used to compare two means to see if they are equal or different. There are two types of *t*-test: the related *t*-test and the unrelated *t*-test. The related *t*-test (sometimes known as the matched or paired *t*-test) is used when comparing the means taken from one group of people at two separate time points or under two different circumstances. This is known as a **within-subjects design**. The unrelated *t*-test (sometimes known as the unmatched *t*-test) is used when comparing the means of two separate groups of people under the same circumstances. This is known as a **between-subjects design**. Knowing which design you have is important in order to decide which test to use.

Related *t*-test	Same group, BUT two different variables
Unrelated *t*-test	Same variable BUT two different groups

While a typical rule of thumb for statistical tests is that there should be at least 30 participants/scores in each group (note that there are advanced ways of working out the minimum sample size needed for research studies, particularly vital when using more advanced techniques, but we do not cover these in this book), the *t*-test can be used with smaller samples than this, but sample sizes should be as equal as possible (for example, if you had 20 scores in one group and 70 in another, then the *t*-test is not a good measure).

Remember, the *t*-test can only be used for comparing the means of two sets of scores.

Student document

Database: SPSS dataset

RUNNING AN UNRELATED T-TEST IN SPSS

Below are instructions on running an unrelated *t*-test, which you should use to familiarise yourself further with SPSS (Figures 11.7 to 11.10). Later in the chapter you'll be asked to run a related *t*-test using the data set on the companion website, and you will be able to find further guidance on running that type of *t*-test on there.

BOX 11.2 RESEARCH EXAMPLE

Tim is a part-time undergraduate criminology student and he also works part-time in a prison. He wants to know whether taking part in a work training programme has any effect on how competent prisoners feel about their work skills. He wants to see if there is any change in the group as a whole. Through discussions with one of his lecturers, Tim has identified an existing scale called the 'Perceived Competence Scale' (PCS) that he plans to ask prisoners to complete both before and after taking part in the training programme.

1   What is the independent variable?
2   What is the dependent variable?

Tim collects scores on PCS from all of the men taking part in the training programme before the programme begins and at the end of the week-long programme. Answers to questions on the scale are collected using a seven-point Likert scale. These scores (1–7) are inputted into SPSS in numerical form.

3   What type of data does Tim have?
4   What statistical test should Tim use to see if there is a statistically significant difference between perceived competence before taking part in the training programme and after taking part in the training programme?
5   Why should Tim use this test?

Answers

1   Taking part in the work training programme.
2   How competent prisoners feel about their work skills (identified by scores on the PCS).
3   Interval data (note that most standardised scales are treated as interval data, although they might at first seem like ordinal data).
4   Tim should use a related t-test.
5   Tim should use this test because: he is testing one group of people, he is looking for change over time (on perceived competence); his data can be classed as interval data; he is testing the participants twice.

If Tim was to test the participants for a third time at a later date he would need to use a different statistical test (a repeated measure ANOVA – these are not discussed in this book).

   If Tim wanted to compare scores from prisoners after completing the training course with scores from a **matched control group**, he could use an independent samples t-test.

Question: Which group of participants has completed more Offending Behaviour Programmes: those recorded as having low or high levels of criminality?

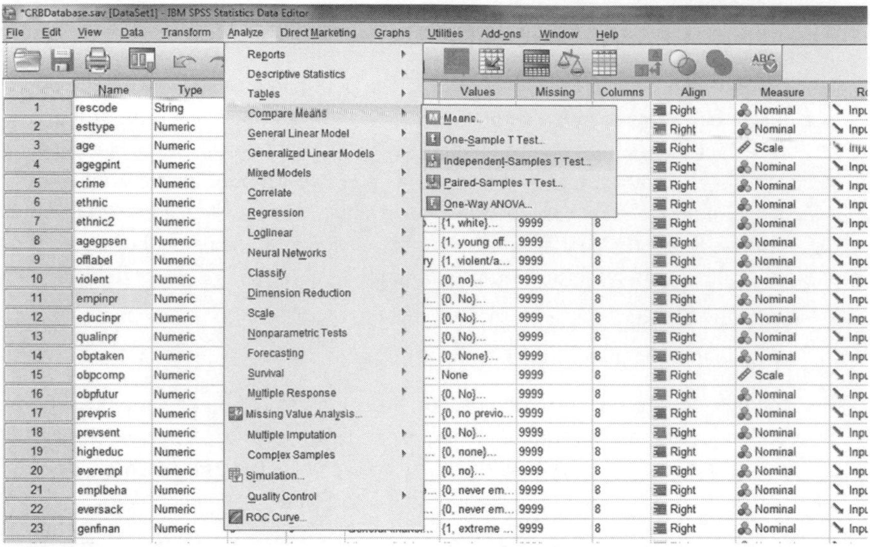

Figure 11.7

This question can be answered using an independent samples *t*-test in SPSS. In order to conduct it, go to:

Analyze > Compare Means > Independent-Samples T Test . . .

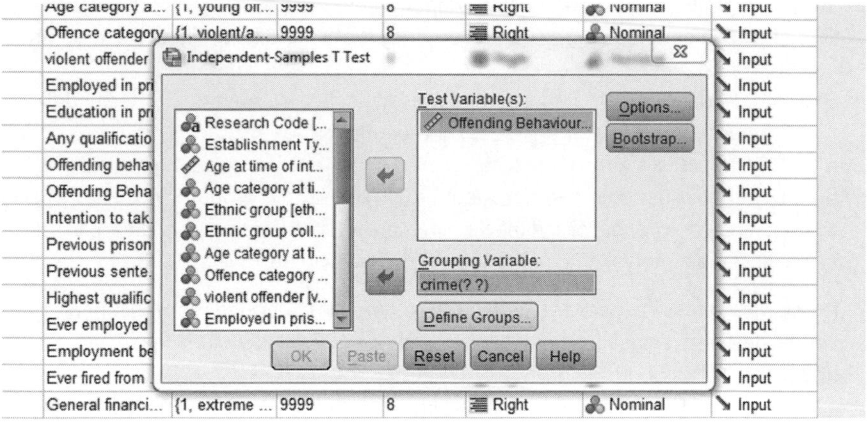

Figure 11.8

First, in the *Independent-Samples T Test* window, select and move the dependent variable [Offending Behaviour courses completed (obpcomp)] to the 'Test Variable(s):' list box and move the independent variable [level of criminality (crime)] to the 'Grouping Variable:' text box.

Second, click on 'Define Groups' to tell SPSS the code numbers for the groups to susbstitute for the question marks.

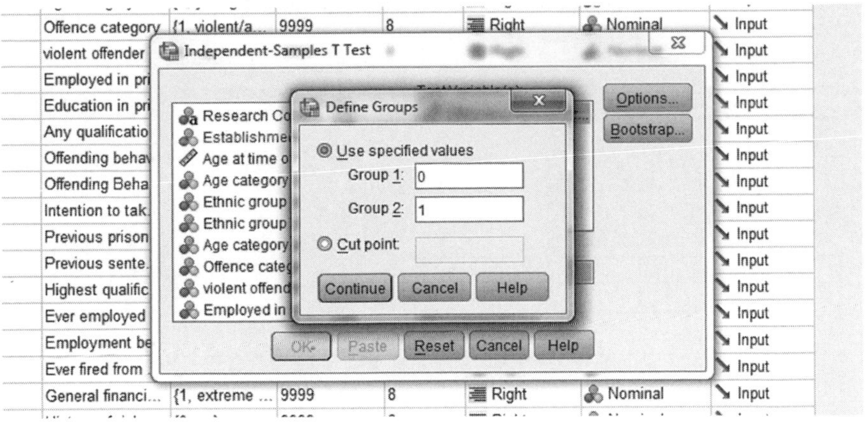

Figure 11.9

0 is the value for 'low' and '1' for the variable [crime]. Type these values in the *Group 1:* and *Group 2:* text boxes.

If you do not recall the code numbers for the groups, look on the Variable View page in the SPSS Data Editor.

Click on the Continue button to close the dialog box.

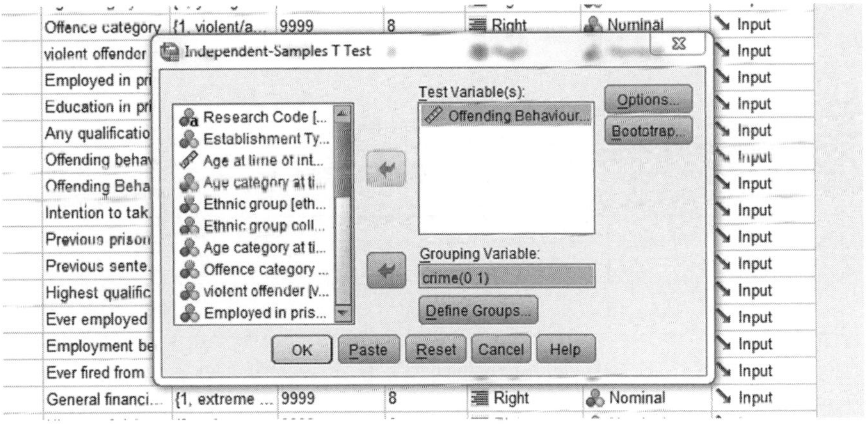

Figure 11.10

Note that the code values for the independent (Grouping) variable replace the question marks that were after the variable name.

Click OK to produce the output.

This is what the results output in SPSS will look like (Figure 11.11):

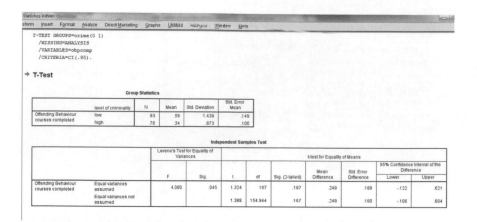

Figure 11.11

This is how to interpret the output (Figures 11.12 to 11.15):

Statistics Viewer

sform   Insert   Format   Analyze   Direct Marketing   Graphs   Utilities   Add-ons   Window   Help

```
T-TEST GROUPS=crime(0 1)
  /MISSING=ANALYSIS
  /VARIABLES=obpcomp
  /CRITERIA=CI(.95).
```

→ T-Test

Group Statistics

	level of criminality	N	Mean	Std. Deviation	Std. Error Mean
Offending Behaviour courses completed	low	93	.59	1.439	.149
	high	76	.34	.873	.100

Independent Samples Test

		Levene's Test for Equality of Variances		t-test for Equality of Means						
									95% Confidence Interval of the Difference	
		F	Sig.	t	df	Sig. (2-tailed)	Mean Difference	Std. Error Difference	Lower	Upper
Offending Behaviour courses completed	Equal variances assumed	4.080	.045	1.324	167	.187	.249	.188	-.122	.621
	Equal variances not assumed			1.388	154.944	.167	.249	.180	-.106	.604

Figure 11.12

The independent samples *t*-test assumes that the different samples you are comparing have similar variance (refer back to the section above on homogeneity of variance to remind yourself what this means). This assumption is tested with *Levene's Test for Equality of Variances*. The *Levene Test* is itself a test of the null hypothesis that the variances of the two groups are equal.

If we fail to reject the null hypothesis because the p-value or sig. for the statistic is greater than 0.05, we satisfy the requirement for equal variances. If we reject the null hypothesis because the p-value or sig. for the statistic is less than or equal to 0.05, we do not meet the requirement for equal variances.

```
T-TEST GROUPS=crime(0 1)
  /MISSING=ANALYSIS
  /VARIABLES=obpcomp
  /CRITERIA=CI(.95).
```

➡ **T-Test**

Group Statistics

	level of criminality	N	Mean	Std. Deviation	Std. Error Mean
Offending Behaviour courses completed	low	93	.59	1.439	.149
	high	76	.34	.873	.100

Independent Samples Test

		Levene's Test for Equality of Variances		t-test for Equality of Means						
									95% Confidence Interval of the Difference	
		F	Sig.	t	df	Sig. (2-tailed)	Mean Difference	Std. Error Difference	Lower	Upper
Offending Behaviour courses completed	Equal variances assumed	4.080	.045	1.324	167	.187	.249	.188	-.122	.621
	Equal variances not assumed			1.388	154.944	.167	.249	.180	-.106	.604

Figure 11.13

If we satisfy the assumption of equal variances, we use the output on the row titled 'Equal variances assumed'.

If we do not satisfy the assumption of equal variances, we use the output on the row titled 'Equal variances not assumed'. This calculation is based on a formula for the *t*-test that takes into account the differences in variance measures.

```
T-TEST GROUPS=crime(0 1)
  /MISSING=ANALYSIS
  /VARIABLES=obpcomp
  /CRITERIA=CI(.95).
```

➡ **T-Test**

Group Statistics

	level of criminality	N	Mean	Std. Deviation	Std. Error Mean
Offending Behaviour courses completed	low	93	.59	1.439	.149
	high	76	.34	.873	.100

Independent Samples Test

		Levene's Test for Equality of Variances		t-test for Equality of Means						
									95% Confidence Interval of the Difference	
		F	Sig.	t	df	Sig. (2-tailed)	Mean Difference	Std. Error Difference	Lower	Upper
Offending Behaviour courses completed	Equal variances assumed	4.080	.045	1.324	167	.187	.249	.188	-.122	.621
	Equal variances not assumed			1.388	154.944	.167	.249	.180	-.106	.604

Figure 11.14

In this problem, the probability associated with *Levene's Test for Equality of Variances* (.045) is less than 0.05.

We reject the null hypothesis that the variances are equal, concluding that the 'Equal variances not assumed' formula for the independent samples *t*-test should be used for the analysis.

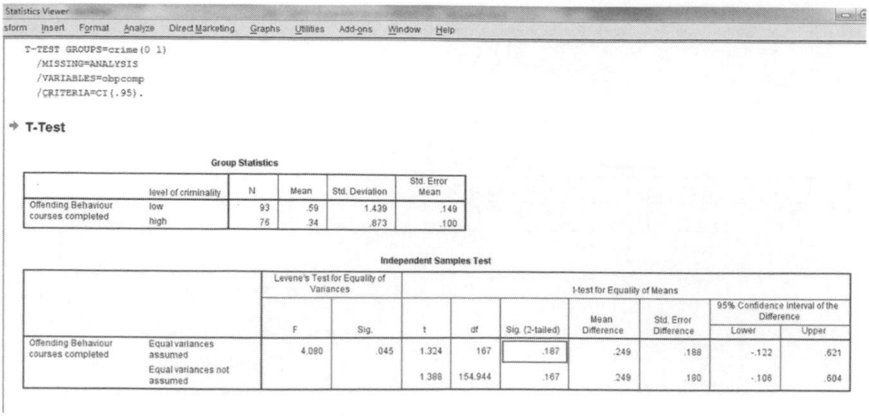

Figure 11.15

Having determined which formula for the *t*-test to base the hypothesis test on, we look to the statistical output for the *t*-test.

The **research hypothesis** implied by the question is that the mean 'number of Offending Behaviour Programmes (OBP) completed' [crime] will be different for participants recorded as having low or high levels of criminality.

The **null hypothesis** for this research hypothesis would state that the mean number of OBP completed by 'low offenders' is equal to the mean for 'high offenders'.

We make our decision about the null hypothesis by comparing the probability of the test statistic (t) to the level of significance (0.05).

Notice that the significance is labelled 'two-tailed'. As the question above did not state a direction to the relationship (i.e. simply stated that there would be a difference in the number of Offending Behaviour Programmes completed by those recorded as having low levels of criminality and those recorded as having high levels of criminality, but did not state which group would have completed more), then we use this value. However, if the research hypothesis stated a direction to the relationship, this would require us to compute the one-tailed probability. This is computed by simply dividing the two-tailed significance in half (so here, for example, this would be $0.187/2 = 0.0935$).

Interpreting the results

As the two-tailed probability of the t statistic (t = 1.324) was p = 1.187, greater than 0.05, the null hypothesis of equal means was not rejected, and we do not have support for the research hypothesis. Based on this analysis, we cannot support that there was any difference between the number of Offending Behaviour Programmes completed by those recorded as having low levels of criminality and those recorded as having high levels of criminality.

BOX 11.3 REPORTING STATISTICAL TESTS

When reporting statistical tests the following information should always be presented:

- value of statistical test;
- degrees of freedom;
- one or two-tailed test;
- the observed p-value;
- whether the test was significant;
- state the direction of the significant finding.

Look at the t-test example above.

You would report the present results as follows:

The mean number of Offending Behaviour Programmes completed by those recorded as having low levels of criminality ($M = 0.59$) was not significantly different to that of those recorded as having high levels of criminality ($M = 0.34$), (t (df 167) $= 1.324$, $p = .19$).

Remember: You should not present the SPSS output tables when writing up your analysis. You should interpret the results and not expect the reader to do this. The only exception to this is when asked to do this by your lecturers to show the details of your workings.

RELATED T-TEST

Now that you are becoming famliliar with SPSS and running basic statistical tests, have a go at running a related t test on the data set found on the companion website, following the brief guidance below. Practise interepreting the output and writing it up. You can find the answers on the companion website.

Run a related t-test to compare the mean scores on participants' assessed levels of motivation to change before and after a course of intervention.

BRIEF INSTRUCTIONS: RELATED T-TEST

Analyze > Compare means > Paired-Samples T-test

Student web links

Stats answers

Before you read the guidance on the website, see if you can identify what you need to know to run the t-test.

SIGNIFICANCE TESTING: CHI-SQUARE (COMPARING DIFFERENCES BETWEEN FREQUENCY DATA)

A Chi-squared test is used when we wish to compare nominal data (to look for a relationship/correlation).

BOX 11.4 RESEARCH EXAMPLE

Siân is a third-year criminology student. As part of her dissertation research she wants to investigate whether the men and women at her university have different attitudes towards people with mental health problems.

Q1. What is the independent variable?
Q2. What is the dependent variable?

She records participants' responses and classifies them as either 'positive attitude', 'neutral attitude' or 'negative attitude' and codes these as 0, 1 and 2 when she inputs them into SPSS.

Q3. What type of data does she have?
Q4. What statistical test should Siân use to test if there is a statistically significant difference between the attitudes towards people with mental health problems of the men and women on her course?
Q5. Why should Siân use this test?

Answers

A1. Gender.
A2. Attitude towards people with mental health problems.
A3. Nominal data.
A4. Siân should use a Chi-squared test.
A5. Siân should use this test because: she has two groups of people (women and men); she wants to do a between groups comparison (of attitudes); she has categorised her data so that it is nominal data; and the variable she is comparing the groups on (the dependent variable – in this case, attitudes) has more than two categories (positive, neutral, and negative).

RUNNING CHI-SQUARE TEST IN SPSS

Using a Chi-square test, we wish to find out if the following statement is true: 'In the sample dataset found on the companion website, levels of criminality [crime] are related to employment behaviour [emplbeha].' (See Figures 11.16 to 11.22.)

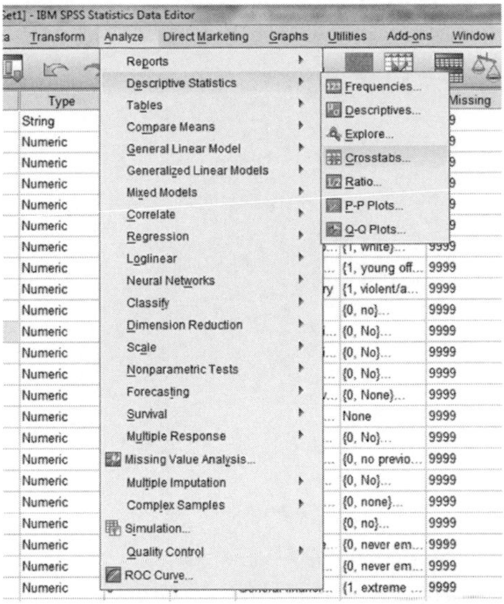

Figure 11.16

You can conduct a chi-square test of independence in crosstabulation of SPSS by selecting:

Analyze > Descriptive Statistics > Crosstabs . . .

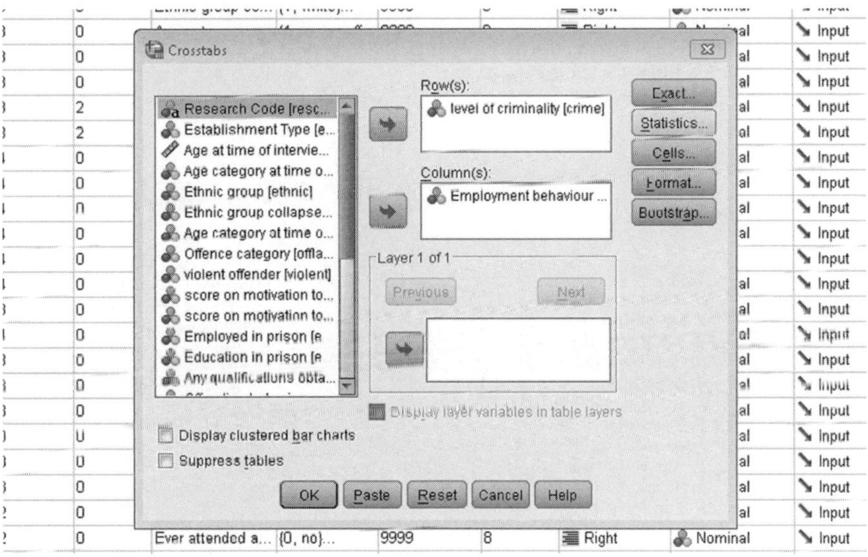

Figure 11.17

First, select and move the variables for the question to the 'Row(s)' and 'Column(s)' list boxes.

The variable mentioned first in the problem, level of criminality, is used as the independent variable and is moved to the 'Column(s)' list box.

The variable mentioned second in the problem, employment behaviour, is used as the dependent variable and is moved to the 'Row(s)' list box.

Second, click on the 'Statistics' button to request the test statistic.

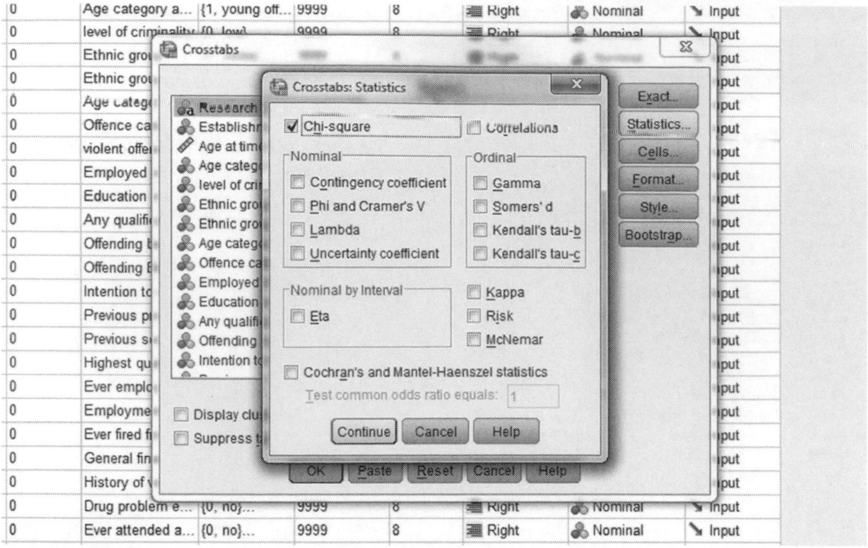

Figure 11.18

First, click on 'Chi square' to request the chi-square test of independence.

Second, click on the 'Continue' button to close the Statistics dialogue box.

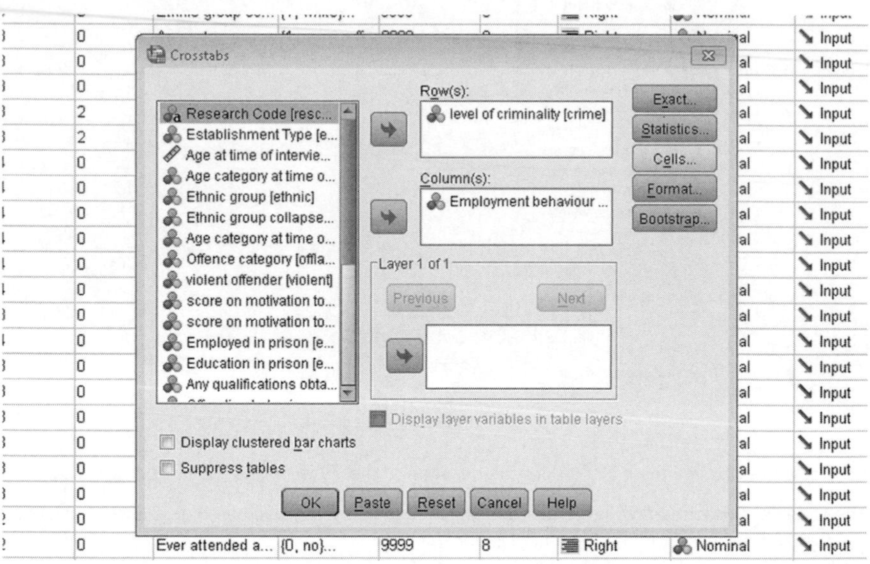

Figure 11.19

Now click on the 'Cells ...' button to specify the contents in the cells of the Crosstabs table.

0	Age category a...	{1, young off...	9999	8	Right	Nominal	Input
0	level of criminality	{0, low}	9999	8	Right	Nominal	Input
0	Ethnic gro						put
0	Ethnic gro						put
0	Age catego						put
0	Offence ca						put
0	violent offe						put
0	Employed						put
0	Education						put
0	Any qualifi						put
0	Offending						put
0	Offending						put
0	Intention t						put
0	Previous p						put
0	Previous s						put
0	Highest qu						put
0	Ever empl						put
0	Employme						put
0	Ever fired f						put
0	General fin						put
0	History of						put
0	Drug problem e...	{0, no}...	9999	8	Right	Nominal	Input
0	Ever attended a	{0, no}...	9999	8	Right	Nominal	Input

Crosstabs: Cell Display

Counts
- ☑ Observed
- ☑ Expected
- ☐ Hide small counts
  - Less than 5

z-test
- ☐ Compare column proportions
- Adjust p-values (Bonferroni method)

Percentages
- ☐ Row
- ☐ Column
- ☐ Total

Residuals
- ☐ Unstandardized
- ☐ Standardized
- ☐ Adjusted standardized

Noninteger Weights
- ● Round cell counts   ○ Round case weights
- ○ Truncate cell counts   ○ Truncate case weights
- ○ No adjustments

[Continue] [Cancel] [Help]

Figure 11.20

Make sure both 'Observed' and 'Expected' in the 'Counts' section in 'Crosstabs: Cell Display' dialogue box are checked and click on 'Continue' and 'OK' buttons.

Click 'Continue' and 'continue' again to run the test (Figure 11.21).

Expected Count	21.0	10.0	20.0	49.0

Chi-Square Tests

	Value	df	Asymp. Sig. (2-sided)
Pearson Chi-Square	19.843[a]	6	.001
Likelihood Ratio	20.803	5	.001
Linear-by-Linear Association	15.520	1	.000
N of Valid Cases	169		

a. 1 cells (8.3%) have expected count less than 5. The minimum expected count is 4.44.

Figure 11.21

The chi-square test of independence requires that the expected frequency for all cells be 5.0 or higher.

The crosstabulated table contains the count and expected counts for each cell in the table.

We can see that one of the expected counts is less that 5. However, chi-square tests are still valid provided none are less than 1, and at least 80 per cent of the expected counts are equal to or greater than 5.

As four out of the five counts in the table above are greater than five, we can still use a chi-squared test (Figure 11.22).

Case Processing Summary

	Cases					
	Valid		Missing		Total	
	N	Percent	N	Percent	N	Percent
level of criminality * Employment behaviour	169	84.5%	31	15.5%	200	100.0%

level of criminality * Employment behaviour Crosstabulation

			Employment behaviour						Total
			never employed	very poor	poor	average	good	very good	
level of criminality	low	Count	6	4	11	22	39	12	94
		Expected Count	11.7	5.6	11.1	27.3	30.6	7.8	94.0
	high	Count	15	6	9	27	16	2	75
		Expected Count	9.3	4.4	8.9	21.7	24.4	6.2	75.0
Total		Count	21	10	20	49	55	14	169
		Expected Count	21.0	10.0	20.0	49.0	55.0	14.0	169.0

Chi-Square Tests

	Value	df	Asymp. Sig. (2-sided)
Pearson Chi-Square	19.843[a]	5	.001
Likelihood Ratio	20.803	5	.001
Linear-by-Linear Association	15.520	1	.000
N of Valid Cases	169		

a. 1 cells (8.3%) have expected count less than 5. The minimum expected count is 4.44.

Figure 11.22

The probability of the chi-square test statistic (chi-square = 19.843) was $p < 0.001$, less than the level of significance of 0.05.

The null hypothesis that differences in employment behaviour are independent of differences in levels of criminality (the actual frequencies are equal to the expected frequencies in the cross-tabulated table) is rejected.

In other words the research hypothesis that differences in employment behaviour are related to differences in levels of criminality is supported by this analysis.

The answer to the question is True.

If the probability of the test statistic is less than or equal to the probability of the alpha error rate (0.05), we reject the null hypothesis and conclude that our data supports the research hypothesis. We conclude that there is a relationship between the variables.

If the probability of the test statistic is greater than the probability of the alpha error rate (0.05), we fail to reject the null hypothesis. We conclude that there is no relationship between the variables, i.e. they are independent. The alpha error rate refers to the probability of what is called a type one error. At this stage we do not suggest you focus on this point but, put simply, this refers to the chances of the results being incorrect and the hypothesis being incorrectly rejected.

CONCLUSION

Analysing your data statistically does not require a natural talent for mathematics. It simply requires logical thought in considering what data you have, or plan to collect, and an ability to consider what statistical tests might be appropriate for your data. It is this point that is the key to conducting quantitative analysis – using tests that are inappropriate for your data will ultimately not tell you anything important or relevant. Once you understand the basics of quantitative analysis and can logically identify appropriate statistical tests, the rest is very straightforward because of the existence of programs like SPSS. This chapter has sought to provide a step-by-step, but very introductory, guide to some of the key concepts in quantitative analysis. The guidance outlined in this chapter provides the first step in seeing how straightforward quantitative analysis can be. We also hope that by completing the tasks in this chapter, using the data set provided on the accompanying website, you will also experience just how satisfying it can be when you see a statistically significant result!

FURTHER READING

We recommend the following texts for those students seeking to work further with quantitative analysis:

Field, A. (2013) *Discovering Statistics using IBM SPSS Statistics*, Thousand Oaks, CA: Sage.

Gau, J. (2013) *Statistics for Criminology and Criminal Justice*, Thousand Oaks, CA: Sage.

Gray, D. and Kinnear, P. (2011) *IBM SPSS Statistics 19 Made Simple*, London: Psychology Press.

Howitt, D. and Cramer, D. (2011) *SPSS in Psychology*, Harlow: Pearson.

We also recommend this online guide from UCLA: http://www.ats.ucla.edu/stat/spss/

✳ KEY LEARNING POINTS

- Understanding statistical concepts and terminology is crucial for you as a researcher so that you can understand and critique other people's quantitative research and so that you can decide which statistical tests are the most appropriate to use with your data.
- Conducting your own statistical analysis allows you to provide much more robust evidence of any relationships between the variables you have measured than simply presenting data from questionnaires in percentage terms or in graphs.
- You do not have to be good at maths to be good at statistical analysis, mainly because programs like SPSS exist. However, you do need to be able to choose an appropriate test for your data, follow instructions on running this in SPSS and interpret the output. This chapter has explained the basics of these processes.

Chapter 12

Analysing the data

Qualitative analysis

GOALS OF THIS CHAPTER

At the end of reading this chapter and by completing the online resources that accompany it, you will be able to:

1 acknowledge the importance of transcription as part of the analysis process;
2 recognise that the work put into data collection is worthless if robust data analysis techniques are not applied;
3 understand the process of conducting a **thematic analysis** and feel confident to put this into practice;
4 write up the process of conducting a thematic analysis;
5 write up the results of a thematic analysis.

OVERVIEW

- While many modes of qualitative analysis exist, thematic analysis is one of the most commonly used methods of qualitative data analysis.
- Having a high level of familiarity with your data is key to conducting a successful thematic analysis, and the transcription process is often fundamental to increasing data familiarity.
- The process of thematic analysis involves applying brief verbal descriptions to the data, known as coding.
- The aim of the thematic analysis is to collate codes into over-arching themes that represent the body of data.
- This chapter provides examples from real research to demonstrate how to conduct and write up qualitative analyses.
- Many researchers now use Computer Assisted Qualitative Data Analysis Software (CAQDAS) software to aid the structure and management of qualitative data sets.

INTRODUCTION

Qualitative research methods have at times been criticised for a lack of robustness. Indeed, it is true that some people see qualitative research as an easy option – these are typically the people who do qualitative research badly. However, when done well, qualitative research can provide a depth and quality of information simply not available using quantitative techniques. As discussed in Chapter 6, choosing appropriate data collection techniques is essential, but all of this is worthless if robust data analysis techniques are not applied.

It is not possible within one chapter to cover the various methods of qualitative analysis in sufficient detail. Therefore, what you will find in this chapter is a focus on one method of qualitative analysis that is widely used by criminological researchers: thematic analysis. Thematic analysis provides a useful introduction to qualitative analysis and is a method that is particularly suited to the analysis of a range of qualitative data when the researcher seeks to allow key themes from the entire body of data to emerge. Other well-documented methods of qualitative data analysis used by criminological researchers include **discourse analysis**, content analysis (see Chapter 13 for discussion of critical discourse analysis and qualitative content analysis), conversation analysis and narrative analysis (among others) and each serves a different purpose. This chapter will provide guidance on how to analyse data using thematic analysis and give real research examples for you to consider. This chapter primarily applies to the data collection techniques discussed in Chapter 8, with most of the examples throughout this chapter relating to interview and focus group data. However, the lessons apply to other forms of qualitative data too.

METHODS OF ANALYSIS

Many novice researchers initially approach qualitative analysis through a process called thematic analysis. Thematic analysis is one of the most commonly used methods of qualitative data analysis, and is a method that is not dependant on specific theory or approaches to data collection. In this way thematic analysis is suitable for most types of qualitative data. However, this is not simply a method for new researchers, but one favoured by many experienced researchers, including the authors of this book.

Like many forms of qualitative data analysis, thematic analysis is easy to do badly. The overall aim of thematic analysis is to identify the key themes from the data and it is important that you do not fall into the trap of identifying superficial themes. Superficial analysis is not an appropriate level of analysis and cannot result in themes that represent sufficiently the data a researcher has collected. To do justice to the data collected, researchers must engage with a rigorous approach to analysis. For thematic analysis, it is vital to be highly familiar with the data before formally beginning the analysis. For this reason we strongly recommend that researchers conduct their own interviews, focus groups, or other methods of data collection, and that they also transcribe their own data. Researchers who do not do this are placed at a significant disadvantage, but to an extent this can be addressed by thoroughly reading the transcripts several times before beginning the analysis. In order to maximise familiarity with the data we suggest all researchers do this, whether they have collected and transcribed the data or not.

TRANSCRIBING YOUR DATA

As noted above, transcribing your own data is one of the best ways of becoming highly familiar with the data you have collected, and this process of familiarisation is vital to successful data analysis. Transcription is the process of transferring recordings into written form and there are a variety of methods of transcribing audio and visual recordings, although generally these methods are more fully documented and better developed for audio recordings. There is no denying that transcription takes a long time, but rather than see this as a chore we encourage you to see the transcription process as a fundamental part of becoming familiar with your data.

Broadly, all methods of transcription can be classed as **naturalism**, where every utterance and pause is transcribed, or **denaturalism**, where pauses are removed, grammar corrected, and even non-standard accents standardised. The method researchers choose will depend upon the mode of analysis they are using. For example, conversation analysis looks at the patterns of speech between people and so requires a naturalised approach. The decision you make about which method of transcription to use must be based on ensuring that your transcriptions are suitable for purpose. For example, if you were investigating the process of conversation between two speakers simply transcribing the literal words used by the speakers would be inadequate. However, if you were interested in how offenders describe a day of their life then a literal transcription including only the words spoken may well be sufficient.

For those seeking a process of transcription where it is important to record pauses and other features of language (also known as paralinguistic features of language), we recommended the Jefferson method of transcription. The Jefferson method is a widely used method of transcription that includes some focus on utterances, pauses and the cross-over of speakers. Howitt and Cramer (2011a) provide a useful guide to Jefferson transcription, and Oliver et al. (2005) take a useful reflective look at transcription more generally. You can also find a number of guides online and some examples on the companion website.

However, many researchers – often including those conducting thematic analysis – do not follow a set method of data transcription, instead opting to devise their own method choosing which features of the speech and language to record. This is typically suitable when it is not essential to record all of the paralinguistic features of a recording.

In the example in Box 12.1 what is spoken by the interviewee is in italics, with a number of short-hand symbols created by the researcher to represent key paralinguistic features of the interviews. For example, (. . .) was used to represent where words were unclear on the recording, pauses such as 'erm' were recorded, and '. . .' was used to denote pauses in speech. This level of detail was sufficient for the thematic analysis that the researcher then conducted.

Student document

Examples of transcriptions

BOX 12.1 TRANSCRIBING INTERVIEWS

The excerpt below provides an example of how one of the authors of this book transcribed 43 interview recordings.

> The 2,277 minutes of interviews were transcribed by the researcher into Microsoft Word. Paralinguistic features of the language within the recordings were not transcribed in full, although, for example, pauses and errors of speech were noted. Some interviews were transcribed in the days directly following each interview. However, due to the time practicalities a larger number of interviews had to be transcribed a considerable amount of time after the interviews had taken place. Transcription of this amount of data is both daunting and immensely time consuming, but necessary if each participant's contribution is to be successfully represented (Atkinson, 1998). Furthermore, transcription is a vital part of the research process, whereby listening, transcription, and reading of the data serve to re-familiarise the researcher with the interview data and the mood and emotional responses of the participants to particular questions. Indeed it is suggested that 'the closer you can get to the text itself, the closer you are to its meaning' (Atkinson, 1998, p. 57). To improve the level of familiarity with the data, interview recordings were listened to again and transcripts read, prior to beginning analysis. (Caulfield 2012: 57)

The above excerpt is taken from research where interviews were conducted with women in prison. The interviews asked women about their lives and histories of offending and did not require a naturalistic approach. The process of transcription described above resulted in transcripts that looked like this:

> So by the time you got your probation order this was before you got ...
> *This was before we got married. I've never told Mum and Dad.*
> But did they find out about ...
> *They did. I told them before we got married. Just before I went to court. Because he was so worried that if I went to court and got sentenced to prison, erm, that he couldn't tell Mum and Dad.*
> Right, ok.
> *Or he wouldn't be able to cope if he didn't know about it.*
> So at this point everyone was then told about the debt?
> *Yeah. They still weren't told about the total amount of debt. (. . .) And, twelve thousand pounds on a wedding. I think about going and buying the wedding dress and like fifteen hundred quid for a dress, five hundred pounds each for bridesmaid's dresses. Now I look back and think 'oh my god, what such a complete waste of money, but at the time I was just in this huge big whirlwind of it all ...*

CONDUCTING A THEMATIC ANALYSIS

Once transcription and data familiarisation are complete, the thematic analysis can begin. The overall aim of thematic analysis is to identify, analyse and report the key themes from the data and this process begins by an initial coding of the data. We will return to this process shortly. First, it is important to be aware of the full purpose and approach of thematic analysis.

Thematic analysis is less dependent on a theoretical approach than other forms of qualitative analysis, and so can be applied to most forms of qualitative data to analyse *what* was said rather than *how* it was said. While researchers conducting a thematic analysis may well have conducted a review of the literature, the process allows findings to emerge from the data and thus the focus is data driven and not theory driven. In this way it is also suitable for approaches such as grounded theory (see the discussion of **induction** in Chapter 2), although there is likely to be some level of theory present even if it is not explicitly acknowledged. Thematic analysis can be a method of examining and reporting the experiences, meanings and the reality of particular groups or individuals, or it can be a method that 'examines the ways in which events, realities, meanings, experiences and so on are the effects of a range of discourses operating within society' (Braun and Clarke, 2006: 81). Fundamentally, thematic analysis encourages close inspection and analysis of text in order to allow the findings to emerge from the data and it is typically used by researchers aiming to explore the views, perceptions and/or experiences of groups or individuals, and any differences or similarities in these.

Coding

The initial coding process should be highly detailed and inclusive. Coding is a process of working though the data line-by-line and applying brief verbal descriptions. For example, we might code the following section of an interview with a woman in prison as follows:

Like, when I was, like, a child my, my brother that I'm close to was always in trouble since he was about six years old. He was always in trouble. We always had the police at the house; always fighting with the family and, oh, everybody, and all.	Sibling delinquency Sibling delinquency
That's from when you were quite young.	
Yeah, he's an alcoholic. So (...) my mom and dad both had affairs by their own business. We had to sell the business. And everything, kind of, went downhill from there.	Parental problems Financial issues
How old were you then?	
I was about 14.	

Right, and that had quite a big impact on, on. . .	
Yeah, it did, yeah.	
In what way?	
In fact I was probably younger than, actually. I don't know because my dad, it is his, it is his life, he's been, like 20-odd years and suddenly, like, he's had, like, six heart attacks, a heart bypass and he couldn't do that anymore. So, he had his driving licence taken off him.	Effects of parental health problems
So, did things, financially, get difficult for the family when that happened or was it just more. . .?	
See, my dad always, like, my dad never really had, I don't know, he never really seemed to be around much. My mum always did. And he never gave my mum much money and she always struggled, like, especially Christmas, and that.	Financial issues
Note: We recommend you use different colour highlights to represent different themes.	

The level of detail of coding typically varies between transcripts and even within sections of transcripts, but our advice is to code as much as reasonably possible at first. It is initially better to be over-inclusive than under-inclusive and risk missing important detail from the data. However, this does not mean that anything and everything should be coded, or indeed that the process should not be systematic. It is likely initially that you will be coding every second or third line of the data, but there are not set rules about this: it depends on the data you have. The words you use for your codes should describe the section of data and be meaningful to you.

The key to successful coding is to be systematic, and also to be transparent in how you explain your approach. We strongly suggest keeping notes on how you conducted your thematic analysis in order to aid the write-up. The coding process is surprisingly intuitive, but does require some practice. There is no 'right' or 'wrong', but the researcher should code all interesting features of the data. As Boyatzis (1998: 63) notes, 'Codes identify a feature of the data which is interesting to the analyst ... and that can be assessed in a meaningful way regarding the phenomenon under investigation'.

Once the entire body of data has been 'coded', the researcher can move on to the next stage of the process, although this is not always a straightforward linear process. It is likely that at every stage of the coding process you will revise your codes as the analysis and your ideas develop, prompted by your increased interaction with, and understanding of, the data. You might adjust the names of codes to better describe the sections of data, and some codes will be merged as inevitably similar points will have initially been given different codes. The aim is to gather all data relevant to each code.

Themes

Once data relevant to each code have been gathered, and codes adjusted to provide a close fit to the data, the next stage is to begin to identify themes from the data. Themes are 'recurrent and distinctive features of participants' accounts, characterising particular perceptions and/or experiences, which the researcher sees as relevant to the research question' (King and Horrocks, 2010: 150). It should be possible to integrate groups of codes to work towards identifying themes that encompass all of the data and the final themes should describe what is going on in the data. For example, when reviewing women offenders' offence-related drug use four key themes emerged from the data:

'Supplying drugs to fund own drug use'
'Theft to fund own drug use'
'Drug importation to fund own drug use'
'Historical drug related offending' (Caulfield 2012: 136–40)

Note that each of these themes is carefully defined in such a way that it describes the content of that theme, allowing the reader to immediately understand what that theme is.

The process of collating codes into over-arching themes that represent the body of data is not an exacting process and you are likely to undergo some trial and error in allowing these themes to emerge. However, you should ensure two key things:

1   That themes represent significant elements of the data – a theme must not be based simply on one or two pieces of interesting data but should exist as a logical way of describing the body of data – codes – underpinning it.
2   That you clearly record how much data each theme consists of – for instance, how many interviewees spoke about issues included in this theme, and on how many occasions? Recording this information means both you and anyone reading about your analysis can see how important this theme may have been in your data.

It is usual to still be defining and redefining the themes even during the write-up of the research. The final themes should be the result of considerable analytical effort and they should be distinct from one another. There should not be too many themes – remember that these themes should represent the analytical effort of the research and not simply re-state all the detail of the data.

Writing up the findings: presenting themes

As noted above, writing up the findings from a thematic analysis can be seen as a part of the actual analysis as it is likely you will continue to refine your themes as you write. When writing up the themes you should describe the theme and provide illustrative examples that highlight the key points within each theme. Let's look at an example. Above we looked at Caulfield's research on women offenders' offence-related drug use. The following section is taken from the theme 'Theft to fund own drug use' (Caulfield 2012: 137):

Other women in this research also talked about how their current offence was carried out in order to fund their drug use. For Sarah,[1] Denise, and Louise this current offence was theft. Sarah explained how all of her past and current offending had been drug-related, either cautions for possession or burglary and theft to fund her drug use. Louise spoke in detail about her history of drug taking that, at its worst, she funded through large amounts of shoplifting.

> 'we'd binge, rob and bring back loads of money and all that kind of stuff and that was for Crack and I just thought, wow, this was not the life I wanted.' (Louise)

Note how the theme is explained, then the data underpinning the theme is outlined, before a quote that illustrates the theme is presented.

BOX 12.2 BRAUN AND CLARKE'S PHASES

The process of thematic analysis discussed above can be viewed in light of Braun and Clarke's (2006) six phases of thematic analysis:

Phase 1: Familiarising yourself with the data
During phase 1 you may listen to the recordings several times, transcribe the data and read through the transcriptions, and note down any items of interest that may inform your analysis.

Phase 2: Generating initial codes
Phase 2 involves working through the data line-by-line noting all interesting features of the data and developing definitions, or codes, to represent these.

Phase 3: Searching for themes
In phase 3 the researcher collates the codes into potential themes. These might represent particular aspects of similarity from across the data. All of the data relevant to a theme is gathered into a theme that effectively describes a distinct aspect of the data.

Phase 4: Reviewing themes
During phase 4 researchers begin to identify and review what a theme includes and doesn't include, and how the theme relates to the other themes from the data.

Phase 5: Defining and naming themes
By phase 5 what each theme represents should be sufficiently clear that a name can be given to each theme. It is also wise at this point to finalise a description or definition of each theme.

Phase 6: Producing the report
Writing up the themes should not simply be a descriptive process, but should provide an analysis of each theme. Within phase 6 specific examples – usually quotes – will be identified to illustrate key aspects of each theme. During this stage the themes should be related back to the research questions and to the literature.

While few descriptions of a set process for conducting a thematic analysis exist, Braun and Clarke's model is respected as one that gives some idea of the processes that a researcher is likely to go through. However, this process is unlikely to be a linear one and it is usual for researchers to move back and forth through the six stages.

Writing about thematic analysis in your research report or dissertation

Howitt (2011) notes that most researchers fail to adequately describe the process of analysis they undertook when using thematic analysis. However, it does not have to be this way. Explaining the process fully in the write-up of qualitative research provides a level of transparency that increases the view of qualitative research as both robust and valid. While the processes that different researchers might take during a thematic analysis may differ, with researchers moving back and forth through the stages, there should be general consistencies to the approach. The important thing is to state what you did and *how* you did it. To fully illustrate this below we have provided a real example of how a thematic analysis was written about in the method section of a research report (see Chapter 14 for further information on writing up criminological research).

BOX 12.3 DESCRIBING A THEMATIC ANALYSIS IN A METHOD SECTION OF A RESEARCH REPORT

While approaches such as conversation analysis or discourse analysis aim to describe the structure of conversational interaction or question the hidden meanings behind text, the aim of this research was to develop understanding of the life experiences and thoughts expressed by the research participants. Furthermore, as the research and interview schedule were based upon areas of interest identified from a review of the literature, a thematic analysis of the interview data was conducted. While 'there is no accepted, standardised approach to carrying out a thematic analysis', 'carried out properly, thematic analysis is quite an exacting process requiring a considerable investment of time and effort by the researchers' (Howitt and Cramer, 2008: 334, 336). Thematic analysis focuses on what is said rather than how it was said, allowing key themes to emerge from the data. Braun and Clarke (2006) have provided perhaps the most systematic account of the process of thematic analysis to date, consisting of six steps to analysis:

1. Familiarising yourself with your data
2. Generating initial codes
3. Searching for themes
4. Reviewing themes
5. Defining and naming themes
6. Producing the report (Braun and Clarke, 2006)

The thematic analysis process broadly followed Braun and Clarke's stages, although did not move through these stages in a straightforward linear process, often returning to previous processes and stages. This is outlined further below. A highly structured approach to the analysis was taken, beginning with an in-depth coding process involving working line by line through the entire body of data. In this context the codes act as 'shorthand devices to *label, separate, compile and organize* data' (Charmaz, 1983: 186).

Braun and Clarke (2006) maintain that the coding process can be done with a *data-led approach* or a *theory-led approach*. While the coding was initially led by themes identified through the literature, noted by the researcher during interviews, when listening to recordings, in the transcription process, and reading transcripts, subsequently a data-led approach was applied to the transcripts. While some researchers taking a data-led approach work within a grounded theory approach and so advocate tackling the data with no prior influences of preconceptions (cf. Glaser, 1992), others encourage the use of relevant knowledge (Hutchinson *et al.*, 2010; Strauss and Corbin, 1998). The latter approach was taken here, primarily as a literature review was essential in identifying an appropriate focus for conducting semi-structured interviews in a time-limited setting where the researcher would be unlikely to be able to return to conduct subsequent interviews.

The initial themes acted as a basis for coding, supplemented by new themes emerging during the in-depth coding process. This first in-depth coding process was, if anything, overly inclusive, identifying all possible codes appearing within the data. Every attempt to give similar data the same codes was made, however with such a large amount of data this was not always possible and code names had to be aligned after the first round of coding.

Next, the list of codes was reviewed in order to search for themes. This involved a process of assessing whether there were any commonalities between codes. Themes therefore represent a coding of the initial coding. Once an initial broad list of themes was highlighted, these were reviewed. At this stage it was important to consider whether there was sufficient evidence in the data to support each of the themes that had emerged. Some themes emerged as key themes, with substantial incidences of the codes from numerous participants. Other groups of codes emerged as sub-themes, relevant to the over-arching themes. As key themes emerged it was essential to add a description to each of these. This process related closely to the data from which the themes had emerged, in order to define the distinctiveness of each theme and what it represented.

Throughout the coding process substantial notes of key themes were made in order to aid the thought process for structuring the write-up of the data. The complexity of dealing with this volume of data, and keeping track of the numerous threads, required a strict logical process of coding, note-taking, naming and revising of codes, and merging codes. These processes were worked through many times, not always sequentially. These notes began to form the basis of the write-up of the data chapters, with the write-up subsequently also informing the data analysis. Indeed, the process of analysis, far from being complete at the write-up stage, instead entered further phases of analysis and revision. In this way the analysis and write-up were intertwined and the entire process developed organically from the data. Indeed, the write-up also formed a fundamental part of the data analysis.

Once the final themes and sub-themes had been identified from the data, and the write-up was underway, an intensive process began of printing the data from each theme and cross-checking the data within each of these to ensure all data relevant to each theme was included within this.

Of note is that the themes that emerged from the data were often unexpected. This is a significant point as it highlights that without a rigorous process of analysis – for example, by relying on memories of 'key points' from interviews that may be largely influenced by more charismatic interviewees – the information taken from the data may not represent the entire body of data, or the voice of all interviewees. It is also important to highlight that the rigorous thematic analysis of such a large body of data was a far more intensive process than it is possible to adequately capture in the description of the process provided above.

To summarise, the thematic analysis brought together data from each interview relevant to a particular theme, in order that through the write-up a clear picture of the experiences of the entire participant group could be given in a coherent way. In this way, the thematic analysis transformed the data from individual life stories, to a body of accessible information concerning a particular life experience. This enabled the data to be presented in four data chapters that present the experiences of this group of women. The data chapters present the overarching themes, with sub-themes presented within each chapter: experiences in childhood and growing up; adult life experiences; alcohol and drug use; mental health and emotional issues.

(Caulfield 2012: 56)

ADVANTAGES AND DISADVANTAGES OF THEMATIC ANALYSIS

Thematic analysis has a number of benefits. It is a flexible method of analysis that is accessible to new researchers and compatible with a number of different schools of thought. It is generally suitable for analysing any forms of qualitative data and in many ways is less demanding than other qualitative methods.

Earlier in this book we discussed the use of mixed methods in research: thematic analysis lends itself to a mixed methods approach where qualitative and quantitative methods can complement one another (although note our discussion in Chapter 6). Thematic analysis, when done well, can provide a rich and detailed account of the data a researcher has collected, and thus give a clear voice to those involved in the research.

However, there are some potential disadvantages to thematic analysis, and it is useful for you to be aware of these. The first of these is the time it takes to do a thematic analysis well. From the time it takes to ensure a high level of familiarity with transcripts,

**Instructor
activity**

Coding

to the rigorous coding process, good thematic analysis does take time. However, as long as you are aware of this you can plan this into your research timetable, and it is a highly rewarding process. Some researchers have been criticised for using thematic analysis in a limited way, with superficial coding that does not truly represent the data. Such criticisms can be avoided in two ways: first, by conducting a thorough analysis; and second, by documenting how thorough the analysis was.

Remember, thematic analysis cannot, for example, be used to analyse what patterns of speech tell us about the power relationships between individuals. Other forms of analysis are more appropriate in such circumstances, as discussed earlier in this chapter.

BOX 12.4 CODING ACTIVITY

Now that you understand the principles of conducting a thematic analysis, have a go at coding the short section of an interview transcript below. Highlight sections of text and use the column on the right to note down codes. You can find this data on the companion website and our suggestions for coding it. Remember, there is no right or wrong, but it may be interesting for you to compare your codes with ours.

A lot of people have problems with sleeping and stuff, especially the first time they come into prison. Has that been an issue for you?	
I think it did to be honest. When I first spent a couple of nights in prison it did seem strange. I was waking up thinking I was at home and that it was over but generally it's been alright, I think I settled in alright. Sad to come back though, I know I've got to come back but it's just nice to go home and have your home comforts.	
How have you experienced prison, how have you felt about things, how you've experienced it?	
I just get on with it. I haven't become bitter, obviously I'm not a lover of my ex-boyfriend because he put me in here but it's an experience in life. I just try to make the most of my time whilst I'm in here.	
What have you been doing whilst here?	
Well I worked in the hairdressers – done hair and beauty, done Indian head massage and I'm working in the gym now because I'm working towards a fitness qualification so it just opens up new doors for when I get out really.	
So if you decide to go into that direction you'll have the qualifications.	
Yes, probably more self-employed.	
Doing what?	
Personal trainer.	

Before you came here I know you said you had some financial difficulties, and I guess that was causing you some stress?

Definitely, probably more stress than I thought at the time.

Can you tell me a bit about your financial troubles and how you got into them?

From the age of 18 it just started off with a credit card and store cards and just building up and getting loans to pay it off and then build the credit up again and...

What sort of things were you spending the money on?

Clothes mainly and going out and holidays. It soon goes.

Was that a problem for you at the time?

At the time no because I always worked and I always thought I'd have the money to pay back. It was only coming towards the end when I was getting jobs and they weren't highly paid and I thought what am I going to do, there's more going out than there is coming in.

If you were juggling with that, in what sort of way, did you have any sleepless nights or ...

Yes, I use to wake up thinking about it and thinking oh God I've got to pay that tomorrow, it would be going around in my head all the time, calculating money all the time.

Did you ever suffer from depression or anyone suggest to you that you might have depression?

Yes. I didn't see it myself but my brother said to me you're depressed, you're thinking too much ...

So were your family aware that you were in financial trouble?

Yes they knew about the debt and I think that's what worried them as well because they didn't have money to bail me out – they could only help me a certain amount because they didn't have money themselves.

Did you ever go to the doctor to discuss any of the stress or the worries?

No.

So you've not seen anyone here about money worries?

No because I'm not in any debt now. Before I came to prison I'd went bankrupt so in a way it's all gone away. When I go out I don't owe anybody anything.

COMPUTER ASSISTED QUALITATIVE DATA ANALYSIS (CAQDAS)

Traditionally, qualitative researchers conducted their analyses by 'cutting and pasting' sections of their data within Word documents, or having all their data physically on paper in front of them. When researchers are working with many pieces of qualitative data this can be difficult to manage. However, in recent years many researchers have begun to use CAQDAS software. A number of CAQDAS programmes exist, with one of the most popular being NVivo (the current version available is NVivo 10). CAQDAS software does not 'do' the analysis for you, but reduces the burden on the researcher in managing the data and can be very helpful in coding and linking data. CAQDAS software supports most types of qualitative analysis and data and some university courses now teach the use of this software as part of their research methods modules.

The decision to use CAQDAS software to aid a thematic analysis is likely to be based upon considerations of time and efficiency. CAQDAS is designed to make the process of coding and the analysis of data more intuitive by reducing the physical effort required to analyse textual data (Lee and Fielding, 1991). It enables data to be stored, coded, retrieved and interrogated with more efficiency than can be achieved using traditional methods or a word processor (Lewins and Silver, 2005; Tesch, 1990; Fielding and Lee, 1998). It is important to be aware that even with CAQDAS software the researcher is still responsible for the cognitive side of the data analysis (Tesch, 1991). Whilst the computer package helps the researcher sort data into meaningful chunks, the software plays no part in the actual analysis or interpretation of results (Weitzman and Miles, 1995). It has been suggested that such packages help enhance creativity through a reduction of the clerical and administrative burden (Tesch, 1991) and the ability to play with the data and explore new analytical perspectives (Tesch, 1990). CAQDAS has been criticised for reinforcing or even exaggerating the fragmentation of data (see Weaver and Atkinson, 1995), but by revisiting the original recordings and full transcripts researchers can go a long way to avoiding these issues. Ultimately, users of CAQDAS remain responsible for analysing the data, but the reduction in the administrative burden associated with large amounts of interview data and the enhanced possibility of objectivity makes the use of such software highly beneficial in many circumstances.

CAQDAS software is particularly useful in aiding the organisational aspects of managing large amounts of qualitative data, and NVivo is thought to retain a greater level of power over the data analysis with the researcher, as opposed to other CAQDAS such as Atlas or NUD*IST (Bringer et al., 2004). However, systematic analysis and rigour through the use of CAQDAS can only be achieved if the researcher is competent in the principles of qualitative research.

BOX 12.5 GETTING STARTED WITH NVIVO

If you want to find out more about NVivo you can watch an introductory video online here:

http://www.qsrinternational.com/products_nvivo.aspx

Keep in mind that NVivo can do some very complex things, including aiding in the analysis of various kinds of qualitative data (including audio and video data, pictures, and websites), but it can also be a very helpful tool when conducting a standard thematic analysis with interview or focus group transcripts.

It is worth enquiring about whether any computers in your university have NVivo or any other CAQDAS software installed. If NVivo is available, you might want to work through the various online tutorials available on the QSR International website:

http://www.youtube.com/watch?v=K3wdeZUZGVY&lr=1

and you can explore an NVivo project by opening up NVivo on your computer and taking a look at the 'Environment project', or begin setting up your own project using this 'getting started' guide:

http://download.qsrinternational.com/Document/NVivo9/NVivo9-Getting-Started-Guide.pdf

If you would like to find out more about CAQDAS, we strongly recommend the 'Introduction to CAQDAS' through the University of Huddersfield's Online Qualitative Data Analysis project: http://onlineqda.hud.ac.uk/Intro_CAQDAS/index.php. This website is also a great resource for learning more about a range of qualitative data analysis techniques.

CONCLUSION

Throughout this chapter, you will have noticed something that we cannot emphasise enough: it is vital to ensure that the analysis of your data is robust. In addition to this, it is vital to ensure that the way you describe and explain the process of analysing your data is clear and sufficiently detailed. Being robust in your data analysis includes ensuring familiarity with your data gained through collecting, transcribing and reading your data. Once researchers are familiar with their data, they can begin the formal process of analysis, potentially using some of the methods outlined in this and other chapters of this book.

✦ KEY LEARNING POINTS

- You should now understand the importance of the transcription process in qualitative analysis.
- While there a number of different approaches to qualitative data analysis, thematic analysis is widely used when researchers wish to understand and explore the ideas, experiences and reality of a group or individuals.
- Conducting a robust thematic analysis requires a high level of analytical effort and a good deal of time from the researcher. This process will allow the findings to emerge from the data via a process of coding.
- Key themes should be presented from the thematic analysis that represent the body of data. When writing up these themes it is important to provide examples from that data that illustrate each theme.
- There is not a 'right' or 'wrong' answer with this type of analysis. The key is to fully document the process and findings to demonstrate that the analysis was robust.

NOTE

1   False names were used in the research in order to protect the identity of participants.

Chapter 13

Analysing the data

Documents, text and other data

GOALS OF THIS CHAPTER

At the end of reading this chapter and by completing the online resources that accompany it, you will be able to:

1 approach the analysis of documents and text in a critical way;
2 plan appropriately prior to the analysis phase of conducting research with **documentary data**;
3 understand the principles and processes involved in qualitative content analysis and critical **discourse analysis**.

OVERVIEW

- As outlined elsewhere in this book, there is a wealth of data available to researchers that does not necessarily involve the collection of new empirical data.
- A structured and consistent approach to analysing documents, employing a robust methodology, will often lead to important insights into relevant criminological issues.
- Before beginning the process of analysis, researchers must do a number of things: plan; consider the best way to access relevant data; and read and reflect.
- There are several approaches that can be used to analyse documents and text-based data. Two popular qualitative methods are qualitative content analysis and critical discourse analysis.
- Qualitative content analysis shares some of the underlying principles of content analysis (a primarily quantitative method of analysis) but allows researchers to ask not simply 'what', but 'why'. There are a number of different approaches to qualitative content analysis, which differ in their level of inductive and deductive reasoning.
- There is no one set approach to critical discourse analysis. However, there are key critical principles that underpin this form of analysis. This chapter sets out some of the ways of thinking and types of questions that should be considered by any researcher seeking to make use of this method in order to understand language as a source of power in their data.

TYPES OF DOCUMENT

Chapter 10 introduced some of the types of documents that researchers might analyse, including personal documents (diaries/autobiographies/letters/photographs), official documents, mass media outputs, internet outputs and more. The type of documents researchers may wish to analyse is large and varied and, as Chapter 10 indicated, researchers can be concerned with both qualitative and quantitative documentary sources. With both types of sources, we should be mindful of the assumptions that underlie the questions that have been asked and the way any data has been collected, analysed and presented. In many ways, therefore, whether data is qualitative or quantitative becomes less important than the assumptions that underpin it. What is important is taking a structured approach to analysing documents and being able to demonstrate a robust methodology. We have seen our own students fail to do this and consequently fail to produce what had the potential to be very strong pieces of work. We have also seen students who have taken a clear and logical approach to analysing documents and produced excellent work. We hope that by reading this chapter you will fall into the latter category.

This chapter will help you identify what you should be thinking about even before you begin your analysis, before moving on to give you guidance on possible methods of analysis that you may wish to use.

WHERE TO BEGIN

Prior to formally beginning any process of analysis we advise that you thoroughly explore your documents, allowing you time to reflect and refine the methodological process you will ultimately employ. While you may wish to delve straight into the analysis, the planning you do beforehand will have a huge impact on how successful your analysis is. Trust us on this!

1   *Plan.* Ensure you know exactly what you are looking for in your data. Have clear research questions.
2   *Consider access.* Where are the documents located? Do you need special access or need to contact particular people? Do this early and ensure you have a contingency plan if you cannot use the data you wanted.
3   *Read and reflect.* Explore what the documents say. What can you find out about the authors and/or organisations that produced them? Why was the document produced? Make notes and reflect on how what you have found in these early stages may influence your approach to analysis.

Whichever approach to analysis you take, you must consider underlying values and subjectivity; both that of the documents you are accessing, and your own. The robustness, reliability and credibility of the analysis you conduct will depend to a large extent on how far you recognise underlying values and subjectivity. What standpoint do the authors take? Whose truth does the document you are reading represent? How does your own theory of knowledge fit with, or oppose, this? Think back to the discussions we had in Chapter 1.

Next, look back at Box 4.2 from Chapter 4.

BOX 4.2 SPECIFYING CONCEPTS AND IDENTIFYING VARIABLES

Using the insights gained from the exercise in Box 4.1 specify what you mean by the concept of family breakdown and jot down some of the crimes that you think might be linked to it. Try to give reasons for the association. Next, try to think of other variables that might help to explain the crimes you believe to be linked with family breakdown (as you have defined it).

Now take a look at the document *Breakthrough Britain* (available at: http://www.centreforsocialjustice.org.uk/publications/breakthrough-britain-family-breakdown). What evidence is provided in the document for the proposition that there is a *strong* (our emphasis) correlation between crime and family breakdown? How would you assess the *strength* of the evidence provided for this theory within the document?

STUDENT ACTIVITY: RECOGNISING THE ROLE OF UNDERLYING VALUES AND POTENTIAL BIAS

Revisit the *Breakthrough Britain* document introduced in Box 4.2 and consider both your own underlying values and those of the authors. Ask yourself the following initial questions:

1   What is the purpose of the document? Does it reflect and/or seek to promote a particular view or political position? Who funded any research presented in the document?
2   What is the background of the authors? Are they credible? Do they have and/or seek to promote a particular view or political position?
3   How might your own values affect the way you plan and conduct an analysis of this document?
4   Do you need to account for your own values or simply recognise and document your own standpoint?

When reviewing your data you should consider – in the context of the questions above – whether there is any attempt to put forward a view that is not backed up with sufficient or convincing evidence. Have the authors explored or highlighted oppositional views, or said why they might reject oppositional views?

Once you have considered the above questions in relation to your data, you should be ready to begin planning the more formal and in-depth process of analysing your data. *Remember* – the method you use should directly work towards addressing your research questions.

CRITICAL ANALYSIS

We have called this section of the chapter 'Critical analysis' as a reminder of one of the key underpinning concepts in good research. Within this section we discuss and provide advice on how to critically analyse text and documents. It is worth reiterating the difference between criticism and critical analysis or critical evaluation. Criticism typically refers to fault-finding and producing negative comments about something. This is not the purpose of critical analysis. While critical analysis can involve fault-finding, the purpose is primarily to assess the assumptions that underpin a piece of work and the methodology employed. What is concealed? What is promoted?

Analysis of documents and text can be done in a variety of ways and, as discussed in Chapter 11, research using documentary sources can be excellent if done well. Doing this sort of research well requires a structured and methodical approach, a clear rationale for the approach taken and a consistency of approach. Researchers who can competently describe the structured and methodical approach they have taken tend to fare well. Critical discourse analysis and qualitative content analysis are two possible approaches to analysing documents and these are discussed more fully below – but do note these are just two of several possible approaches. **Thematic analysis**, for example, is another method it is possible to apply to textual data and you can find this explained fully in Chapter 12.

QUALITATIVE CONTENT ANALYSIS

Qualitative content analysis is perhaps the most widely used qualitative approach to analysing documents. Like thematic analysis, which we outlined in Chapter 12, qualitative content analysis involves a process of searching for themes in the data. Again, like thematic analysis, this method can be managed very well with Computer Assisted Qualitative Data Analysis Software (CAQDAS: see below). Qualitative content analysis allows researchers to elicit patterns from the data that represent a social reality (or realities), as opposed to critical discourse analysis – discussed below – that is primarily concerned with language as a source of social power.

You may have heard of content analysis, and at this point it is worth noting how this differs from qualitative content analysis. Content analysis is an approach to data analysis that seeks to categorise and quantify documents and text in a systematic way. This is a quantitative approach to data analysis, which involves coding data to relatively strict coding schedules in order to ascertain and statistically test the occurrence of specific variables. There are many benefits to content analysis – not least that, done well, it is a highly transparent research method – but also limitations. It allows us to ask 'what' but not 'why'. As criminological researchers it is very often the 'why' that we are most concerned with. Qualitative content analysis allows us to ask more of the 'why' by allowing a detailed exploration of key themes that occur within the data we wish to analyse. Just like traditional content analysis, there are a number of approaches to qualitative content analysis. These approaches primarily differ in the extent to which they involve inductive reasoning, i.e. the extent to which the analysis is data led (inductive) or theory driven (deductive). Hsieh and Shannon (2005) discuss three approaches to qualitative content analysis:

1   Conventional qualitative content analysis – inductive. Coding categories are derived directly from the raw data. Aligned with grounded theory approaches.
2   Directed content analysis – allows for both **induction** and **deduction**. Initial coding begins with theory and/or relevant research findings. Researchers also immerse themselves in the data during the process of analysis and allow further themes to emerge from the data. This approach is most often used to validate or extend a conceptual framework or theory.
3   Summative content analysis – largely deductive. Researchers begin by counting the words and main content before extending the analysis to include underlying meanings and themes. While this approach may begin as quantitative and in-line with traditional content analysis, its goal is to explore the usage of the words/indicators in an inductive manner.

We favour an approach that retains many of the systematic elements of traditional content analysis, but that allows the researcher to constantly revise the themes as the analysis progresses. This is closest to what Hsieh and Shannon term 'directed content analysis'. The process should move back and forth between the formulation of ideas, the process of analysis, and the interpretation of the data. Of course, the approach you decide to take will depend upon your aims, research questions, methodological standpoint and the data you have.

Altheide (2004) outlines the steps he takes in qualitative content analysis:

- Generate a research question.
- Become familiar with the context within which the documents were/are generated.
- Become familiar with a small number of documents (6–10).[1]
- Generate some categories that will guide the collection of data and draft a schedule for collecting the data in terms of the generated categories.
- Test the schedule by using it for collecting data from a number of documents.
- Revise the schedule and select further cases to sharpen it up.

By schedule, Altheide essentially means a set of rules about the categories that will be used in the data analysis process. Initially, these categories may be determined by existing theories, ideas and research. This is also referred to as a coding scheme or coding manual. Developing a coding manual is a good idea, especially where more than one researcher is working on a project. While you are likely to be working independently on your dissertation project, for example, there may be assignments during your research methods course that require you to work on data in groups. We suggest your coding manual consists of at least the following: category names (codes), definitions or rules for assigning codes, and examples. You may also wish to include a space for notes. It is a good idea to make notes as your analysis progresses as this will help you when you come to write up your research and will remind you (and help you explain to anyone reading your research) how and why your coding scheme developed. As we have discussed in various places in this book, providing a clear and comprehensive methods section in research reports/dissertations is very important. The more transparent your methods, the better. Having a coding manual will help you be transparent and help you to demonstrate the robustness of your process of analysis. It is good practice to include your coding manual in the appendix of your research report or dissertation.

BOX 13.1 SUGGESTIONS FOR A QUALITATIVE CONTENT ANALYSIS CODING MANUAL

1. Label/name for each category	e.g. offending
2. Definition	e.g. mention of crimes committed, whether arrested, convicted, or not
3. Rules for assigning	e.g. each time offences committed by any individual are mentioned in the text
4. Exclusions?	e.g. where the offences of someone other than the speaker are being referred to
5. Examples	e.g. '*I committed a crime. I hit him with an iron in the head'* (quote from Caulfield, 2012: 104)
6. Notes	e.g. code each occurrence, even where several mentions are made of the same offence in the text
Add columns to the right for each new category	

Student document

Suggestions for a qualitative content analysis coding manual

The process of coding or categorising material is fundamental to any form of content analysis. The coding process should be highly detailed and inclusive. As outlined in Chapter 12, coding is a process of working though the data line by line and applying brief verbal descriptions. Take this page from a report by Johnson, Keen, and Pritchard (2011) that looks at the economic benefit of the arts in criminal justice. We might code/categorise it as such:

A lack of evidence

The most recent and comprehensive UK research on the effectiveness of the arts in criminal justice was completed in 2005 by the Centre for Applied Theatre Research.[1] The resulting report, *Doing the Arts Justice*, concluded that too little high-quality evaluation exists for arts interventions, and that the sector is lacking a solid theory from which to demonstrate its impact.

Six years on, the number and quality of evaluations has increased. As illustrated in Box 1, individual charities' evaluations are contributing to a growing body of evidence. Yet the sector continues to face significant challenges in demonstrating its effectiveness. The conclusion of *Doing the Arts Justice* still applies: the sector has not yet done enough to talk coherently and comprehensively about how arts projects work towards targets in the criminal justice system. Several factors contribute to this.

Firstly, although long established, the delivery of arts projects in the criminal justice sector remains fragmented. Few organisations have the scale required to carry out the thorough and long-term evaluation required to demonstrate fully the value of using arts projects in this context.[2]

Secondly, gathering good-quality follow-up data on participants is difficult. Charities struggle both to access government data on re-offending and to follow up with participants themselves. Ex-offenders often live chaotic lives and may not be able or willing to stay in touch with an organisation once the programme has finished. It is therefore difficult to link interventions directly with outcomes such as re-offending and understand the lasting impact of interventions.

Box 1: How the arts can help to rehabilitate offenders

There is a growing body of evidence from individual organisations that indicates how the arts can help to rehabilitate offenders.

Engagement

Good Vibrations uses Gamelan (Indonesian bronze percussion) workshops to help prisoners to develop life and work skills. An evaluation by Birmingham City University found that the workshops act as catalysts for change in the lives of offenders, and this change is sustained as offenders move through the prison system and out into the community.*

New skills

Dance United uses dance to engage young people who have offended and are at risk of offending. Its Academy offers an intensive 12-week programme in which young people are treated as trainee professional dancers. An evaluation by the University of Manchester shows that Academy participants have higher rates of transfer into education, training and employment than their peers and are less likely to re-offend.†

Responsibility

Geese Theatre's Insult to Injury project uses drama to explore anger, aggression and violence. Participants have '*an acknowledged and persistent history of violent offending*'. An evaluation by the University of Birmingham found that anger levels are reduced after participation in the project, and participants report that they are less likely to express anger either physically or verbally.‡

Positive relationships

Safe Ground's Family Man programme uses drama to develop participants' social skills and help participants improve their relationships with family members, peers and staff. Extensively evaluated, one study found the programme particularly encourages personal development through the use of drama-based, interactive ingredients that promote individual insight and reflection. There is also evidence that the course supports prisoners to re-evaluate their attitudes and beliefs, stimulating improved communication, especially with families and children.^

* Wilson, D. et al (2008) *Promoting positive change*. Centre for Applied Criminology, Birmingham City University.
† Miles, A. and Strauss, P. (2008) *The Academy: A report on outcomes for participants*. ESRC Centre for Research on Socio-cultural Change, University of Manchester.
‡ Blacker, J. et al (2008) *A combined drama-based and CBT approach to working with self-reported anger and aggression*. University of Birmingham.
^ McGuire, J. (2009) *Family Man: An outline of the theoretical basis of the programme*. University of Liverpool.

	Evidence (lack of)		Theory (lack of)		Issues with data

Figure 13.1

Note that we recommend you use different colour highlights to represent different themes.

Head back to Chapter 12 for more detailed information on the process of coding data. Once you have developed your initial coding manual, test it on some of your data. Refine it. Keep updating it. The process of coding is the process of analysis and in qualitative content analysis this should be a continually evolving process.

BOX 13.2 WHAT TO DO WHEN YOU HAVE DEVELOPED YOUR INITIAL CODES

Test your coding scheme on a sample of text – 'The best test of the clarity and consistency of your category definitions is to code a sample of your data.' Code a sample, check for consistency (do your codes fit your data?) and revise your coding scheme where needed.

Code all the text – 'When sufficient consistency has been achieved, the coding rules can be applied to the entire corpus of text.' Keep developing your coding themes while you code your data and add these to your coding manual. Be responsive to your data.

Assess your coding consistency – 'It is not safe to assume that, if a sample was coded in a consistent and reliable manner, the coding of the whole corpus of text is also consistent.' Researchers are human. We get tired. Sometimes we lose focus and make mistakes. Check that the categories and codes you now have in your coding manual make sense.

Draw conclusions from the coded data – 'This is a critical step in the analysis process, and its success will rely almost wholly on your reasoning abilities.' This is where you begin to make sense of your categories. You should be seeking out relationships in the data and uncovering patterns. Review how well these patterns account for the whole body of data.

Report your methods and findings – 'Qualitative content analysis ... uncovers patterns, themes, and categories important to a social reality.' You must report your decisions and practices in developing the coding process. When presenting your results, you should strive for a balance between description and interpretation and it is common practice to use typical quotations to represent themes and justify conclusions.

(Adapted from Zhang and Wildemuth, 2009: 4–5)

Remember: in order to develop (and also to write about) a robust qualitative content analysis, you should be clear about where your categories come from. What theory and existing data influenced the categories you started with? How did the categories develop as the process of analysis began? All too often researchers fail to fully document the process of analysis, yet doing this well is critical to the quality and validity of the research. Through careful preparation and thorough coding and interpretation, qualitative content analysis can be used to provide considerable insight, validate or challenge existing theories, and develop new theories.

CRITICAL DISCOURSE ANALYSIS

Most basically, 'discourse' refers to talk and conversation. However, within social science the word takes on a broader meaning, and includes all elements of communication. As Worrall (1990: 8) states, discourse embraces 'not only its content, but its author (who says it?), its authority (on what grounds?), its audience (to whom?), its objective (in order to achieve what?)'.

Critical discourse analysis (CDA) primarily seeks to review how social power is reproduced, represented and resisted in text and talk. In this form of analysis, language is viewed as a source of power. Such analyses stem from the critical works of social theorists including Foucault, Bourdieu and the Frankfurt School, and you will find that many texts discuss CDA in this context. However, it should be noted that CDA as a process of analysis was not necessarily practised by these thinkers and no single method of CDA exists. Instead, it is a broad approach to the critical analysis of language, text and communication that developed out of the critical thinking and theoretical approaches of these social scientists. CDA involves exploring why some elements of conversation, documents or text may become privileged while others are underplayed or even disregarded.

The main principles of CDA have been described by Fairclough and Wodak (1997: 271–80):

1   CDA addresses social problems.
2   Power relations are discursive.
3   Discourse constitutes society and culture.
4   Discourse does ideological work.
5   Discourse is historical.
6   The link between text and society is medialed.
7   Discourse analysis is interpretative and explanatory.
8   Discourse is a form of social action.

While there are many forms of CDA, Jupp and Norris (1993) outline a CDA agenda for analysing documents. Although this agenda is now relatively old, it asks some important questions and we recommend you use these questions as a starting point in analysing the documents you might be including in your own research.

We do not suggest that you follow each and every one of the questions in Box 13.3 completely, but rather use them as a guide in developing your own agenda. We strongly recommend that you refer back to Chapter 1 of this book where we discuss assumptions about knowledge and power. This will help shape your thinking in answering questions like those posed by Jupp and Norris.

BOX 13.3 JUPP AND NORRIS' DISCOURSE ANALYTIC RESEARCH AGENDA

1   What public and/or institutional discourses are important in terms of know-ledge of what is 'right' and what is 'wrong'?
2   In what kinds of documents and texts do such discourses appear?
3   Who writes or speaks these discourses and whom do they represent or purport to represent?
4   What is the intended audience of such writing or speech?
5   What does a critical reading of these documents uncover in terms of:

    a   what is defined as 'right' and 'wrong' and therefore what is seen as problematic;
    b   what explanation is offered for what is seen as problematic;
    c   what, therefore, is seen as the solution?

6   What does a critical reading of these documents tell us about:

    a   what is not seen as problematic;
    b   which explanations are rejected or omitted;
    c   which solutions are not preferred?

7   What alternative discourses exist?
8   How do these relate to 'internal differentiation' within and between semi-autonomous realms of control?
9   What does a critical reading of these alternative discourses tell us?
10 Is there evidence of negotiation with, or resistance to, dominant discourses?
11 What is the relationship between the discourses and social conflict, social struggle, hierarchies of credibility, order and control, and, most of all, the exercise of power?
12 Are discourses, knowledge and power pervasive or reducible to class, class conflict and struggles refracted through one source, the state?

(Source: Jupp and Norris, 1993: 50)

BOX 13.4 ACTIVITY

Read Lockyer and Chambers' (2013) report on plans to reform the prison estate.

Now read it again, but consider how Jupp and Norris' questions could be applied to this piece of research.

In addition to these questions, what else might you want to consider? For example, what can you ascertain about the political standpoint of the authors and the organisation they represent (from either the report or from conducting some wider research)? How might this influence and inform your answers to the questions above?

PAUSE TO THINK . . .

Spend a few minutes reflecting on how far your own thinking about this report has changed since employing the sorts of questions posed by Jupp and Norris. Compare this with how you first read the document. Has your thinking changed?

We know that CDA can at first appear a challenging process, but by employing questions such as those above and by reading the suggestions we make on the companion website on employing this method to analyse Lockyer and Chambers' report, we hope you will gain a fuller appreciation of the value of CDA.

ANALYSING OTHER KINDS OF DOCUMENTS

In reality, almost anything text based can be analysed using qualitative content analysis, following the processes outlined in this chapter, and it is also possible to work with pictures, video and audio data. If you are using a range of web-based sources you may need to spend more time in the planning stages of the research in bringing your sources together ready for analysis. As highlighted below, computer software such as NVivo can be invaluable in these circumstances.

CDA can be an insightful method to analyse a variety of documents. The work of Teo (2000) is a good example of how this method can be applied to newspaper articles. Teo used CDA to explore issues of racism in the reporting and structures of Australian newspapers. If you are likely to be analysing either transcripts or recordings of television or radio interviews or programmes, the methods described in this chapter on CDA are wholly applicable.

You should also note there are other suitable methods of analysing documents, web sources and various types of media. We have covered two popular approaches here but this chapter is not intended as exhaustive. We recommend that if you plan to conduct research on documentary and media sources and are not entirely comfortable that the approaches to analysis outlined here will allow you to address your research questions, that you seek out alternatives, including thematic analysis (Chapter 12). Other examples include narrative analysis – a process sometimes employed by those reviewing television programmes and films. Wilson and O'Sullivan (2004) provide an interesting example of a narrative analysis of prison films.

USING CAQDAS TO AID THE ANALYSIS OF DOCUMENTS

In Chapter 12 we introduced you to the use of Computer Assisted Qualitative Data Analysis Software (or CAQDAS). The benefits of using CAQDAS with qualitative data primarily revolve around the management of relatively large amounts of data. As with the types of qualitative analysis outlined elsewhere in this book, the methods discussed in this chapter typically involve working with several large documents and this can be difficult to manage in a program like Microsoft Word (or indeed having all your data physically on paper in front of you). CAQDAS works particularly well with qualitative content analysis.

In recent years many researchers have begun to use CAQDAS software. A number of CAQDAS programs exist, with one of the most popular being NVivo (the current version available is NVivo 10). CAQDAS software does not 'do' the analysis for you, but reduces the burden on the researcher in managing the data and can be very helpful in indexing data in particular. CAQDAS software supports most types of qualitative analysis and data and some university courses now teach the use of this software as part of their research methods modules.

It is worth remembering that, ultimately, users of CAQDAS remain responsible for analysing the data. The reduction in the administrative burden associated with large amounts of qualitative data and the enhanced possibility of objectivity makes the use of such software highly beneficial in many circumstances. CAQDAS software is particularly useful in aiding the organisational aspects of managing large amounts of qualitative data, and NVivo is thought to allow the researcher to retain a greater level of power over the data analysis, as opposed to other CAQDAS such as Atlas or NUD*IST (Bringer *et al.*, 2004). However, systematic analysis and rigour through the use of CAQDAS can only be achieved if the researcher is competent in the principles of **qualitative research**. For further discussion of CAQDAS see Chapter 12.

NVivo is particularly useful if you are analysing non-traditional forms of data. See Box 13.4 below for more information.

BOX 13.5 GETTING STARTED WITH USING NVIVO TO HELP YOU MANAGE DOCUMENTS

If you want to find out more about NVivo you can watch an introductory video online here:

http://www.qsrinternational.com/products_nvivo.aspx

Keep in mind that NVivo can do some very complex things, including aiding in the analysis of various kinds of qualitative data (including audio and video data, pictures and websites), but it can also be a very helpful tool when conducting analysis of traditional text-based data.

This video explains how NVivo can be used to work with images, audio and visual data:

http://www.youtube.com/watch?v=domX-waoadA

and here you can find information on working with data from web pages, Twitter and YouTube:

http://www.qsrinternational.com/products_nvivo.aspx

It is worth enquiring about whether any computers in your university have NVivo or any other CAQDAS software installed. If NVivo is available, you might want to work through the various online tutorials available on the QSR International website:

http://www.youtube.com/watch?v=K3wdeZUZGVY&lr=1

and you can explore an NVivo project by opening up NVivo on your computer and taking a look at the 'Environment project', or begin setting up your own project using this 'getting started' guide:

http://download.qsrinternational.com/Document/NVivo9/NVivo9-Getting-Started-Guide.pdf

If you would like to find out more about CAQDAS, we strongly recommend the 'Introduction to CAQDAS' through the University of Huddersfield's Online Qualitative Data Analysis project: http://onlineqda.hud.ac.uk/Intro_CAQDAS/index.php. This website is also a great resource for learning more about a range of qualitative data analysis techniques.

CONCLUSION

We have highlighted the following point throughout this section of the book, and we do so again here: it is vital to ensure that the analysis of your data is robust. Being able to analyse your data in a thorough and appropriate way using the methods outlined in this chapter to a large extent depends on how you approach the data. Employing a critical approach and considering the role of underlying values – both your own and those of the authors of the data you are analysing – is a crucial stage in your research. Consideration of the types of questions we pose around values and bias must be done before you begin the formal process of analysis. Once you begin your formal analysis, you must ensure you plan and document the process and apply set rules and questions relevant to the form of analysis you have employed. This structure is critical to gaining a full understanding of your data.

 **KEY LEARNING POINTS**

- The method of analysis you use to analyse your data should directly work towards addressing your research questions.
- Prior to beginning the data analysis phase of your research with documents, text-based data and other sources, you must spend time planning, reading and reflecting on your data.
- Whichever approach is taken, good analyses of documents, text-based data and other sources take a systematic, consistent, and robust approach. Good researchers ensure their methodology, methods and processes of analysis are clear to anyone reading about their research;
- Computer Assisted Qualitative Data Analysis Software (CAQDAS) can be particularly useful in managing large amounts of data.

NOTE

1   We note that student researchers may well be working with fewer documents than professional researchers such as Altheide, and so may develop their schedule based on fewer documents than he suggests.

Chapter 14

Writing up criminological research

GOALS OF THIS CHAPTER

At the end of reading this chapter and by completing the online resources that accompany it, you will be able to:

1   appreciate the importance of clearly and comprehensively writing up criminological research;
2   understand the differences between writing up qualitative and quantitative research;
3   present an appropriate account of each stage of the research process;
4   acknowledge the importance of providing an interesting, concise and descriptive title for your research report of dissertation;
5   write a clear, concise and informative summary of your research, known as an abstract.

Instructor PPoint Slides

Writing up criminological research

OVERVIEW

- Your primary duty when writing up research is to communicate clearly enough that a naive reader could replicate your study using the information you have provided.
- There is not necessarily a right or wrong way of writing up criminological research. Many of the decisions you take about how to best write up your research will be informed by the nature of your research.
- Depending on the type of research you have conducted you might include a literature review, methods section, discussion and conclusion.
- As a rule of thumb the title and abstract of a dissertation or research report should be written last. As the abstract and the title create the first impressions of research for the reader it is important that they are written clearly and concisely.
- It is a good idea to work through a checklist (such as the one at the end of this chapter) once you have written your dissertation or research report, to ensure you have included everything important.

BEFORE YOU BEGIN

It is important to be aware that there is not necessarily a right or wrong way of writing up criminological research. In many ways there is little difference between writing up criminological research and other social sciences research, and many of the decisions you take about how best to write up your research will be informed by the nature of the research. For example: did you use primary or **secondary data**? Was your research qualitative or quantitative, or did you use a mixed methods approach?

Your own university department tutors may offer guidance on how they expect dissertations and research reports to be presented, so you should check this. Where specific guidance is provided by your university you must follow it. At a minimum the university will almost certainly provide guidance on word limits. Presented below is general basic guidance on good practice in writing up and presenting criminological research, but this is not meant to be prescriptive. Please note that we have used the words dissertation and research report interchangeably throughout this chapter.

> ### TIP
>
> One of the best ways to improve your own academic writing style is to read research reports, journal articles and past student dissertations. In this way you can pick up tips on style from professional criminologists and good dissertations to help you structure your work and understand the required style. Why not have a look at articles written by your own lecturers – who better to learn from than the people you know!

TOP TIPS ON SUCCESSFULLY WRITING UP CRIMINOLOGICAL RESEARCH

First, remember that your primary duty as an author (because that's what you are when writing your dissertation or research report) is to communicate to the reader.

All of us can tell when an author has failed to communicate clearly, so your dissertation or research report should enable you to tell the reader:

- what was carried out;
- how it was carried out;
- why it was carried out;
- what was found;
- what the results actually mean.

An important thing to remember when writing up research is that it should be written in such a way that a naive reader could replicate it. As you write, ask yourself whether you have provided sufficient information for a person who knows nothing about your research to understand what you have done. If you suspect the answer is 'no', you need to address this. Your supervisor may know everything about your research, but when s/he is marking your work s/he will expect to see the depth of information that would be required by a naive reader.

Arguably, the abstract and conclusions are the most important sections of the dissertation. Your research should 'do what is says on the tin': that is, your title and abstract should accurately reflect the content of your research report. You can read more on this later in this chapter.

Your university may provide guidance on basic things like formatting, but a general rule of thumb is that your work should be double-spaced with all pages numbered. Each major section (for example, abstract, literature review, method and so on) should start on a new page with the title of the section in bold. Each minor section (for example, subsections in your methodology) should be in italics. The last section is the Appendices and includes things such as a blank consent form, ethics approval form and other relevant information.

Almost always in academic writing, you are expected to write in what is known as the 'third person'. You will probably have experience of this from essays and other assessments you have done throughout your course. The third person avoids the use of 'I' and 'we'. For example, instead of writing 'I decided' you might use 'It was decided' or 'The investigator(s) chose to'.

BOX 14.1 OUR TOP THREE TIPS FOR SUCCESSFULLY WRITING UP CRIMINOLOGICAL RESEARCH

1   Start writing early – we often forget important details about the research if the write-up is left to the last minute. Keeping a journal of the research process will also help here.
2   Get feedback – get this from your supervisor as you go, and reflect on this. Feedback is provided to help you, so don't leave seeking this until the last minute!
3   Remember – a naive reader should be able to follow your report and replicate your findings.

STRUCTURING YOUR DISSERTATION OR RESEARCH REPORT

Spot the difference?

Note the fairly subtle differences between the two contents pages below. These are indicative of the differences often seen in these two types of report. For example, you can see that the qualitative dissertation is 32 pages long, while the quantitative dissertation is only 22 pages long (minus appendices). This could reflect the guidance of different universities on dissertation word length, but in this instance this actually reflects a common difference between qualitative and **quantitative research**: the

a)

Contents	Pages
	4–6
	7–13
	14–19
1. Introduction	
2. Review of Literature	20–26
3. Research Methodology	27–28
4. Discussion of Findings	29–32
5. Conclusion	
6. References	

b)

Literature Review	
Methodology	
Findings	3
Discussion	8
References	11
Appendices	14
	18
	22

Figure 14.1 a) Example contents page from a qualitative dissertation; b) Example contents page from a quantitative dissertation

results sections of quantitative research tend to be shorter, reporting numbers and tables, while qualitative reports typically include much more text.

The other difference you may have spotted relates to the way the findings in each of these dissertations were presented. While the quantitative dissertation included both a findings (or as it is more commonly known, results) section and a discussion section, the qualitative report instead had a 'discussion of findings'. The merits of these two approaches are discussed later in this chapter.

We like to think about the structure of research reports and dissertations a bit like a Victoria sponge cake:

Report Structure

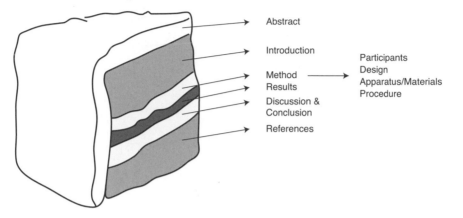

Abstract

Introduction

Method ——————→ Participants
                Design
Results   Apparatus/Materials
                Procedure
Discussion &
Conclusion

References

Figure 14.2 A traditional report structure

The structure above represents a traditional approach to presenting research, based on scientific and quantitative approaches. You may find – particularly if you have conducted a dissertation based on existing data sources, or a qualitative piece of research – that this structure is not appropriate for your work. Instead, you might like to consider the following examples:

EXAMPLE STRUCTURE: SECONDARY RESEARCH-BASED RESEARCH REPORT

Abstract

Introduction

Overview of approach to secondary data selection and analysis

Critical review of secondary data

Final discussion and conclusion

References

Appendices

EXAMPLE STRUCTURE: **QUALITATIVE RESEARCH REPORT**

Abstract

Literature review

Methodology

Discussion of results

Conclusions

References

Appendices

If you have conducted a dissertation based on secondary research, you may wish to follow the structure set out above alongside the guidance in Chapters 5, 10 and 13. We consider each section of the dissertation or research report under the sub-headings below. Remember, you might not include all of these sections as this will depend on the type of research you have done. The key thing is to ensure that your research is presented in a logical way and that a naive reader could follow your report and replicate your findings.

While you should always present your abstract first, this should in fact be the last thing you write as it provides an overview of your research. Because of this you will find details of how to write an abstract after the sections below on writing other sections of your dissertation.

LITERATURE REVIEW

What is it? The literature review provides the rationale for conducting a piece of research including previous research in the area and the current research questions or hypotheses.

The literature review should contain a critical review of (relevant) background material including existing theories and key findings, providing an outline of the exact problem to be researched. Chapter 5 considered the detail of critiquing the literature, and here we provide a brief overview in the context of writing up the dissertation or research report. The literature review section in the write-up should provide a rationale for, and lead directly to, the research questions or hypotheses. You should start broad and become narrower as you reach your research questions or hypotheses. We suggest you think of this like a funnel or upside-down triangle, a bit like this:

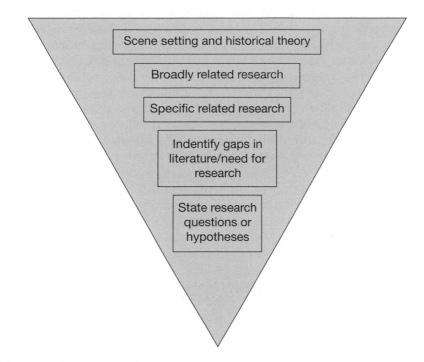

Figure 14.3 Structuring your literature review

You should ensure you explain sufficiently the relevant literature and theory and give a clear picture of why the research is important. Coverage of the literature should be thorough and include the major studies that have been conducted on the topic of interest. A reader will in part judge whether you have covered relevant literature by looking at whether you have cited recent journals articles and whether suitable sources have been used. As you will no doubt already know, references from peer-reviewed journals and books are more credible and add more 'weight' to your arguments than internet-based sources. Key terms should be explained rather than making assumptions about the reader's knowledge.

The literature review should demonstrate a clear and logical development of ideas and it should support the need for the research presented in this dissertation or report. This need for new research – be this primary or secondary research – should be linked to the explicit aims and objectives of your research. The research report does not have to include a formal **hypothesis**, but it should be clear what the purpose of the research is.

METHOD

The method section for qualitative and quantitative research reports will include different things, but should always provide enough detail for the reader to be able to understand

and, in theory, replicate the research. Whether qualitative, quantitative or both, the method section should provide the reader with details of why the research was conducted, what was done, how this was done and with whom. It is also usual to provide details of any ethical considerations and ethics committee approvals. When reporting your research you should always write in the past tense and ensure it is clear what data were used and why, how and why the data were collected, and that the analysis is explained and appropriate. The method should contain sufficient information for the reader to understand and replicate the study exactly as you did it. However, note that it is often very difficult to fully replicate **qualitative research**. For qualitative research the primary importance of providing a detailed methodology is to demonstrate the quality of the data collection and analysis.

The method should be one of the first sections of the report that is written up immediately after the study has finished. It is important to do this as details of what happened in the research can easily be forgotten. In traditional quantitative reports the method is split into the following four principle sections:

- *Design*
  This section should state the type of design that was used (independent measures, repeated measures, mixed or matched subjects), the **independent variables** (IV), and **dependent variables** (DV). This section is not used in qualitative research reports. Instead a qualitative research report may explain the approach to data collection and why this approach was appropriate for this research, and if relevant referencing where such an approach has been used in this way in the past.
- *Participants*
  This section should include the number of participants, the sampling method used, any demographic information (such as age, gender, educational level, occupation) and any other information about the participants specific to the research (for example, offence history).
- *Materials*
  This section describes the materials or tool used to collect the data. In quantitative research this section may include a description of any questionnaires or other data collection tools used. If these are pre-existing (i.e. have been developed and used in other research) then this section should explain this. If they have been designed for this current research the way they were designed should be explained and a link provided to the full version as an appendix. In qualitative research this section might instead be called 'Data collection methods'. Qualitative research using semi-structured interviews might include a description of the interview topics in this section (rather than a list of the questions – these should be included as an appendix).
- *Procedure*
  You should think about the procedure like the instructions for baking a cake (you might have guessed by now that we like cake!). It should describe exactly what was done in the research, how communication with participants was undertaken (including participant recruitment and informed consent). The procedure should be logical and insightful and contain sufficient information for the reader to follow.

It is also useful – vital in qualitative research – to provide details of the approach to data analysis. One risk with qualitative research is that researchers fail to provide sufficient detail of the data analysis methods used. For example, stating 'a **thematic analysis** of the interview transcripts was conducted' does not give the reader anywhere near enough information to understand what was done. The reader should be given details of *how* the analysis was done and what stages the researcher worked through. We suggest you refer back to Chapters 11, 12 and 13 of this book when writing up your approach to data analysis.

RESULTS

Writing up the results section is often one of the most feared parts of the dissertation process. However, this need not be the case, and most students find that once they begin writing this section they actually quite enjoy it! The results section may well differ depending on the type of research you have conducted. As discussed earlier, if you have conducted primary research of a quantitative nature you are likely to have separate results and discussion sections, while if you have conducted qualitative research you may wish to combine these two sections (although you do not have to).

A traditional results section will report the key findings but will not discuss the findings or attempt to explain why these results may have occurred. It will provide a clear and concise summary of the data that was collected and the results of the analysis. In quantitative research the results section should start with descriptive (summary) statistics (e.g. mean, median, range) before reporting any statistical tests. The statistical tests used in the research must be reported.

Remember: each statistical test has its own format for reporting that should be adhered to. This is vital. You should refer back to Chapter 11 for guidance on presenting quantitative analysis.

The results sections of qualitative research may also include some numbers, for example, the number of times that a particular theme occurred in the data. Given this, in both qualitative and quantitative research you may wish to include some graphs and tables. However, only use these where they are meaningful and add something to the overall dissertation and ensure you discuss them clearly.

In qualitative research the results often include examples and quotes from the data. You will know from Chapter 12 that it is vital to provide illustrative examples that highlight the key points within each theme from the data. Refer back to Chapters 12 and 13 for information on presenting qualitative analysis. As mentioned above, qualitative research reports may combine the results and discussion (in a section called 'Discussion of results') and this is covered below.

DISCUSSION

Most research reports have a distinct discussion section. The purpose is to discuss the results of the research, explaining exactly what was found, how we might account for the research findings, and relating the findings back to the literature and theories highlighted in the introduction and/or literature review. Summarising this can help the reader to draw together the different threads of the research and enables the interpretation and explanation of the results. The discussion can also be a place to introduce other research relevant to your findings.

It is often useful to begin the discussion by briefly summarising the findings (if you have conducted quantitative research you should avoid putting any numbers in this section). You should re-explain what was observed and/or examined and/or studied in the research. Discussing the results in the context of existing literature and theory comes next, although how you tackle this will depend upon the nature of your research. If you have conducted secondary research the main part of your dissertation will be a critical discussion. Whatever method of research you adopted, a critical review of your findings in light of the evidence is crucial.

Notice how the examples below (taken from a real undergraduate student dissertation) relate a finding from this qualitative research to the existing literature.

BOX 14.2 EXAMPLE OF RELATING THE FINDINGS TO THE EXISTING LITERATURE

An analysis of the experience of female therapy staff in a therapeutic community prison (Neelama Kumari, 2011)

'Most of the prisoners became infuriated by these situations, and were over-protective of the female staff. Indeed, Petrillo (2007) has found that female staff are perceived to be at high risk. However, Stanko (1990) identified that female staff have knowledge concerning reasonable measures to take for their safety.'

'The participants ensure their clothes 'are not revealing or low necked, and accessories cover bare skin' (Participant 3). Lupton (2000) has found that in just the same way that women prevent discriminatory issues at work, men in 'feminine' jobs will take measures to avoid inappropriate situations.'

Once the results have been summarised and discussed in the context of existing literature and theory, it is good practice to outline the limitations of the current study and provide ideas for future research. When writing this part of the discussion students often fall into the trap of stating things like 'lack of time to conduct the research was a limitation to the study'. Avoid these kinds of statements and instead focus on discussing more thoughtful limitations and ideas. For example, consider whether other data could have been collected to support/add to the findings. You might also want to consider whether the results are likely to be generalisable or restricted to your participant group and how future research might increase generalisability. Generalisation is achieved differently in quantitative and qualitative approaches to research – in the latter it is usually achieved as a result of others picking up where one researcher has left off. The discussion should contain ideas for where future work might be directed.

You should always end your discussion with a conclusion. This might form the end of the discussion, or might even be a separate sub-heading. Look at the example below, taken from a real student dissertation. Note how this conclusion immediately highlights the key finding from the research, before outlining the main results in a clear and concise way. The conclusion then briefly states the relevance of this in light of other research (or the lack of it), and how these results might be applied in the future.

BOX 14.3 EXAMPLE CONCLUSION

Female Alcohol Consumption, Motivations for Aggression and Aggressive Incidents in Licensed Premises (Nikki Williams, 2011)

The most crucial implication resulting from this research is that results suggest that whilst fighters both drink more heavily and spend more time in licensed premises than non-fighters, it is likely that alcohol consumption is the greatest factor involved in licensed premises aggression. Essentially it was also found that women were likely to be intoxicated at the time of licensed premises aggression suggesting that an effective way to reduce these incidents would be an attempt to limit alcohol consumption; for example pubs and clubs could cease very cheap drinks promotions such as happy hours and put greater focus on the promotion of ideas such as spacers and non-alcoholic cocktails. Another chief consideration from this research is that the number of women found to have been involved in licensed premises aggression suggests that women have the potential to be equally aggressive as males, however these women were found to be motivated to acts of aggression by different reasons than those motivators previously reported by men. Research specifically focusing on women's involvement in licensed premises aggression is limited even now and should be developed further. Future research should aim to investigate a wider and more **representative sample** of women than for example solely university students to provide greater levels of ecological validity and could investigate how these implications could be used to reduce licensed premises aggression.

REFERENCES

Your references section should be at the end of the report, before the appendices. As you may already know, criminological researchers use the Harvard referencing system. You will probably find that your own university or university library has a guide to Harvard referencing that you can access. However, you can consult the 'How to write references' guide from Birmingham City University: http://library.bcu.ac.uk/references.pdf

TITLE

We have left discussion of the title towards the end of this chapter because in most circumstances it is best to leave finalising your title until near the end of writing your dissertation or research report.

A title should be both concise and provide the reader with an insight to the research being reported. The key aim of the title is to entice the reader into looking further into the report. The title is the first part of the report a reader will see, therefore it has to be interesting, concise and descriptive.

BOX 14.4 EXAMPLE TITLES: DOMESTIC VIOLENCE

'An investigation of university students' attitudes towards men as the victims of domestic violence'

or

'*Does gender make a difference?* – A study into the effects of victim gender on perceptions of domestic violence'

Either of the above titles is appropriate, although the first is the most conventional form of title writing. This study included an independent variable (IV: victim gender) and a dependent variable (DV: participants' perceptions), and both of these are clear in the title.

The title of a qualitative piece of research might highlight the research question or might relate to key themes from the analysis. The examples below are from an exploratory piece of qualitative research. Again, both titles are appropriate and both provide the reader with sufficient insight into the research.

BOX 14.5 EXAMPLES TITLES: FEMALE PRISON STAFF

'An investigation of the experiences of women working in a therapeutic community prison'

or

'Women in men's prisons: Women's experiences of working in a therapeutic community prison'

ABSTRACT

As mentioned earlier in this chapter, although the abstract is presented as the first section after the title, it should be the last thing you write.

What is it? The abstract is a brief summary of the key points from the research. Like the rest of your dissertation or research report, the abstract should be written in the third person. Abstracts are usually between about 150 and 250 words and should contain:

- a brief statement of the problem being investigated;
- the design used (for experimental research only);
- relevant participant details (e.g. 20 males and 20 females);
- the key measures used (e.g. questionnaires, semi-structured interviews – for primary research only);
- the main results;
- the main conclusions and nature of the discussion;
- reference to a key theory or piece of research if the study is based partly on a replication.

This is a lot to say in not very many words, so you must write the abstract clearly and concisely. Remember, the abstract and the title create the first impressions of your research for the reader.

BOX 14.6 WRITING ABSTRACTS

Below is a real abstract from a student who received a very high mark for her quantitative dissertation.

Example abstract: *Female Alcohol Consumption, Motivations for Aggression and Aggressive Incidents in Licensed Premises* (Nikki Williams, 2011)

Research into the relationship between alcohol and aggression has previously focused on men. However, in recent years there has been an increase in binge drinking and violent crime among women, behaviours which have been labelled 'ladette' culture in the UK. The current study advances the literature in this area by investigating the relationship between alcohol consumption and aggressive behaviour of females in licensed premises, including the type of aggression and motivations for aggressive incidents. Ninety-three female university students completed the Student Alcohol Questionnaire (SAQ; Engs, 2002), the Aggression Questionnaire (Buss & Perry, 1992) and a questionnaire developed to measure self-reported aggressive incidents. Females who had been involved in an aggressive incident reported spending more time on average in licensed premises per week and higher levels of aggression as well as consuming significantly more alcohol on the day or evening of the incident than females who had not been involved in an aggressive incident. Contrary to expectations, however, those who had been involved in an aggressive incident did not report drinking more beer (a male-orientated drink) than those who had not. Verbally aggressive incidents were reported more than physically aggressive incidents, and the most common motivation for becoming involved in an aggressive incident was to address a grievance. The finding that average alcohol consumption per week was a significant predictor of female aggression in licensed premises highlights the importance of developing interventions to reduce alcohol consumption among young females.

This abstract contains all the information we need to know to understand what this article is about and whether it is relevant to us. Let's break this down to take a look at what makes this a good abstract.

Problem being investigated/aims of the study

Research into the relationship between alcohol and aggression has previously focused on men. However, in recent years there has been an increase in binge drinking and violent crime among women, behaviours which have been labelled 'ladette' culture in the UK. The current study advances the literature in this area by investigating the relationship between alcohol consumption and aggressive behaviour of females in licensed premises, including the type of aggression and motivations for aggressive incidents.

This clearly and concisely highlights this area as both a societal issue and an area requiring further research.

Participant details

Ninety-three female university students completed the Student Alcohol Questionnaire (SAQ; Engs, 2002), the Aggression Questionnaire (Buss & Perry, 1992) and a questionnaire developed to measure self-reported aggressive incidents.

This concisely says what the reader needs to know initially about the participants.

Key measures used

Ninety-three female university students *completed the Student Alcohol Questionnaire (SAQ; Engs, 2002), the Aggression Questionnaire (Buss & Perry, 1992) and a questionnaire developed to measure self-reported aggressive incidents.*

Again, note how clear and concise this is. There is no need for any extra information in this abstract on the measures used.

Key results

Females who had been involved in an aggressive incident reported spending more time on average in licensed premises per week and higher levels of aggression as well as consuming significantly more alcohol on the day or evening of the incident than females who had not been involved in an aggressive incident. Contrary to expectations, however, those who had been involved in an aggressive incident did not report drinking more beer (a male-orientated drink) than those who had not. Verbally aggressive incidents were reported more than physically aggressive incidents, and the most common motivation for becoming involved in an aggressive incident was to address a grievance.

This tells us all of the key results from the study, including what the student researcher did not expect to find.

Nature of discussion

The finding that average alcohol consumption per week was a significant predictor of female aggression in licensed premises highlights the importance of developing interventions to reduce alcohol consumption among young females.

This hints at the wider social relevance of the findings, which we can expect to see discussed at the end of the dissertation.

NOW THAT YOU'VE WRITTEN YOUR RESEARCH REPORT . . .

Now that you've written your research report, we suggest you work through the ten-point checklist below. If you answer 'no' to any of these questions, you should revisit the relevant part of your report, and perhaps discuss this with your supervisor. Keep in mind that some of these questions do not apply unless you have conducted primary research.

	Checklist	Yes	No
1	Do the title and abstract clearly reflect the content of the dissertation?		
2	Is the 'problem' that the research addresses clearly stated? *This might be a societal issue that led to the research, or a gap in the research literature.*		
3	Is there a clearly defined purpose? *Usually the purpose leads directly on from the 'problem'. This is usually expressed either through a testable hypothesis (quantitative research) or clear research questions (qualitative and secondary research).*		
4	Were the data-gathering techniques you used appropriate and fully explained?		

	Checklist	Yes	No
5	Was the sample included in the research appropriate and able to provide information relevant to investigating the 'problem'?		
6	Were the data analysis techniques you used appropriate and suitably explained? *Ensure it is clear why these were the best methods and provide references for this.*		
7	Do the results you have reported fully reflect the analysis? *You should not have included anything that is not supported by the analysis.*		
8	Does your interpretation of the results really make sense and fully reflect the data?		
9	Have you discussed your findings in light of the existing, relevant literature?		
10	Have you highlighted any significant limitations to the research, how these could be overcome in future research, and – if appropriate – the relevance of this research to wider society?		

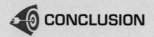 CONCLUSION

Conducting robust, methodologically sound research is vital. However, the value of robust research can be lost if the research is not written up well. If a reader cannot follow why the research was done, what was done, what was found and the meaning of this, then the researcher has failed in their duty. Following a clear structure – usually provided by your university department, and likely similar to what you have read in this chapter – will help you go a long way towards producing a good research report or dissertation.

⚜ KEY LEARNING POINTS

- The primary duty of researchers when writing up research is to communicate effectively to the reader. A failure to clearly communicate the research conducted can render even the most high quality research almost worthless.
- There are some subtle – and some not so subtle – differences in the structure and reporting of primary and secondary research. Within primary research differences also exist in how researchers can best write up quantitative and qualitative research.
- Each distinct section of the research report or dissertation is important to the overall piece of work. Each section should fulfil its purpose and provide a clear link to the other sections in the write-up.
- It is useful to work through a 'research checklist' after you have written up your research report or dissertation to help you think critically about the quality and appropriateness of what you have written.

The student dissertations discussed in this chapter were of such high quality that they were written up as journal articles with the students' supervisor and a lecturer from another university. If you would like to read these articles you can find them using the following references:

Kumari, N., Caulfield, L. S. and Newberry, M. (2012) 'The experiences of women working in a therapeutic community prison', *Prison Service Journal*, 20: 7–11.

Newberry, M., Williams, N. and Caulfield, L. S. (2013) 'Aggression in Females: Does Alcohol Consumption Make a Difference?', *Aggressive Behaviors*, 38: 1844–51.

GLOSSARY

Absolute relativism   When used in the context of research ethics this term refers to the view that there are no moral rights and wrongs, that is, what is right for some people can be understood to be wrong by others. Absolute relativism can be very problematic as it can lead to the position where oppressive practices can be justified.

Bivariate relationship   A relationship between two variables.

Classicism   A school of criminological thought based upon the work of Beccaria (1738–94) which assumes that people have free will to choose criminal or lawful solutions to their problems. It advocates swift punishment as a deterrent in order to make crime unattractive and illogical.

Closed questions   Questions that can only be answered from a set of specified answers.

Common sense   Knowledge that is generally taken for granted and which, therefore, is the most difficult to disrupt.

Consequentialism   A branch of ethics that highlights the need to consider the consequences of our ethical decisions in order to weigh up benefits against harms.

Correlation   A relationship between one phenomenon and another/others such that one impacts the other in either a positive or negative direction.

Critical criminological research   This is a theory of knowledge which aims to provide theoretical understanding of the mechanisms through which we make sense of crime in society in order to bring about changes to policy or to our modes of thinking about crime.

Deduction   An approach to data gathering associated with logical positivism that begins with theories and reaches conclusions by testing out these theories (hypothesis testing).

Denaturalism   A mode of transcription where pauses are removed, grammar corrected and even non-standard accents standardised.

Dependent variable   A term used in research to describe a phenomenon, such as theft, that might be brought about by something else (an **independent variable)** such as unemployment.

Determinism   A philosophical position that asserts a necessary relationship between one thing (e.g. biology) and another (e.g. criminal behaviour).

Dialectical analysis   A process of looking beyond surface appearances in order to attempt explanations of why some things are not questioned. The process requires researchers to ask questions and provide answers that demonstrate the contradictions within the surface appearance in order to effect change in thinking and or policy.

Dialogic interview   A technique used by feminist researchers that gave the participants more control of the interview process by allowing them to lead the 'conversation' and challenge the privileged voice of the researcher by asking questions of the interviewer.

Discourse analysis   The analysis of many forms of verbal and written materials with the purpose of examining how meanings can be hidden or how meanings function.

Documentary data   Secondary data that is derived from official documents such as government or company records; newspapers; journals, books or social media, etc.

Epistemology   The study of knowledge and how knowledge can be gained.

Ethnography   Usually the term used to describe complete participant observation in which the researcher takes on a covert role and becomes part of the community to be studied.

Ethnomethodology   An approach to research that is based on the work of the American sociologist Garfinkel. It entails the study of people's methods of making sense of their everyday lives in a variety of social contexts. In criminological research this type of research has been used to make sense of sentencing decisions.

Hegemony   The dominance or leadership of one social group, nation or set of ideas over others.

Hypothesis   A provisional theory or proposition that can be tested.

Independent variable   a term used in research to describe a phenomenon that may explain another social phenomenon (e.g. poverty might explain some types of crime).

Induction   An approach to data gathering that claims to begin with facts and derive theories from those facts.

Interpretivism   In the study of crime this term refers to a theory of knowledge (or epistemology) that is concerned with people's subjective understanding of their life experiences.

Interval data   This term refers to the relationships between values. For example, the temperature difference between 29 and 30 degrees Centigrade is the same size as the difference between 4 and 5 degrees Centigrade. While data from attitudinal scales and Likert scales are typically ordinal, they are often treated like interval data in statistical analysis.

Marketisation   A process through which market forces are imposed upon services that were previously public.

Naturalism   A mode of transcription where every utterance and pause are transcribed.

Nominal data   This term refers to categories that are separate to others, such as the name of your university, the gender of your participants, the name of a research methods book, or hair colour. You can remember this easily as nominal sounds like name.

Non-parametric test   Statistical procedures that do not rely on assumptions about the shape or parameters of the underlying population distribution and which is less powerful than the parametric test.

Ontology   The study of the nature of 'being', reality or existence.

Open questions   Questions that provide research participants with the freedom to answer in their own words.

Ordinal data   This term refers to numerical data, usually quantities that have a natural order. The easiest example of this is the place runners finish in a race   first, second, third and so on. The most usual type of ordinal data we deal with in criminological research are choices on a Likert scale.

Parametric tests   Statistical procedures suitable for use when assumptions about the distribution of the underlying population from which the sample was taken are met   typically that data are approximately normally distributed. Parametric tests are more powerful than non-parametric tests and allow us to have more confidence in our statistical analysis.

Plagiarism   The appropriation of someone else's words or ideas as your own.

Positivism   In the study of crime this term refers to a theory of knowledge that follows closely a deductive natural science approach to research.

Qualitative research   An approach to research that focuses upon the gathering of in-depth data through which meaning can be derived.

Quantitative research   A systematic approach to research that relies upon statistical analysis.

Reflexivity   A process through which researchers reflect upon their own beliefs and values in order to elucidate their role in the process of gaining knowledge.

Representative sample   A small group of research participants whose characteristics accurately reflect those of the larger population from which it is drawn.

Secondary data   Data that is not derived from original sources but rather from the work of others. This data is unlikely to have been collected for the same purpose as the criminological researcher.

Social construction   A concept that appears obvious to those who accept it but that may be open to question. For example crime is a social construct and what is to count as crime in our society is embodied in the law. However, there may not always be agreement as to what actions should be defined as criminal.

Spurious relationship   A claimed relationship between two variables that turns out to be false or misleading

Symbolic Interactionism   A theoretical approach in sociology or social psychology which focuses upon the ways in which human beings behave towards things in ways that reflect the meanings that they give to them. Meanings are derived socially and will be modified through processes of interpretation.

Thematic analysis   This is one of the most commonly used methods of qualitative data analysis, and a method that is not dependant on specific theory or approaches to data collection. Through in-depth analysis this method allows for key themes from the data to emerge. In this way thematic analysis is suitable for most types of qualitative data.

Universalism   When used in the context of research ethics this term refers to the idea that there can be agreement amongst all about ethical decision-making.

Vignette   A research technique which involves the researcher presenting a short summary of a scenario that is designed in such a way as to invite comment from the participant/s. Vignettes are often followed by some questions that are designed to draw out the participants' views.

REFERENCES

Alexander, C. (2000) *The Asian Gang Ethnicity, Identity, Masculinity,* Oxford: Berg.

Alexander, V. D., Thomas, H., Cronin, A., Fielding, J. and Moran-Ellis, J. (2008) 'Mixed Methods', in N. Gilbert (ed.) *Researching Social Life*, third edition, London: Sage, pp. 125–44.

Altheide, D. (2004) 'Ethnographic Content Analysis', in M. Lewis-Beck, A. Bryman and T. Futing Liao (eds) *Encyclopedia of Social Science Research Methods*, Thousand Oaks, CA: Sage.

American Correctional Association (1990) *The Female Offender: What Does the Future Hold?*, Washington: American Correctional Association.

Andrews, D. A. and Bonta, J. (1995) *The Level of Service Inventory – Revised,* Toronto: Multi-Health Systems Inc.

Becker, H. S. (1963) *Outsiders: Studies in the Sociology of Deviance*, London: Macmillan.

Beins, B. C. (2004) *Research Methods: A Tool for Life,* London: Pearson Education.

Bell, J. and Opie, C. (2002) *Learning from Research,* fifth edition, Buckingham: Open University Press.

Bennett, T. and Holloway, K. (2004) 'Gang Membership, Drugs and Crime in the UK', *British Journal of Criminology,* 44(3): 305–23.

Berg, B. L. (2004) *Qualitative Research Methods for the Social Sciences,* fifth edition, London: Pearson.

Blagden, N. and Pemberton, S. (2010) 'The Challenge in Conducting Qualitative Research with Convicted Sex Offenders', *Howard Journal of Criminal Justice,* 49(3): 203–13.

Blauner, R. and Wellman, D. (1988) 'Toward the Decolonization of Research', in J. A. Ladner, *The Death of White Sociology: Essays on Race and Culture,* Baltimore: Black Classic Press.

Box, S. (1983) *Crime, Power and Mystification,* London: Routledge.

Boyatzis, R. (1998) *Transforming Qualitative Information: Thematic Analysis and Code Development,* Thousand Oaks, CA: Sage.

Braun, V. and Clarke, V. (2006) 'Using thematic analysis in psychology', *Qualitative Research in Psychology,* 3(2): 77–101.

Bringer, J. D., Johnston, L. H. and Brakenridge, C. H. (2004) 'Maximising Transparency in a Doctoral Thesis: The Complexities of Writing About the Use of QSR*NVIVO Within a Grounded Theory Study', *Qualitative Research,* 4(2): 247–65.

Bryman, A. (2008) *Social Research Methods,* third edition, Oxford: Oxford University Press.

Burman, E., Smailes, S. L. and Chantler, K. (2004) *Critical Social Policy,* 24(3): 332–57.

Burnett, J. (2011) 'Reshaping the Criminal Justice System After the Riots' (available at: http://www.irr.org.uk/news/reshaping-the-criminal-justice-system-after-the-riots/).

Burrell, G. and Morgan, G. (1992) *Sociological Paradigms and Organisational Analysis,* Aldershot: Ashgate Publishing.

Calvey, D. (2008) 'The Art and Politics of Covert Research: Doing Situated Ethics in the Field', *Sociology*, 42(5): 905–18.

Cameron, A. (2006) 'Stopping the Violence: Canadian Feminist Debates on Restorative Justice and Intimate Violence', *Theoretical Criminology*, 10(1): 46–96.

Carlen, P. (1992) 'Criminal Women and Criminal Justice: The Limits to, and Potential of, Feminist and Left Realist Perspectives', in J. Young and R. Matthews, *Issues in Realist Criminology*, London: Sage.

Carlen, P. and Worrall, A. (2004) *Analysing Women's Imprisonment*, Cullompton: Willan.

Carrabine, E., Lee, M., South, N., Cox, P. and Plummer, K. (2009) *Criminology: A Sociological Introduction*, London: Routledge.

Caulfield, L. S. (2012) *Life Histories of Women Who Offend: A Study of Women in English Prisons*, PhD thesis, Loughborough University.

Caulfield, L. S. and Twort, H. (2012) 'Implementing change: Staff experiences of changes to prison mental healthcare in England and Wales', *International Journal of Prisoner Health*, 8(1): 7–15.

Caulfield, L. S. and Wilkinson, D. J. (2014) *Forensic Psychology*, Harlow: Pearson.

Centre for Social Justice (2007) 'Breakthrough Britain: Ending the Costs of Social Breakdown,' Volume 1 available at: http://www.centreforsocialjustice.org.uk/client/downloads/family%20 breakdown.pdf (accessed 14 August 2012).

Chalmers, A. F. (2004) *What is This Thing Called Science?*, third edition, Buckingham: Open University Press.

Charmaz, K. (1983) 'The Grounded Theory Method: An Explication and Interpretation', in R. M. Emerson, *Contemporary Field Research: A Collection of Readings*, Boston, MA: Little Brown.

Colman, A. M., Norris, C. E. and Preston, C. C. (1997) 'Comparing Rating Scales of Different Lengths: Equivalence of Scores from 5-point and 7-point Scales', *Psychological Reports*, 80(2): 355–62.

Cowburn, M. (2004) Quote cited in Mills, J. (2004) '"There's a Lot in Those Keys Isn't There?" The Experience of a Female Researcher Researching Rape in a Male Prison Undertaking the Research as a Key Holder', in G. Mesko, M. Pagon and B. Dobovsek (eds) *Policing in Central and Eastern Europe – Dilemmas of Contemporary Criminal Justice*, Ljubljana: Faculty of Criminal Justice, University of Maribor.

Cowburn, M. (2007) 'Men Researching Men in Prison: The Challenges for Pro-Feminist Research', *Howard Journal*, 46(3): 276–88.

Crighton, D. (2006) 'Methodological Issues in Psychological Research in Prisons', in G. J. Towl, *Psychological Research in Prisons*, Oxford: BPS Blackwell.

Currie, E. (2007) 'Against Marginality: Arguments for a Public Criminology', *Theoretical Criminology*, 11(2): 175–90.

Daly, K. and Stephens, D. J. (1995) 'The Dark Figure of Criminology: Towards a Black and Multi-ethnic Feminist Agenda for Theory and Research', in N. H. Rafter and F. Heidensohn, *International Feminist Perspectives in Criminology: Engendering a Discipline*, Buckingham: Open University Press.

Daly, K. and Stubbs, J. (2006) 'Feminist Engagement with Restorative Justice', *Theoretical Criminology*, 10(1): 9–28.

Darlington, Y. and Scott, D. (2002) *Qualitative Research in Practice: Stories From the Field*, Buckingham: Open University Press.

Denscombe, M. (2002) *Ground Rules for Good Research: A Ten-Point Guide for Social Researchers*, Buckingham: Open University Press.

Denzin, N. K. (1989) *Interpretive Biography*. Newberry Park: Sage.

Ditton, J. (1977) *Part-Time Crime,* London: Macmillan.

Dodd, V. (2012) 'Metropolitan Police "Buried" Report in 2004 Warning of Race Scandal', *Guardian,* 6 April.

Downes, D. and Rock, P. (2007) *Understanding Deviance,* fifth edition, Oxford: Oxford University Press.

Durkheim, E. (1970) *Suicide: A Study in Sociology,* London: Routledge and Kegan Paul.

Durkheim, E. (1982) *The Rules of Sociological Method,* ed. Stephen Lukes, London: Macmillan.

Edwards, A. and Sheptycki, J. (2009) 'Third Wave Criminology: Guns, Crime and Social Order', *Criminology and Criminal Justice,* 9(3): 379–97.

Enosh, G. and Buchbinder, E. (2005) 'The Interactive Construction of Narrative Styles in Sensitive Interviews: The Case of Domestic Violence', *Qualitative Inquiry,* 11(4): 588–617.

Fairclough, N. L. and Wodak, R. (1997) 'Critical discourse analysis', in T. A. van Dijk (ed.) *Discourse Studies. A Multidisciplinary Introduction, Vol. 2. Discourse as Social Interaction,* London: Sage, pp. 258–84.

Fielding N. G. and Lee R. M. (1998) *Computer Analysis and Qualitative Research,* London: Sage.

Fine, M. and Weis, L. (1998) 'Crime Stories: A Critical Look Through Race, Ethnicity and Gender', *Qualitative Studies in Education,* 11(3): 435–59.

Firestone, S. (1970) *The Dialectic of Sex: The Case for Feminist Revolution,* New York: William Morrow and Company.

Flick, U. (2009) *An Introduction to Qualitative Research,* fourth edition, London: Sage.

Galton, F. (1883) *Inquiries into Human Faculty and its Development,* London: Macmillan.

Garland, D. (1994) 'Of Crimes and Criminals: The Development of Criminology in Britain', in M. Maguire, R. Morgan and R. Reiner (eds) *The Oxford Handbook of Criminology,* Oxford, Clarendon Press.

Garland, D. and Sparks, R. (2000) 'Criminology, Social Theory and the Challenge of our Times', *British Journal of Criminology,* 40(2): 189–204.

Gau, J. (2013) *Statistics for Criminology and Criminal Justice,* Thousand Oaks, CA: Sage.

Genders, E. and Player, E. (1995) *Grendon: A Therapeutic Prison,* Oxford: Clarendon Press.

Giddens, A. (1979) *Central Problems in Social Theory,* London: Macmillan.

Giddens, A. (1990) *Essays in Social Theory,* Cambridge: Polity.

Gill, M. and Spriggs, A. (2005) 'Assessing the Impact of CCTV', *Home Office Research Study 292,* Development and Statistics Directorate, www.cctvusergroup.com/downloads/Martin%20gill.pdf

Glaser, B. G. (1992) *Basics of Grounded Theory: Emergence vs. Forcing,* Mill Valley: Sociology Press.

Gold, R. (1958) 'Roles in Sociological Field Observation', *Social Forces,* 36(3): 217–23.

Gray, D. and Kinnear, P. (2011) *IBM SPSS Statistics 19 made simple,* London: Psychology Press.

Groombridge, N. (2008) 'Stars of CCTV? How the Home Office Wasted Millions – A Radical "Treasury Audit Commission" View', *Surveillance and Society,* 5(1): 73–80.

Hall, S., Critcher, C., Clarke, J. and Roberts, B. (1978) *Policing the Crisis: Mugging, The State and Law and Order,* London: Macmillan.

Harding, S. (1991) *Whose Science? Whose Knowledge?: Thinking From Women's Lives,* Buckingham: Open University Press.

Harvey, J. (2008) 'An Embedded Multimethod Approach to Prison Research', in R. D. King and E. Wincup (eds) *Doing Research on Crime and Justice,* Oxford: Oxford University Press.

Harvey, L., MacDonald, M. and Hill, J. (2000) *Theories and Methods,* London: Hodder and Stoughton.

Heidensohn, F. (1985) *Women and Crime,* New York: New York University Press.

Herek, G. M., Cogan, J. C. and Gillis, R. J. (2003) 'Victim Experiences in Hate Crime Based on Sexual Orientation', in B. Perry (ed.), *Hate and Bias Crimes: A Reader,* London: Routledge, pp. 243–59.

Herrnstein, R. J. and Murray, C. (1994) *The Bell Curve: Intelligence and Class Structure in American Life,* New York: Free Press Publications.

Hill, J. (1999) *The Discourse of Inter-agency Co-operation: Towards Critical Understanding of the Theory and Practice of Child Protection Work,* University of Keele, PhD thesis.

Hill, J. (2007) 'Daring to Dream: Towards an Understanding of Young Black People's Reflections Post-custody', *Youth Justice,* 7(1): 37–51.

Hillyard. P., Sim, J., Tombs, S. and Whyte, D. (2004) 'Leaving a Stain Upon the Silence: Contemporary Criminology and the Politics of Dissent', *British Journal of Criminology,* 44(3): 369–90.

Holdaway, S. (1983) *Inside the British Police: A Force at Work,* Oxford: Blackwell.

Howitt, D. (2011) *Introduction to Qualitative Methods in Psychology,* Harlow: Prentice Hall.

Howitt, D. and Cramer, D. (2008) *Introduction to Research Methods in Psychology,* Harlow: Pearson.

Howitt, D. and Cramer, D. (2011a) *Introduction to Research Methods in Psychology,* third edition, Harlow: Prentice Hall.

Howitt, D. and Cramer, D. (2011b) *SPSS in Psychology,* Harlow: Pearson.

Hsieh, H.-F. and Shannon, S. E. (2005) 'Three Approaches to Qualitative Content Analysis', *Qualitative Health Research,* 15(9): 1277–88.

Humphreys, C. and Thiara, R. K. (2003) 'Neither Justice nor Protection: Women's Experiences of Post-separation Violence', *Journal of Social Welfare and Family Law,* 25(3): 195–214.

Hutchinson, A. J., Johnston, L. H. and Breckon, J. D. (2010) 'Using QSR-NVivo to Facilitate the Development of a Grounded Theory Project: An Account of a Worked Example', *International Journal of Research Methodology,* 13(4): 283–302.

Jacobs, B. J. (2006) 'The Case for Dangerous Fieldwork', in Hobbs, D. and Wright, R. (eds) *The Sage Handbook of Fieldwork,* London: Sage.

Jansson, I., Hesse, M. and Fridell, M. (2008) 'Validity of Self-reported Criminal Justice System Involvement in Substance Abusing Women at Five-Year Follow-Up', *BMJ Psychiatry,* 8(2): 1–8.

Jewkes, Y. (2011) *Crime and the Media,* second edition, London: Sage.

Johnson, H., Keen, S. and Pritchard, D. (2011) *Unlocking Value: The Economic Value of the Arts in Criminal Justice,* London: New Philanthropy Capital.

Jones, S. (2008) 'Partners in Crime: A Study of Female Offenders and their Co-defendants', *Criminology and Criminal Justice,* 8(2): 147–64.

Juby, H. and Farrington, D. P. (2001) 'Disentangling the Link Between Disrupted Families and Delinquency', *British Journal of Criminology,* 41(1): 22–40.

Jupp, V. and Norris, C. (1993) 'Traditions in Documentary Analysis', in M. Hammersley (ed.) *Social Research: Philosophy, Politics and Practice,* London: Sage.

Katz, J. (1988) *Seductions of Crime,* New York: Basic Books.

Kelly, L. with Bindel, J., Burton, S., Butterworth, D., Cook, K. and Regan, L. (1999) *Domestic Violence Matters: An Evaluation of a Development Project,* London: Home Office.

King, N. and Horrocks, C. (2010) *Interviews in Qualitative Research,* London: Sage.

King, R. D. (2000) 'Doing Research in Prisons,' in R. D. King and E. Wincup (eds) *Doing Research on Crime and Justice,* Oxford: Oxford University Press.

King, R. D. and Leibling, A. (2008) 'Doing Research in Prisons', in R. D. King and E. Wincup (eds) *Doing Research on Crime and Justice,* Oxford: Oxford University Press.

King, R. D. and Wincup, E. (2008) 'The Process of Criminological Research', in R. D. King and E. Wincup (eds) *Doing Research on Crime and Justice,* Oxford: Oxford University Press.

Kirby, S. L., Greaves, L. and Reid, C. (2006) *Experience, Research and Social Change: Methods Beyond the Mainstream,* Toronto: Broadview.

Kitsuse, J. (1962) 'Social Reaction to Deviance: Problems of Theory and Method', *Social Problems,* 9: 247–56.

Klein, D. (1973) 'The Etiology of Female Crime' reproduced in J. Muncie, E. McLaughlin and M. Langan (eds) (1996) *Criminological Perspectives: A Reader,* London: Sage.

Kumari, N., Caulfield, L. S. and Newberry, M. (2012) 'The Experiences of Women Working in a Therapeutic Community Prison', *Prison Service Journal,* 201: 7–11.

Lacombe, D. (2008) 'Consumed with Sex: The Treatment of Sex Offenders in Risk Society', *British Journal of Criminology,* 48(1): 55–74.

Lankford, A. (2013) 'Mass Shooters in the USA, 1966–2010: Differences Between Attackers Who Live and Die', *Justice Quarterly,* Online First.

Lee, R. M. and Fielding, N. G. (1991) 'Computing for Qualitative Research: Options, Problems and Potential', in N.G. Fielding and R. M. Lee, *Using Computers in Qualitative Research*, London: Sage.

Leibling, A. (1992) *Suicides in Prison,* London: Routledge.

Leigey, M. E. and Reed, K. L. (2010) 'A Woman's Life Before Serving Life: Examining the Negative Pre-Incarceration Life Events of Female Life-Sentenced Inmates', *Women & Criminal Justice,* 20(4): 302–22.

Lewins, A. and Silver, C. (2005) *Choosing a CAQDAS Package: A Working Paper,* University of Surrey: CAQDAS Networking Project.

Lilly, J. R., Cullen, F. T. and Ball, R. A. (2011) *Criminological Theory: Context and Consequences*, London: Sage.

Lincoln, Y. S. and Cannella, G. S. (2004) 'Qualitative Research, Power and the Radical Right', *Qualitative Inquiry,* 10(2): 175–201.

Lloyd, A. (1995) *Doubly Deviant, Doubly Damned: Society's Treatment of Violent Women,* London: Penguin Books.

Lockyer, K. and Chambers, M. (2013) *Future Prisons: A Radical Plan to Reform the Prison Estate,* London: Policy Exchange.

Lombroso, C. (1876) *L'Uomo Delinquente,* fifth edition, Turrin: Bocca.

Lombroso, C. (1920) *The Female Offender,* New York: Appleton.

Lukes, S. (2005) *Power: A Radical View,* second edition, Basingstoke: Palgrave Macmillan.

MacLeod, M. and Saraga, E. (1988) 'Challenging the Orthodoxy: Towards Feminist Theory and Praxis', *Feminist Review,* 28, Spring: 16–55.

McNeil, P. (1997) 'Paying People to Participate in Research: Why Not?', *Bioethics,* 11: 390–6.

Mann, N. (2012) 'Ageing Child Sex Offenders in Prison: Denial, Manipulation and Community', *Howard Journal of Criminal Justice,* 51(4): 345–58.

Matthews, B. and Ross, L. (2010) *Research Methods: A Practical Guide for the Social Sciences,* London: Longman.

Matza, D. (1964) *Delinquency and Drift,* New York: Wiley.

Mawby, R. C. and Gisby, W. (2009) 'Crime Fears in an Expanding European Union: Just Another Moral Panic?', *The Howard Journal,* 48(1): 37–51.

May, T. (2001) *Social Research: Issues, Methods and Process,* Buckingham: Open University Press.

Mead, G. H. (1934) *Mind, Self and Society,* London and Chicago: Chicago University Press.

Milgram, S. (1963) 'Behavioral Study of Obedience', *Journal of Abnormal and Social Psychology,* 67(4): 371–8.

Mills, J. (2004) 'There's a Lot in Those Keys Isn't There?' The Experience of a Female Researcher Researching Rape in a Male Prison Undertaking the Research as a Key Holder, National Criminal Justice Reference Service: US Department of Justice.

Moore, L. (2011) 'The Convention on the Rights of the Child Comes of Age: Assessing Progress in Meeting the Rights of Children in Custody in Northern Ireland', Northern Ireland Legal Quarterly, 62(2): 217–34.

Morgan, S. (1999) 'Prison Lives: Critical Issues in Reading Prisoner Autobiography', Howard Journal of Criminal Justice, 38(5): 328–40.

Muncie, J. (1998) 'Reassessing Competing Paradigms in Criminological Theory', in P. Walton and J. Young (eds) The New Criminology Revisited, Basingstoke: Macmillan.

Nancarrow, H. (2006) 'In Search of Justice for Domestic and Family Violence: Indigenous and Non-Indigenous Australian Women's Perspectives', Theoretical Criminology, 10(1): 87–106.

Nee, C. (2004) 'The Offender's Perspective on Crime: Methods and Principles in Data Collection', in A. Needs and G. Towl (eds) Applying Psychology to Forensic Practice, Oxford: BPS Blackwell.

Neuman, W. L. (2006) Social Research Methods, sixth edition, Boston, MA: Pearson International.

Neuman, W. L. (2011) Social Research Methods, seventh edition, Boston, MA: Pearson International.

Newberry, M., Williams, N. and Caulfield, L. S. (2013) 'Aggression in Females: Does Alcohol Consumption Make a Difference?', Aggressive Behaviors, 38(3): 1844–51.

Nicholas, S., Kershaw, C. and Walker, A. (2007) Crime in England and Wales 2006/7, fourth edition, London: Home Office.

Noaks, L. and Wincup, E. (2004) Criminological Research: Understanding Qualitative Methods, London: Sage.

Nutt, D. (2009) 'Estimating Drug Harms: A Risky Business?', Eve Saville Lecture Centre for Crime and Justice Studies, October 2009, http://citeseerx.ist.psu.edu/viewdoc/download?doi=10.1. 1.183.2355&rep=rep1&type=pdf (accessed 12 August 2012).

O'Leary, Z. (2010) The Essential Guide to Doing Your Research Project, London: Sage.

O'Mahony, P. (2009) 'The Risk Factors Prevention Paradigm and the Causes of Youth Crime: A Deceptively Useful Analysis?', Youth Justice, 9(2): 99–114.

O'Malley, P. (2010) Crime and Risk, London: Sage.

Oakley, A. (2002) Gender on Planet Earth, Cambridge: Polity.

Oliver, D. G., Serovich, J. M. and Mason, T. L. (2005) 'Constraints and Opportunities with Interview Transcription: Towards Reflection in Qualitative Research', Social Forces, 84(2): 1273–89.

Parker, H. (1974) View from the Boys, Newton Abbott: David and Charles.

Parton, N. (1991) Governing the Family, London: Macmillan.

Phoenix, J. (2000) 'Prostitute Identities: Men, Women and Violence', British Journal of Criminology, 40(1): 37–55.

Piper, H. (2005) 'Ethical Responsibility in Social Research: Stories From the Field' in B. Somekh and C. Lewin (eds) Research Methods in the Social Sciences, London: Sage.

Pole, C. and Lampard, R. (2002) Practical Social Investigation: Qualitative and Quantitative Methods in Social Research, Harlow: Prentice Hall.

Popper, K. R. (1980) The Logic of Scientific Discovery, tenth impression (revised) edition, London: Unwin Hyman Ltd.

Prison Link (2007) Prison link homepage (available at: http://prisonlink.co.uk/).

Punch, M. (2009) *Police Corruption: Deviance, Accountability and Reform in Policing,* Cullompton: Willan.

Qureshi, F. and Farrell, G. (2006) 'Stop and Search in 2004: A Survey of Police Officers Views and Experiences', *International Journal of Police Science and Management,* 8(2): 83–103.

Ramesh, R. (2012) 'Winterbourne View Abuse: Last Staff Member Pleads Guilty', *Guardian,* 12 August.

Rumney, P. (2008) 'Policing Male Rape and Sexual Assault', *Journal of Criminal Law,* 72(1): 67–86.

Sanders, B. (2005) 'In the Club: Ecstasy Use and Supply in a London Nightclub', *Sociology,* 39(2): 241–58.

Sapsford, R. and Jupp, V. (1996) *Data Collection and Analysis,* London: Sage.

Scheper-Hughes, N. (2004) 'Parts Unknown: Undercover Ethnography of the Organs-trafficking Underworld', *Ethnography,* 5(1): 29–73.

Simmel, G. (1908) *The Metropolis and Mental Life*, Dresden: Peterman.

Smart, C. (1989) *Feminism and the Power of the Law*, London: Routledge.

Smith, C. and Wincup, E. (2000) 'Breaking In: Researching Criminal Justice Institutions for Women', in R. D. King and E. Wincup (eds) *Doing Research on Crime and Justice*, Oxford: Oxford University Press.

Smith, R. (2006) 'Actuarialism and Early Intervention in Contemporary Youth Justice', in B. Goldson and J. Muncie, *Youth Crime and Justice,* London: Sage.

Somekh, B. and Lewin, C. (2009) *Research Methods in the Social Sciences,* London: Sage.

Sparks, R., Bottoms, A. E. and Hay, W. (1996) *Prisons and the Problem of Order*, Oxford: Clarendon Press.

SRA (2003) *Ethical Guidelines,* http://the-sra.org.uk/wp-content/uploads/ethics03.pdf (accessed 18 November 2013)

Stout, B., Yates, J. and Williams, B. (2008) *Applied Criminology,* London: Sage.

Strauss, A. L. and Corbin, J. (1998) *Basics of Qualitative Research: Grounded Theory Procedures and Techniques,* London: Sage.

Taylor, I., Walton, P. and Young, J. (1973) *The New Criminology: For a Social Theory of Deviance,* London: Routledge.

Teo, P. (2000) 'Racism in the News: A Critical Discourse Analysis of News Reporting in Two Australian Newspapers', *Discourse and Society,* 1(1): 7–49.

Tesch, R. (1990) *Qualitative Research: Analysis Types and Software Tools*, London: Falmer Press.

Tesch, R. (1991) 'Software for Qualitative Researcher's Analysis Needs and Program Capabilities', in N. G. Fielding and R. M. Lee, *Using Computers in Qualitative Research*, London: Sage.

Tewksbury, R. and Gagne, P. (1997) 'Assumed and Presumed Identities: Problems of Self-presentation in Field Research', *Sociological Spectrum,* 17: 127–55.

Tierney, J. (2010) *Criminology: Theory and Context,* Harlow: Longman.

Tierney, W. (1999) 'Writing Life's History', *Qualitative Inquiry,* 5(3): 307–12.

Tombs, S. and Whyte, D. (2006) 'Corporate Crime', in E. McLaughlin and J. Muncie (eds) *The Sage Dictionary of Criminology*, second edition, London: Sage.

Valier, C. (2002) *Theories of Crime and Punishment,* Harlow: Longman.

Weaver, A. and Atkinson, P. (1995) *Microcomputing and Qualitative Data Analysis*, Aldershot: Avebury.

Weitzman, E. A. and Miles, M. B. (1995) *Computer Programs for Qualitative Data Analysis*, Thousand Oaks, CA: Sage.

White, R. and Haines, F. (2004) *Crime and Criminology: An Introduction,* third edition, Oxford: Oxford University Press.

Williams, L. M. (1994) 'Memories of Child Sexual Abuse: A Response to Lindsay and Read', *Applied Cognitive Psychology,* 8: 379–87.

Wilson, D. (2010) 'News of the Screws: A Critical Analysis of Some Recent Prison Officer Autobiographies', *The Prison Service Journal,* 188: 3–9.

Wilson, D. and Jones, T. (2008) 'In My Own World: A Case Study of a Paedophile's Thinking and Doing and His Use of the Internet', *Howard Journal of Criminal Justice,* 47(2): 107–20.

Wilson, D. and O'Sullivan, S. (2004) *Images of Incarceration: Representations of Prison Film and Television Drama,* Winchester: Waterside Press.

Wilson, D., Yardley, E. and Lynes, A. (2013) 'A Taxonomy of Male British Family Annihilators, 1980–2013', *The Howard Journal,* online early view.

Wilson, J. Q. and Herrnstein, R. (1985) *Crime and Human Nature,* New York: Simon and Schuster.

Worrall, A. (1990) *Offending Women,* London: Routledge.

Wright, G. and Hill, J. (2004) 'Victims, Crime and Criminal Justice', in J. Muncie and D. Wilson, *Student Handbook of Criminal Justice and Criminology,* London: Cavendish.

Yates, J. (2004) 'Criminological Ethnography: Risks, Dilemmas and their Negotiation', Document 208043, National Criminal Justice Reference Service (accessed online 3 March 2013).

Young, J. (1971) *The Drugtakers: The Social Meaning of Drug Use,* London: Paladin.

Zhang, Y. and Wildemuth, B. M. (2009) 'Qualitative Analysis of Content', in B. Wildemuth (ed.), *Applications of Social Research Methods to Questions in Information and Library Science,* Westport, CT: Libraries Unlimited, pp. 308–19.

INDEX

absolute relativism 32, 227
abstracts 209, 211, 214, 220–3
access: documentary data analysis 196; gaining 3; gatekeepers 6; official reports 101; 'real-world' criminological research 90, 92; secondary data sources 143
accuracy 17
administrative criminology 66, 67, 88
Alexander, Claire 22
Altheide, D. 199
anomie theory 76
anonymity 35–6, 103
ANOVA (Analysis of Variance) 161, 165
anti-discrimination 82–3
the arts 142, 201
Atkinson, P. 182
autobiographies 140

balance 7
BBC *Panorama* programme 38
Beccaria, Cesare 71
Becker, Howard 78
Belns, B. C. 34
Bell, J. 56
Bentham, Jeremy 71
Berg, B. L. 36, 115
between-subjects design 164
biological determinism 17, 61, 88
biological positivism 72–3, 75, 76
bivariate relationships 77, 227
Blagden, N. 60–1
Bourdieu, Pierre 203
Box, S. 76
Boyatzis, R. 184
Braun, V. 183, 186, 187–8
Breakthrough Britain 45, 47, 48–9, 50, 197
British Crime Survey *see* Crime Survey for England and Wales
British Journal of Criminology 50
British Society of Criminology 27, 28

British Sociological Association 28
Bryman, A. 30
Buchbinder, E. 116
Burman, E. 25
Burrell, G. 66, 68

'call-in system' 100
Calvey, D. 32–3, 35, 38
Cannella, G. S. 21
capitalism 80
CAQDAS *see* Computer Assisted Qualitative Data Analysis Software
Carlen, P. 85, 92, 102
Carrabine, E. 9, 33, 57, 76
Caulfield, Laura 95, 142, 143, 185–6, 187–9
causation 76–7, 78, 83, 85
CCTV 5
CDA *see* critical discourse analysis
census categories 134
Chambers, M. 204, 205
change 67–8, 69, 85, 86, 87
Chi-square 161, 172–6
children 34, 35, 36, 37
Clarke, V. 183, 186, 187–8
class 21, 79, 83
classicism 71–2, 73, 227
closed questions 125, 130–2, 227
coding manuals 199–200
coding of data: qualitative content analysis 199–202; quantitative analysis 159, 198; thematic analysis 179, 183–4, 186, 188, 190–1
common sense 3, 13, 26, 85, 87, 227
Computer Assisted Qualitative Data Analysis Software (CAQDAS) 179, 192–3, 198, 205–6, 208
conclusions 211, 219
confidentiality 29, 34, 35–7, 134
conflict theory 80
consent 29, 33–5, 40, 94, 101, 103

consequentialism 32, 40, 227
content analysis 195, 198–9; *see also*
    qualitative content analysis
contents pages 211–12
convenience sampling 128–9
conversation analysis 181, 187
corporate crime 10, 12, 76, 80
correlation 17, 227
correlations 77–8
covert research: ethics 32–3, 34, 35–6, 38,
    40; observation 117–18, 120, 121, 122
Cowburn, Malcolm 23–4, 32, 33, 34, 57–60,
    61, 101, 116
Cramer, D. 181, 187
credibility 64, 139, 143, 147, 148, 149
Crighton, D. 92, 101
crime: defining 26, 45; as social construction
    46, 86, 230–1
crime prevention 72, 73, 88
Crime Survey for England and Wales 101,
    124, 125–6, 134, 136, 146
criminal justice system: gatekeepers in the 6;
    'real-world' criminological research 90,
    91–2, 97; *see also* prison
critical analysis 198
critical criminological research 15, 19–21, 26,
    69, 70; anti-discrimination 83;
    deconstruction 53; definition of 227;
    dialectical analysis 79, 82; in-depth
    methods 87; meaning and structure 123;
    statistics 86
critical discourse analysis (CDA) 195, 198,
    203–5
critical ethnography 111, 120
critical reading 55, 57, 64
cultural criminology 76, 79
Currie, E. 11

Darlington, Yvonne 84
data analysis *see* quantitative data analysis;
    thematic analysis
Data Archive (UK) 146
data collection: ethnographic approaches
    109–23; observation 117–18; positivism
    16; questionnaires and surveys 124–37;
    'real-world' criminological research 94–7,
    99; researcher safety 99; time and costs 4;
    use of secondary data 138, 139, 144, 149;
    writing up the method section 216; *see
    also* methodology
data entry 159–60
data-led approach 188
data protection 29
deception 29, 31, 32, 34, 40

deconstruction 53
deduction 16–17, 199, 227
denaturalism 181, 227
Denscombe, M. 49, 64
Denzin, N. K. 93 4
dependent variable 77, 119, 155, 156, 216,
    220, 227
descriptive statistics 161, 162–4, 217
determinism 15, 67, 68, 86; biological 17, 61,
    88; classicism 71, 73; definition of 228;
    positivism 17, 73, 77–8, 84
deterrence 9, 10
dialectical analysis 79, 82, 86, 228
dialogic approach 115, 228
diary entries 140
directed content analysis 199
discourse analysis 187, 195, 198, 203–5,
    228
discussion section 217–19
dissertations *see* writing up research
documentary data 139–44, 195–207, 228;
    see also secondary data
domestic violence 8–9, 12, 23, 25, 51, 83–4,
    115, 134
drug use 45, 77, 78–9
Durkheim, Emile 74–5, 76, 80, 85

Economic and Social Research Council
    (ESRC) 32
Edwards, A. 21
empirical studies 56
Enosh, G. 116
epistemology 15, 20, 50, 68, 73, 228; *see
    also* knowledge
ethics 27–40; ethical dilemmas 30, 31–2, 36,
    37; ethical stances 32–3; ethics
    committees 33, 37, 39; key ethical
    principles 28–9; observation 117–18, 119;
    payment for research participants 103;
    secondary data sources 139, 144, 148;
    writing up the method section 216
ethnography 22, 109–23; critical 111, 120;
    definition of 228; in-depth interviews 87,
    110–17, 121; interpretivist 119–20, 123;
    observation 117–23
ethnomethodology 118, 228
eugenics 72
evidence 49
ex-offenders 95–7, 103
Excel 154

Fairclough, N. L. 203
familiarisation with data 179, 180, 181, 182,
    186, 193

family breakdown 45–6, 47–9, 50, 197
Farrell, G. 130
Farrington, D. P. 50
feminism 15, 25, 61, 84; anti-discrimination 82–3; biological determinism 17; black crime 86; Cowburn's work 58, 59, 60; dialogic approach 115, 228; domestic violence 8; rape within marriage 19; subjectivity 22–3; *see also* gender; women
Fine, M. 7–8
focus groups 97, 110, 113
Foucault, Michel 203
Frankfurt School 203
free will 67, 68, 71, 73, 79, 86
Freud, Sigmund 74
functionalism 67, 69, 76
funding 3, 4, 5, 11, 13, 29

Gagne, Patricia 115
Galton, F. 71, 72
Garland, D. 66
gatekeepers 5–7, 13, 97–8
gender: anti-discrimination 82–3; biological determinism 17; inequalities 21; literature reviews 61–2; male and female victims of domestic violence 134; oppression 22; social construction of 51; *see also* feminism; women
generalisation 86–7, 218–19
Giddens, Anthony 68–9
Gill, M. 5
Gisby, W. 140–2
Goffman, E. 57, 58
Gold, R. 118
Gramsci, A. 81
Groombridge, N. 5
grounded theory 183, 188
group interviews 97, 110
guided interviews 110, 113

Hall, S. 81, 86
Haraway, Donna 22
Harding, Sandra 21–2, 23
harm, avoidance of 29, 30, 37–9, 40
Harvard referencing system 219
Harvey, J. 97
Harvey, L. 15, 82
Hearn, Jeff 61–2
hegemony 58, 81, 228
Heidensohn, F. 82
Herrnstein, R. J. 75, 85
Hill-Collins, Patricia 23
Hill, Jane 6, 111, 114
Hinchcliffe, David 62

Home Office research 4–5, 10
homogeneity of variance 157
hooks, bell 23
Horrocks, C. 185
Howitt, D. 181, 187
Hsieh, H.-F. 199
human nature 68, 73
humanism 67, 86
hypotheses: definition of 228; ethnography 119; quantitative analysis 156, 158, 170; questionnaires 125, 137; translating ideas into questions 52–3; writing up research 215

idealism 67, 80, 84
in-depth interviews 82, 87, 110–17, 121; *see also* interviews
independent variable 52–3, 77, 155, 156, 176, 216, 220, 228
indigenous people 23
induction 16, 199, 228
inequalities 21, 23, 71
inferential statistics 162
informed consent 29, 33–5, 40, 94, 101, 103
Integrated Research Application System (IRAS) 92
interactionism 57, 58, 78, 230
internet 4, 47; questionnaires 127; secondary data 141, 147
interpretivism 15, 18–19, 51, 78–9, 85–6; definition of 228; ethnography 119–20, 123; qualitative methods 16; subjective/objective continuum 67, 69
interval data 155–6, 161, 228
interviews 6, 50, 68, 82, 103; ethnographic approaches 109, 110–17, 121; phone 127; secondary data sources 143; thematic analysis 180–91; transcription of data 181–2; vulnerable groups 94–7; writing up the method section 216; *see also* qualitative research
Intimate Partner Violence (IPV) *see* domestic violence
introductions 62
'inverted pyramid' approach 63
IRAS *see* Integrated Research Application System

Jefferson method of transcription 181
Johnson, Alan 45
Johnson, H. 201
Jones, T. 60, 61
journals 46, 47, 50, 51, 52, 215

Juby, H. 50
Jupp, V. 93, 203–4

Katz, Jack 79
Keen, S. 201
Kelly, Liz 83–4
keys, in prison 101–2
King, N. 185
King, R. D. 4, 94
Kitsuse, J. 78
knowledge 12, 14; epistemology 15, 20, 50,
    68, 73, 228; functionalism 69;
    interpretivism 18; objectivity 22; positivism
    18, 26, 77; theories of 70

labelling perspective 78, 79, 86
Lacombe, D. 60
Lampard, R. 6, 7, 110, 117, 122
language 198, 203
Lankford, A. 146
laws 73, 76
leading questions 133
left realism 81, 84–5
lesbian, gay, bisexual or trans-sexual (LGBT)
    people 83; see also sexual orientation
Levene's Test for Equality of Variances 168,
    169
life histories 58, 62, 111, 113, 140
Likert scale 132, 165
Lilly, J. R. 9–10, 73, 88
Lincoln, Y. S. 21
literature reviews 43, 55–64, 188; case study
    60–2; critiquing the literature 55–60,
    63–4, 154; informal 46–52, 53; writing up
    research 62–4, 214–15
Lockyer, K. 204, 205
Lombroso, C. 16, 71, 72, 73–4
Lukes, S. 5

MacLeod, M. 61
Mann, N. 60–1
marketisation 5, 229
Marxist approaches 15, 47, 71, 80–2, 83
matched control groups 165
Matza, D. 62, 92
Mawby, R. C. 140–2
May, T. 11, 28, 38, 118
Mead, George Herbert 78
media 13, 45; data analysis 205; drug crime
    78; secondary data sources 140–2; street
    crime 81
Merton, Robert 76, 84
methodology 53, 63, 66, 68, 69; choice of
    methods 70; documentary data 144, 196;

literature review 56; mixed methods 83–4,
    189; positivism 73; writing up the method
    section 215–17; see also ethnography;
    qualitative research; quantitative research
Milgram, S. 31–2, 34
Mills, J. 101
mixed methods 83–4, 189
Moore, Linda 34
Morgan, G. 66, 68
mugging 81
Muncie, J. 80
Murray, C. 75, 85

narrative analysis 205
National Health Service (NHS) 92
naturalism 181, 229
Nee, C. 93, 94, 97
neo-conservatives 85
network sampling 129
Neuman, W. L. 45
neutrality 14–15, 21, 60, 70, 80, 114–15;
    see also objectivity
newspapers 140–2, 205
NHS see National Health Service
Nicholas, S. 84
nominal data 155, 159, 172, 229
non-parametric tests 157, 229
normal distribution 157
Norris, C. 203–4
null hypothesis 168, 170, 176
Nutt, D. 45
NVivo 103, 192–3, 205, 206–7

Oakley, A. 19
OASys see Offender Assessment System
objectivity 21–5, 69–70; observation 118;
    subjective/objective continuum 67, 68,
    85
observation 58, 68, 117–23
Offender Assessment System (OASys) 93,
    94, 101, 143
offenders: 'real-world' criminological research
    92–4, 95–7, 99–100; sex offenders
    57–9, 60–2; young black offenders
    111, 114; see also prison
official documents 48–50, 101, 141,
    142–3, 146
O'Leary, Z. 140
Oliver, D. G. 181
O'Mahony, P. 51
O'Malley, P. 79
ontology 15, 18, 20, 68, 73, 229
open questions 125, 130, 132–3, 229
operationalisation of concepts 46

Opie, C. 56
oppression 19, 20, 53, 83; Cowburn's work
58, 60; gender 22; researchers 23–4, 25
order 67–8, 69
ordinal data 155, 161, 229
organisational communication and documents
141
O'Sullivan, S. 205
overt observation 117–18, 121, 122

p-values 158, 168, 171
Panorama 38
paralinguistic features 181, 182
parametric tests 157, 229
participant observation 117–18, 119–20,
121–2
Parton, Nigel 62
payment for research participants 103
Pemberton, S. 60–1
personal communication and documents 141
phone interviews 127
Piddick, Brian 25
pilot studies 90, 95–7, 103, 105, 125
Piper, H. 36, 37
plagiarism 56, 229
planning 43–54; background reading 46–52;
documentary data analysis 196; research
ideas 44–6, 52; research questions 52–3
Pole, C. 6, 7, 110, 117, 122
police 6, 18, 25
policy 11, 48, 87
policy documents 48–50
politics 11, 13, 14, 21, 45, 48
Popper, Karl 16–17, 85
positivism 15, 16–18, 26, 51, 75–8, 84, 85;
biological 72–3, 75, 76; definition of 229;
interviews 114–15; Marxist critique 80;
objectivity 21, 69; quantitative methods 16
post-modernism 15
postal questionnaires 126, 127
poverty 7, 50, 77, 84
power relations 12, 53, 69, 85; critical
discourse analysis 198, 203, 204;
gatekeepers 5–7; Marxist approaches 80
prison 10, 12; Cowburn's work 57–60;
exceptions to confidentiality 37; Offender
Assessment System 93, 94, 101, 143;
'real-world' criminological research 90, 92,
94, 95–7, 99–105; secondary data
sources 140; *see also* offenders
Prison Link 95–6
prison officers 58, 140
Pritchard, D. 201
privacy 94

psychoanalytic criminology 66
psychology 66, 67
public and private domains 143, 144
public opinion 11, 45
Punch, M. 18
punishment 9–10, 13, 72, 73
purposive sampling 129

qualitative content analysis 140–2, 195,
198–203, 205, 206
qualitative research: CAQDAS 179, 192–3,
198, 205–6, 208; critical criminological
research 21; definition of 229; example
report structure 211–12, 213, 214;
generalisation 218–19; inequalities 21;
interpretivism 16, 18–19; method section
216, 217; mixed methods 83–4, 189;
political imperatives 45; results section
217; secondary data sources 142, 143;
subjective/objective continuum 67;
thematic analysis 179–94, 198, 217, 230;
titles 220; *see also* ethnography; interviews
quantitative data analysis 153–78; basic
concepts 154–8; Chi-square 161, 172–6;
choice of test 161–2; data entry 159–60;
descriptive statistics 161, 162–4, 217; *t*-
test 161, 164–71; writing up research 217
quantitative research: content analysis 198–9;
critical criminological research 21;
definition of 229; example report structure
211–12, 213; informed consent 33;
method section 216; mixed methods 83–4,
189; observational methods 118;
operationalisation of concepts 46;
positivism 16, 17, 77; results section 217;
secondary data sources 142, 143, 146;
subjective/objective continuum 67; *see
also* questionnaires
questionnaires 124–37; advantages and
disadvantages 126–7; design of 129–35,
137; missing data 159; offenders 94;
selection of participants 127–9; sensitivity
in using 136, 137; variables 155; writing
up the method section 216
quota sampling 129
quotations 54, 56, 202
Qureshi, F. 130

race 7–8, 11, 12, 22, 25; anti-discrimination
82; black feminism 86; black women 23,
24–5; critical criminological research
19–20; inequalities 21; social construction
of 51; street crime 81; young black
offenders 111, 114

racism 21, 23, 24–5, 34, 73–4, 82
radical structuralism 67
Ramesh, R. 38
random sampling 127–8
rape 18, 19, 24, 115
rating scales 131
ratio data 156, 161
rational choice theory 72
reading, critical 55, 57, 64
'real-world' criminological research 89–105;
    data collection 94–7; practical issues
    100–4; reasons for doing 91; recruiting a
    sample 97–8; research design 92–4;
    researcher safety 99–100; settings 91–2
realism 67, 80, 84–5
recruitment of research participants 97–8,
    105, 126, 127–9
references 52, 219
reflexivity 19, 24, 35, 58, 229
regression 161
regulation 67–8, 69, 85, 86, 87
related t-test 161, 164, 171
relativism 15, 32, 227
reliability 17, 139, 148, 149
reporting of crime 11
representative samples 145, 229
representativeness 17, 139
'research buddies' 100
research ideas 43, 44–6, 52
research participants 90, 101, 102; abstracts
    222; management of 99; payment and
    feedback 103–4; recruitment of 97–8,
    105, 126, 127–9; writing up the method
    section 216
research questions 52–3, 129, 137, 140,
    208
researchers: background of 3; black 25;
    data from other 145; ethics 27, 28, 30,
    39; in-depth interviews 114–16; neutrality
    14–15; observation 121–2; oppressive
    practices 23–4; research ideas 43; safety
    of 90, 99–100, 105, 121; social location of
    12; thematic analysis 180–1
responsibility 76
results section 217
Risk Factors Prevention Paradigm (RFPP) 51

safeguarding 29
sampling 126, 127–9, 137; representative
    samples 145, 229; sample size 164;
    sampling error 77; secondary data sources
    144
Sanders, B. 36
Sapsford, R. 93

Saraga, E. 61
science 16, 21–2, 26, 67, 68, 73, 78, 85, 88;
    see also positivism
secondary data 138–49; advantages and
    disadvantages 143–4; analysis of 144,
    145, 147–8, 195–207; critical discussion
    218; data sets 144, 145–6; definition of
    229; example report structure 213–14;
    reasons for using 139; types of sources
    140–3, 196
self-report data 93–4, 125, 126
sex offenders 57–9, 60–2
sexism 21, 34, 82; black women 23;
    Cowburn's work 24, 58–9; Lombroso 73–4
sexual orientation 21, 82, 83, 117
Shannon, S. E. 199
Sheptycki, J. 21
Simmel, George 78
situated ethics 32
situational crime prevention 72
Smart, Carol 61
social artefacts 142
social class 21, 79, 83
social construction 46, 51, 78, 86, 229–30
social context 76, 78, 120
social control 73, 80
social structures 19, 20, 26, 86
social workers 6, 110
sociological criminology 66, 67
Spriggs, A. 5
SPSS (Statistical Package for the Social
    Sciences) 103, 153, 155, 158–78
spurious relationships 77, 230
standard deviation 157
statistical analysis 153–78, 217; basic
    concepts 154–8; Chi-square 161, 172–6;
    choice of test 161–2; data entry 159–60;
    descriptive statistics 161, 162–4, 217; t-
    test 161, 164–71; writing up research 217
statistical significance 77, 156, 158, 170, 171
statistics on crime 10–11, 13, 50, 86, 145
stereotypes 12, 14, 78
Stout, B. 9, 67
strain theory 76, 84
street crime 11, 12, 45, 81
structural functionalism 67
structuralism 15, 67
structure 68–9, 123; see also social
    structures
subjectivity 22–3, 69–70; observation 118;
    subjective/objective continuum 67, 68, 85
suicide 74
summaries 218
summative content analysis 199

surveys 68, 112, 124–37; advantages and disadvantages 126–7; design of 129–35, 137; observational methods 118; secondary data sources 144; selection of participants 127–9; sensitivity in using 136, 137; see also questionnaires
symbolic interactionism 57, 58, 78, 230

t-test 161, 164–71
Taylor, I. 80
Teo, P. 205
thematic analysis 179–94, 198, 217; advantages and disadvantages 189–90; CAQDAS 192–3; coding 183–4, 186, 188, 190–1; definition of 230; themes 185, 186, 188, 189, 194; transcription of data 181–2, 188; writing up the findings 185–9
theory 44–5, 65–88; deductive method 16–17; dimensions of criminological research 66–70; early criminology 70–6; Marxist approaches 80–2; methods and 66; role of 11; theoretical triangulation 121; theory-led approach 188; see also critical criminological research; interpretivism; positivism
'third person' writing style 211
thrill of crime 79
Tierney, J. 11, 76, 84
Tierney, W. 111
time issues 4
titles 209, 211, 220
Tombs, S. 47
transcription of data 180, 181–2, 188
triangulation, theoretical 121
Twort, H. 142

UK Data Archive 146
universalism 32, 230
unrelated t-test 161, 164–71
unstructured interviews 110, 113

validity 17, 19, 203
Valier, C. 78–9

values 3, 9–11, 22, 26; biological positivism 75; critical criminological research 20; documentary data analysis 197, 207; ethics underpinned by 28; facts mediated by 17; post-modernism 15; secondary data 143, 144
variables 155, 156, 158, 159, 173, 176
victims of crime 10
vignettes 116–17, 230
violence: domestic 8–9, 12, 23, 25, 51, 83–4, 115, 134; gender roles 83; race and 8, 25; sexual 61, 62

Weis, L. 7–8
Whyte, D. 47
Wilson, D. 60, 61, 142, 205
Wilson, J. Q. 75
Wincup, E. 4, 94
within-subjects design 164
Wodak, R. 203
women: biological determinism 17; domestic violence 8–9, 12, 23, 25, 51, 83–4, 115, 134; feminist criminological research 15, 82–3; interviews with ex-offenders 95–7, 103; Lombroso on 74; prison officers 58; rape victims 24–5; rape within marriage 18, 19; sexual abuse 61; subjectivity 22–3; see also feminism; gender
working classes 79, 81, 84–5
Worrall, A. 92, 102, 203
writing up research 209–25; abstracts 220–3; checklist 223–4, 225; discussion 217–19; example report structures 211–14; guidance on 210; literature reviews 62–4, 214–15; method section 215–17; references 219; results 217; thematic analysis 185–9; titles 220; top tips 210–11

Yates, J. 117
Young, J. 78–9
Youth Justice System 51
Youth Offending Teams 6